GLOBAL IPO

The Great Rewiring of Capital Markets

By Jeffrey Stewart

Published by Urgent Books, a Division of Urgent Publishing, Inc., USA.

Pre-release printing.

ISBN 979-8-218-87743-9

Printed in the United States, U.K., Australia, and Europe.

For my children,
our investors,
and the founders we back.

Table of Contents

Introduction

Once upon a time, venture-backed companies went public. Entrepreneurs used the public market to fuel their vision. Investors allocated resources. Employees were rewarded. Whole new industries were created.

The system worked.

In the 1980s and '90s, hundreds of venture-backed companies went public every year. This didn't necessarily involve an enormous amount of capital; these companies often raised just tens of millions of dollars. But once they'd gone public, the companies could easily access more capital, talent and customers as their performance, reputation and ambitions grew.

Venture capitalists would fund A, B and C rounds. D rounds were rare, as this was the zone of the public market. In fact, the best VCs would say "*D is for Dead. Great companies go public after C. You don't even want to know what 'F' is for.*"

Both individual citizens and institutional investors had direct access to the fastest-growing and most important innovative companies. Fortunes were made. It was transparent. Incentives were aligned.

But then, everything changed around the year 2000.

Structural, cultural and regulatory shifts caused the public markets to shrink. Around the world, fewer companies went public. The U.S. market became a mega-cap market—the U.S. stock exchanges became geared to the needs of only the biggest companies and most active traders. Small companies were ignored. Going public became harder while starting a company became easier. At first hundreds, and then thousands, of venture-backed companies stayed private. The backlog of private innovative venture-backed companies grew. The top of the venture funnel got bigger while the bottom of the funnel shrunk.

There were further knock-on effects. Capital stopped being recirculated. Only the biggest companies went public. Fees grew, incentives diverged, and opacity spread like fungus in a wet forest. Sub-optimal outcomes ensued as selling a company became acceptable. Monopoly-sized tech and private equity grew fat on acquisitions. Power and access became concentrated. Bad for founders, bad for early investors, and bad for society.

This book is about what comes next, the return of the IPO, and this time it is *Global*. Thanks to the interconnected nature of markets, regulatory diversity and the global proliferation of wealth, Global IPOs are now possible. IPOs that are faster, cheaper, less distracting and, once again, occur much earlier in a company's lifecycle. Companies can go public earlier, publicly list, and then grow into a decacorn, using the many benefits of being public to accelerate growth, just like the generation-defining companies of the past.

Currents of technology, geopolitics and economics are all converging. The result: the public markets rising again, not as they were, but reborn—bigger, bolder and not bound by the size of their city or country.

The best owners and managers have already learned the benefit of accessing talent and customers globally. It builds better companies. Now they're waking up to the fact that accessing international capital also has benefits. It's a game-changer.

It turns out that not all capital is the same. Diverse perspectives, aligned investment horizons, stakeholder diversification, shared vision, regional credibility and, most importantly, local knowledge are all elements that cross-border investors can bring to a fast-growing company. All this with the added benefit of embedding the option to go public sooner.

Global Talent. Global Customers. Global Capital. Each one is a powerful force multiplier. But when you bring them together, the impact is explosive! It's not just about growth; it's about building generation-defining companies: It reshapes industries, creates markets, and builds legacy. This is the future, and this book seeks to give you an edge. Those who get it will ride this next wave of wealth and innovation. We call it a "**Global IPO.**" *Surf's up!*

Rise of the Global IPO

What is a "Global IPO?" The simple answer is that it is a financing strategy that involves a company, customers, management, regulations and investors in more than one country. That answer is technically correct, but it is insufficient. A "Global IPO" is shorthand for a strategy that has three characteristics:

- multi-national execution
- a global mindset
- it is relationship-oriented

Teams that are global in mindset build out global operations, revenue and capital. Embedding the option to go public and attract global investors is part of their strategy. Teams that are relationship-oriented view their investors as long-term partners, not as transaction counterparties. They are willing to do the work needed to build trust, sometimes over many years, and often in multiple jurisdictions. In many parts of the world, relationships trump transactions. As a senior executive at the Dubai Exchange said: "Confusing an IPO with being public is like confusing a wedding party with a marriage."

Exactly! The Global IPO strategy is about building a dynamic, resilient and significant company that has evergreen investors who want to support the company's long-term vision. Founders can build more resilient capital bases, and, once again, have greater control of their destiny. They have the power to define their category, and acquire others, not be acquired themselves.

This is also a story about a huge new pool of modern investors. It is about how billions of people are moving into the middle class, and how that transformation is creating vast new pools of capital.

It is also about how a new generation of portfolio managers are looking beyond their backyard for that next crop of generation-defining companies. This book is about an emerging set of investors, from every corner of the earth, who are willing to do the work needed to outperform the market.

This is a dramatic opportunity to turn human ambition, error, and diversity into progress: better products, lower prices, and higher standards of living.

This book aims to be more than just a guidebook for founders, investors and policymakers. Hopefully it will become a parable for management teams who want to change the world and a treasure map for investors.

This book was years in the making. In 2018, Key Compton and I co-founded the Global Public Offering Fund, the first venture fund designed to support ambitious founders who wanted to accelerate their international expansion and grow in the public market. Turns out our thesis resonated with both founders and investors. Since 2018, my team and I have met hundreds of entrepreneurs, board members, investors, exchanges and advisors. These diverse discussions helped us to develop our fund playbook, which then enabled our team to better screen and support our founder-led, globally-scaling portfolio companies. These many discussions also laid the foundation for this book.

This book is not just a guide for the modern, multi-jurisdictional IPO. It is about building companies, portfolios and the future. It is about connecting management teams with investors who match their vision, agency and timing. All that sounds sweet, but to be clear: this book is designed for war. It is a weapon for the disruptors, bold investors and all those who battle the "complacents."

I hope you enjoy reading it as much as I enjoyed researching it. May you be victorious in your battles!

Global IPO

Chapter 1
Rise of the Global IPO

Why Global?

Capitalism: "It must nestle everywhere, settle everywhere, establish connections everywhere... In one word, it creates a world after its own image."
Karl Marx, *Communist Manifesto*, 1848

It might seem odd to start a book about capital markets with a quote from Karl Marx, but although he was an idiot on many things, that quote about capitalism proved prescient. Walter Wriston's quote from his 1992 book, *The Twilight of Sovereignty: How the Information Revolution Is Transforming Our World,* would be more contemporary, and comforting: "Capital goes where it is welcome and stays where it is well-treated."

Both men were right. Capitalism seeks to be global. Like air into a vacuum or water into a crack, it spreads naturally. Unfortunately, some people are slow to grasp the following simple, undeniable truth: *The biggest pools of customers, talent and capital are outside your borders.*

If you're a founder, investor or regulator, failing to understand that simple truth will result in sub-optimal outcomes.

No country has a monopoly on talent. Even if you combine the vast talent pools of India and China, it is a minority of talent relative to the world. Combining the purchasing power of Japan and Europe, still a minority. Combining the vast wealth of America with Saudi-Arabia, still a minority. All over the planet, hundreds of millions of people are moving into the middle-class,[1] causing huge changes in where talent resides, products are consumed, and wealth is created.

To be a globally-significant, category-leading, company, you must have a strategy for regions beyond your border. This strategy must include customers, talent and capital.

Customers Everywhere

Founders, and the venture capitalists who backed them, were once satisfied focusing on their home market. That began to change around 2010, when Groupon merged with the Samwer brothers's CityDeal.[2] The key issue here was that Groupon had ignored massive opportunities outside its home U.S. market. That had worked well enough before the world wide web, but not in a world where potential competitors can monitor your progress from a far away screen. Conversely, CityDeal had seized their market opportunity overseas. The companies merged to improve scale and be more global in advance of a 2011 U.S. IPO. Founders and Investors took note; ignore "the rest of world" and risk being a regional also-ran.

Since then, much has been written on how to localize your marketing and product to attract globally diverse customers. Today, most founders and early-stage investors understand the importance of having a strategy to attract international customers. The under-appreciated added benefit of a global customer base is that it also opens new listing venues. Investors in other parts of the world are more likely to buy your equity if they also use your product, or have first-hand knowledge of your customers.

If a company's customers are global, why limit its listing venue to the one that happens to be closest?

Talent Everywhere

You would expect talent-hungry start-ups to be quick to understand the value of sourcing talent globally. Yet, ironically, staffing best practices were first widely adopted in the 1990s by big companies, and start-ups were slower to realize the benefit of global talent[3]. Despite a large percentage of start-ups being founded by immigrants, the team they hired tended to be local.

I remember the skepticism in the venture community in the early 2000s when my start-up was setting up teams in Argentina, Ukraine, China and the Philippines. Back then, my founder peers thought I was being frugal, just trying to save money. They missed the point entirely! Opening up our talent funnel globally allowed us to hire faster, acquire a different type of talent, and in many cases attract more professional and engaged talent. As an example, top engineers are almost impossible to find, so you can't afford the luxury of only looking in your neighborhood. And it's not just engineers; there are many roles to fill in a startup to fuel explosive growth. For example, the top talent in New York City does not want to tag data to train algorithms, but I found this role is viewed as a "high-prestige position" with "important multinational companies" in sunny Manila. By tapping into these cultural differences, you can build a more effective workforce. Building a hybrid global team enabled us to build powerful AI algorithms over a decade before the practice became commonplace.

When entrepruners think about the global sourcing of labor, cost savings are often what comes to mind. But this is a limited outlook, which overlooks the true value inherent in this process. It's about great talent. It's about getting exceptional people on your team. As management guru Jim Collins says: "The right people in the right seats[4]."

There was logical resistance to remote teams in the start-up community. Management can be harder, especially in a new and rapidly growing organization. Despite the advantages and potential remote teams offer, for many years the perception was that it's hard for them to innovate as quickly as a team sitting in the same room. But that all changed with COVID in 2020, and by 2024, most founders and VCs had learned to be deliberate in where they sourced talent[5]. Today, it is hard to find a venture-backed company at scale that does not have at least some distributed workforce.

If a company's team is global, why should it limit its listing venue to the one that happens to be closest?

Capital Everywhere

Top entrepreneurs and their investors are also waking up to the fact that capital, just like talent and customers, is increasingly global. Already between 10-20% of all IPOs are cross-border[6], meaning that the location of incorporation is different from the stock exchange. Family offices also tend to be multinational, and are becoming an increasingly important source of innovation capital.

It just makes sense. Well-run companies are very deliberate in where they operate, all the way down to where they're incorporated, which is often Delaware, Singapore or the United Arab Emirates. They are deliberate about where they set up operations, whether it be factories, R&D centers, or sales offices. They are deliberate about where they house their IP, the jurisdictions of their contracts, and the jurisdiction of their data centers.

So why wouldn't they also be deliberate in which exchange they choose and which regional investors they target? Ambitious leaders must design their global capital strategy to match their vision.

Today's disruptors can learn from Rod Drury and Hamish Edwards, the founders of Xero, headquartered in New Zealand. They did not wake up and say, "Let's build the biggest cloud based accounting software in New Zealand." Instead, they sought customers, talent and investment on a scale that matched their ambition. They went public on Australia's ASX in 2007. As a consequence of these decisions, Xero was a decacorn by the mid-2020s.[7] Xero still had a global investor base.

When done right, public capital is global capital and global capital is strategic capital.

Why Now?

"If something cannot go on forever, it will stop."
Herbert Stein

The above idiom, also known as Stein's Law, is an inexorable reality of the known universe. Herbert Stein was an economist who served as Chairman of the Council of Economic Advisers in the 1980s. Stein's Law is one of the best ways to describe the need for the return to the IPO. The public markets can not shrink forever.

In my firm's estimation, far too many start-ups stayed private for far too long between 2000 and 2020. Public markets became more cumbersome while unprecedentedly low interest rates provided big pools of private capital. As a consequence, the median IPO age jumped from four years (1999) to 12+ years (2020).[8] The result of this was a dearth of exits and a huge overhang of venture-backed companies. Businesses were under pressure to go public for several reasons:

- Employees needing liquidity and a morale boost
- Cap tables requiring cleaning up to unlock value and flexibility
- Pressure from LPs growing tired of the "stay private forever" playbook
- VCs needing to show exits as a pre-condition for raising a new fund

Liquidity alternatives, such as continuation funds, management buy-outs and secondary transactions, are not meeting the needs of founders and LPs. Pricing is seen by LPs as opaque, slow, rife with conflicts and usually at a significant discount to supposed value. Yet, these liquidity events have proven lucrative for finance insiders, while sophisticated institutions worry that these efforts are just a push to extend fee generation.

The era of endless private capital is ending. LPs have woken up to the difference between DPI (Distributions to Paid-In Capital) and TVPI (Total Value to Paid-In Capital). DPI is cash returned and TVPI is only on paper. Paper returns can't fund scholarships, pensions, or operating budgets. The fund "extend and pretend" game eventually stops.

The good news is we are about to see a new era of IPOs, but this time better. A confluence of technological, cultural and geopolitical forces are converging to support a new type of IPO: the Global IPO, an IPO that is multijurisdictional, yet possessing a frictional cost that is appropriate for a high-potential company still early in its journey. Something that works for a company that is not yet worth multiple billion dollars.

The move away from local IPOs and toward Global IPOs is driven by geopolitics, demographics, cultural shifts and technological change. Let's first look at how technology is changing the IPO landscape, by examining several disruptive areas.

Internet

Perhaps the biggest impact on the IPO landscape is from the internet. Hundreds of millions of people are now connected to the global economy, which has enabled the proliferation of education, opportunity and wealth. There is a global middle-class building vast pools of capital that are seeking investment. In the U.S., the investment institutions have become so big that it is not worth the effort for them to look at any IPO unless it is a mega-listing. But in much of the world, pensions resemble the U.S. pensions of the 1980s—small enough that investing in a smaller IPO can move the needle.

Smartphone/Mobile/Social

There has been a global proliferation of smartphone-based investment apps and super-apps. Most readers are familiar with RobinHood, but there are hundreds of fast-growing, consumer-facing investing apps now available globally. These engaged investors can be socially connected to form swarms capable of setting prices. Our fund generally advises our portfolio companies to focus on institutional investors, for reasons elaborated later in the book. But for a new IPO issuance more eyes are better. No institution has a monopoly on insights and access is being democratized. Smartphone-empowered investors increasingly play an important role in helping set prices, especially in the first few days and weeks around an IPO.

Artificial Intelligence

The race is on among equity investors to unlock meaningful value using generative AI tools. Sophisticated investors know that fundamental stock valuation, when done right, is a lot of work. It is therefore important to note that AI is lowering the barrier for stock discovery, analysis, and research[9], resulting in an increased appetite for publicly-traded companies. This comes at a time when AI is also being used to lower the administrative cost of both listing and going public.

AI is also improving how software is developed and markets are connected—the "plumbing" is rapidly improving. Standard Protocols, APIs, and good old-fashioned greed are driving us to a world where investors can trade anything, anytime, anywhere.

BlockChain

Just as tokenized systems have evolved to trade tokens backed by currency, increasingly there are tokens backed by stocks held at a regulated custodian. The rate of innovation in the crypto-industry is high, and is rapidly spilling into the equity markets. The impact on the IPO process is inevitable. Soon, a whole new class of exchanges will be helping companies list their equity.

Awareness

Increasingly, investors and founders are realizing they can list globally on an exchange that is appropriate for the stage of the company. Finance has a history of major shifts driven by awareness. One example: Michael Milken did not invent high yield "junk" bonds; what he did was raise awareness and showed that they were legitimate financial tools. As a result, his work at Drexel Burnham Lambert in the late 1970s and 1980s reshaped U.S. capital markets[10]. Drexel simply repositioned "junk" as "high yield," while raising awareness. Today, about 20% of all IPOs are cross-border, but awareness in the founder and VC community more closely resembles the debt markets of the early 1980s.

VCs Under Pressure

There has never been a better time to make investments, yet this might also be the worst time to raise a venture fund. Scientific knowledge that was once siloed by language, geography and academic discipline is increasingly connected. Diverse fields such as energy, transportation, manufacturing, materials and biological sciences are all on the cusp of radical phase change. At first, this acceleration was driven by the internet, and now it is moving into hyperspeed due to AI. Innovation no longer seeds slowly—the world has become a digitally connected, thriving ecosystem. Each breakthrough enriches, inviting ever-faster ingenuity. Opportunities sprout like desert flowers after the rain. Investors will profit handsomely!

Yet for many venture capitalists, there has never been a harder time to raise a fund. Their LPs are finally waking up to the corrosive impact of 25 years of the "Stay private forever" mindset. Turns out that not going public and relying on M&A or selling to PE is not a winning long-term strategy for most companies. Consequently, LPs are demanding an approach that results in actual cash returns.

VCs are under pressure to show Distributions to Paid-In Capital (DPI) to their LPs. DPI refers to the ratio of cash or stock that a fund has actually returned to its LPs, divided by the capital those LPs have invested. Paper gains don't count, only actual distributions. LP patience has run out. DPI, not promises, now determines whether new funds get raised. For many venture managers, returning capital is no longer just a performance metric—it is existential. That urgency is rippling through portfolios, reviving the IPO as a central instrument once again.

Reduced M&A

M&A has become harder; even routine tuck-ins now trigger antitrust reviews. The U.S. Department of Justice, the UK's Competition and Markets Authority, the FTC, and various regulators in the EU are taking a harder line on acquisitions[11].

Higher interest rates in the mid-2020s also caused strategic buyers to become more selective about valuations. This pushes companies toward IPOs as the only scalable liquidity option[12]. This is especially true in categories such as fintech, cyber security, healthtech or AI infrastructure, where the number of realistic acquirers is limited.

Private Equity

PE is not the answer for exits; they are having their own problems. Besides, most VCs will privately tell you that a PE sale usually has an inferior valuation. PE is inherently valuation-sensitive, and is therefore not the preferred exit path for VCs. That is because PE is usually looking to pay the lowest price possible, especially given their battery of financial headwinds.

Performance Issues

By almost all accounts, PE returns have underperformed the

S&P 500 for the better part of a decade[13]. PE was expected by LPs to overperform, showing a "illiquidity premium." Private Fund Managers are having increasing difficulty attracting capital for new funds. Limited Partners are frustrated. Their distributions of capital have been hobbled, from a typical 30% of assets down to around 10% today according to a Bain study[14].

Interest Rates

PE faces additional strain because the industry typically relies on debt. Sharp interest-rate increases in the early 2020s caught many funds flat-footed, pushing down valuations, borrowing costs up, and leverage ratios far outside the assumptions made at purchase.[15]

Lack of PE Exits

PE firms are struggling to profitably sell the portfolio companies they have accumulated in the go-go years of near zero interest rates. By the mid-2020s, there were nearly 12,000 companies accumulated by PE, according to a 2025 study by accounting firm Cherry Bekaert.[16]

Public market investors have learned to be skeptical of PE firm-backed IPOs, as too many firms have used the public markets to dump their losers. PE firms adapted, and for over a decade PE firms turned to other PE firms to exit. Burger King, for example, changed hands four times since 1997.[17] But all PE buyers care about is the purchase price. PE firms have become more selective, as bad managers were unable to raise more capital, and good managers were disciplined in what they're willing to pay. As a result, the game of musical chairs seems to be coming to an end.

Supply Chain Uncertainty

The global threat of a trade war, kicked off by a new administration in the U.S. in the mid-2020s, has also introduced uncertainty into the fate of many PE-backed companies. Investors don't want to deploy more capital into the asset class until they see capital returned, and it's hard to exit a company when the tariffs on their supply chain and the underlying business economics are in flux.

New Pressure on U.S. Universities

U.S. universities have historically been big backers of PE. For them, these changes in the industry could not have come at a worse time. They are under a new form of pressure, driven by policy changes that are negatively impacting their ability to raise revenue in the form of international student tuition, as well as government grants. There is even talk of revoking their tax-exempt status, potentially kicking off a PE selloff by LPs looking to exit before their gains become taxable. Trendsetters Yale and Harvard are already turning to the secondary market to sell, and their actions have fueled discussion about over allocation amongst professional LP allocators.

Policy Toward Public Markets is Changing

Private markets reduce transparency, increase fees and move the economic mobility associated with investment away from the mom-and-pop investors, and into the hands of fund managers. Stable democracies should want dynamic capital markets and broad and direct equity ownership.

Part of this transition to private markets is driven by regulation. Well-intentioned regulators everywhere have added new layers of rules, regulations and disclosures. Taken individually, they are just small inconveniences that add costs of both time and money—costs that are ultimately borne by investors. These rules add up. Each one is like plaque in a society's arteries, slowing performance until eventually becoming fatal. Policymakers are waking up to the benefits of a public market, and starting to rightsize regulation, in order to support innovation.

Skepticism toward private markets is rising among both the public and policymakers. Across the political spectrum, large private companies are increasingly viewed as "shadow giants" that wield enormous economic and social influence while operating with limited transparency. Stripe offers a clear example: it employs thousands, processes a meaningful share of global online payments, and functions as critical financial infrastructure, yet remains privately held with minimal public disclosure. This has intensified calls for greater accountability, often summarized as: *If a company employs thousands and affects millions, it should be public.* Proposed legislation such as the U.S. Enhancing Public Markets Act reflects this sentiment by encouraging, or requiring earlier public listings, creating another structural tailwind for the return of the IPO.

Impact of Geopolitics on Capital

Top-down globalization is fading. Bottoms-up internationalization is rising. Markets are changing. The world's largest investors are seeing a seismic shift. In short, the Era of Globalization is waning. So what's rising? One word: internationalization. A multi-polar decentralized world built from the ground up.

Globalization is the process of increasing worldwide interconnectedness, which in turn creates interdependencies across economies, cultures, and political systems. Globalization is often top-down, and with a mindset that governments are there to support the individual and their entities.

Internationalization, by contrast, is the expansion of activities across national borders by individuals or entities. It's more bottom-up when it comes to mindset, adaptation and resilience. Operations, products or services designed with foreign markets as they uniquely exist. Customized bottom-up, as opposed to standardized top-down.

The mid-2020s witnessed a string of assaults on global frameworks. A new administration in Washington statements signaled a change away from business as usual. Trust in multilateral institutions such as NATO and NAFTA were called into question, as a string of policy changes were unilaterally proposed. The transition from global to international accelerated. The ways companies go public is changing in lock-step.

Beyond Multi-polar, International and Distributed

This transition is not from a uni-polar world to a multi-polar world; this is a world where each jurisdiction looks out for its own interests. Businessmen have realized some governments can no longer be counted on for driving a common rule standard, but instead may take the role of "chaos monkey," throwing wrenches into smooth operations in the form of unpredictable tariffs, regulations or taxes.

Governments everywhere are living beyond their means, and politicians have proven unwilling to make hard choices. The result will either be a reduction of services, or confiscation of assets, or some combination of both.

Businesses and investors adapt. International businesses are designed to be resilient, in the same way arctic equipment is designed for the cold. It is just the nature of the environment. They need a diversified footprint, and to be prepared to move operations and investment to where they are treated well.

The movement from top-down centralized globalization to bottom-up decentralized internationalization creates many new business opportunities, including in how those opportunities are financed.

Capital Markets in an Internationalized World

This leads us to the capital markets. Let's start with banking and payments infrastructure, and then move to the central topic of this book, equity markets.

The payments portion of the banking industry is built on trust—in a globalized world, you can count on a multinational standard of fairness. Property rights are respected across nations, and you can broadly trust in the rule of law. "Might does *not* make right" and "Possession is *not* nine-tenths of the law." It makes no difference if you store your gold in a vault in New York or Berlin. Your cash is just as safe in a bank in Tokyo or London. Your government bonds will be repaid whether you are a grandmother in Ohio, or a sovereign wealth fund in Beijing.

A globalized world is dependent on trust, and that trust has been eroded. Many believe this diminution in trust began with the general erosion of privacy. Excessive surveillance of private relationships. For hundreds of years, the best bankers got to know their clients. As J.P. Morgan said under oath in 1912, "The first thing is character... before money or anything else. Money cannot buy it... A man I do not trust could not get money from me on all the bonds in Christendom. I think that is the fundamental basis of business."

Banking is, at its core, a reputational business. Knowing who you take deposits from and lend to is not a formality; it is the foundation of risk management. Trust and risk management are inseparable, much like much like an immune system and health: invisible when functioning, catastrophic when ignored. Everyone can agree that knowing your client (KYC) is a good idea, but regulators wanted a seat at the table.

In 1970, the U.S. government introduced the Currency and Foreign Transactions Reporting Act, commonly referred to as the Bank Secrecy Act (BSA).[18] This well-intentioned law had the noble goal of deterring financial crimes, and the U.S. used its influence to push this standard globally. Over time, the objectives were expanded and new regulations include more jurisdictions, transaction types and counterparties. The narrow goal of reducing financial crimes was gradually expanded to encompass all sorts of undesirable mischief.

In 2001, after 9/11, the United States launched an aggressive push to expand financial transparency. Bankers, instinctive custodians of trust and risk, understood immediately that transparency, while valuable, introduces its own set of vulnerabilities. Every disclosure is a trade-off. Asset owners have long known that privacy can be a form of protection: against competitors, estranged partners, extremists, and criminals alike. Even the most junior risk manager learns this early; information cuts both ways. The more data you collect or share, the harder it becomes to ensure that it stays out of the hands of the careless, the compromised, or the malicious.

The question of what is the optimal trade-off between transparency and privacy is outside the scope of this book. What is in our scope is how it impacted financial market participants.

By 2017, many international bank policy professionals felt the U.S. had pushed too far. The phrase I kept hearing was "bureaucrat imperialism." As an American, the charge stings, but it is difficult to claim that policymakers in Washington D.C. possess the cultural context, local knowledge or experience required to design banking systems for societies as different from the U.S. as they are distant.

By 2018, the foundation was laid for a world in which the political class everywhere could see who owns what. "Disconnecting" parties from the financial system became increasingly common. As a manifestation of this, in that same year of 2018, the Bank of England refused to return Venezuela's gold reserves stored in London.[19]

And then, in February 2022, everything changed. First, Canada evoked the Emergencies Act, freezing the bank accounts supporting the "Freedom Convoy," a group of mainly truckers, who had a range of political grievances with Ottawa.[20] And in the very same month, the European Union,[21] the U.S.,[22] Canada,[23] Britain[24] and Japan[25] blocked the transfer of assets owned by the Russian Central Bank, with Switzerland[26] and Australia[27] following suit soon thereafter. This was an enormous precedent—the globalized world threatened to seize about $300 billion of holdings.

Whether this was a good or bad idea is a topic for another book. As a businessman, my opinion of the merit of the idea matters no less than a farmer's opinion on the merit of the weather. Like it or not, this is the world. As an investor and businessman doing business globally, I can confirm that the nature of trust has changed, businessmen and investors now care about custody. Where something is held now matters. As one investor put it, "I used to say, Not my keys, not my crypto; Now I say, Not my vault, not my asset."

Arguably, the threat alone broke the trust. It all boils down to risk management. Once a proposal is taken seriously, it introduces a new potential risk, regardless of whether it is implemented "*this time*"—just the presence of the idea in the zeitgeist quickly erodes trust. In risk management, the mere identification of a credible threat often carries greater weight than the event itself. The critical shift occurs when stakeholders recognize that a once-unthinkable outcome has entered the realm of possibility. The realization alters behavior. Yet governments have not dispelled the seizure idea, just the opposite. Governments have continued to impinge assets. Some Russian bank assets are frozen, while other Russian accounts have their interest payments redirected to Ukraine.

The impingement of assets is not limited to bank deposits. Commodities such as gold and silver are experiencing a wave of reshoring as central banks look to reduce risk. Physical custody again matters. Even payments on debt and productive assets have been called into question. For example, the U.S. Congress proposed Section 899, which would give the U.S. government the power to withhold payments to parties "perceived as unfair."[28] Again, it is the uncertainty that destroys trust, regardless of whether legislation is ever implemented. Even the proposal of such legislation is destabilizing.

Internationalization of Equity Markets

Exchange operators, like bankers, are dependent on trust, and its cousin, risk management. For banks and exchanges, their obsession with risk management is rivaled only by that of insurance companies.

The same winds ruffling banking and payments are also affecting equity capital markets. Exchanges, like banks, move and store value, and in the case of banks, the assets are cash, and the rules are driven by the location of the bank. In the case of exchanges, the assets are shares, and the process is more complex, as there are more parties involved; thus, the potential exists to impact more jurisdictions. But before we examine this in more depth, we need to understand the background of exchanges.

For hundreds of years, exchanges were owned by their members, kept in check by the brutally efficient force of self-interest. If they screwed over investors, they went out of business, screwing over companies... the same result! This was predictable behavior enforced by the checks and balances of a properly functioning market.

Member-run exchanges were also quick to adopt technology. The telegraph, the telephone, the networked computer all changed the nature and geographic footprint of exchanges.

At the dawn of the last century, it seemed that every growing city had an exchange. In the UK, Sheffield, Leeds, Newcastle, Liverpool, Manchester, Birmingham, Glasgow, Edinburgh, and Belfast all had vibrant exchanges The U.S. had exchanges in Baltimore, Philadelphia, Boston, San Francisco, Denver and Cincinnati, to name but a few. By the 1980s, technology had driven country-level centralization. In the U.K. and U.S., the benefactors were London and New York.

Over time, the ownership of stock exchanges also became increasingly centralized, while the influence of regional government regulators expanded.[29] In the U.S., a wave of regulatory and structural reforms in the early 2000s triggered significant shifts in the market.[30] A short timeline of this involves the New York Stock Exchange (NYSE) and Nasdaq converting from mutual or member-owned organizations into for-profit, publicly traded firms; part of a broader wave of demutualization and consolidation.[31] As part of this restructuring, in 2006 NYSE merged with electronic exchange Archipelago Exchange, and soon after NYSE became part of NYSE

Group, Inc., reflecting a transformation from a traditional floor-based exchange to a modern, corporate-structured, cross-venue trading group. Furthermore, regulatory and market-structure reforms, such as Regulation NMS (2005), reshaped the U.S. equities market infrastructure, promoting automated, electronic trading, inter-market competition, and a national market system.[32]

Driven by a variety of factors, the new rules fundamentally altered the economics of going public. Suddenly, it only made sense for very large companies to go public, and, as a consequence, U.S. exchanges were forced to adapt their business model. U.S. exchanges increasingly focused on the needs of the largest companies and the most active traders, and the small cap IPO market withered.

Over time, exchange ownership became more centralized, and the role of regional external government regulators grew. In the U.S., the public markets substantially restructured in the early 2000s.[33] The reasons were many, but the wave of new rules forced U.S. exchanges to change their business model. Suddenly, it only made sense for very large companies to go public. U.S. exchanges focused on the needs of the largest companies and the most active traders, and the small cap IPO market withered.

But withering doesn't mean "dead." Businesses evolve. They always do. It turns out that where a company is incorporated need not be the same country where it lists. In fact, about 20% of all IPOs have a HQ in a different jurisdiction than their exchange.[34] "Exchange shopping" was a well-worn path, just one forgotten by the natives of Silicon Valley, who had grown accustomed to the exchanges in New York.

Business leaders are re-discovering that incorporation is just one element of a business. Management can be in another jurisdiction. Customers a third. Intellectual property another. Shareholders yet another. And the places where equity shares trade, exchanges, they too can be located elsewhere.

Equity Exchange transactions often involve many jurisdictions. Think layers. At the top is the company, in the middle the exchange, and at the bottom is the register and custodian. Somewhere in-between are the buyers and sellers. This multi-jurisdictional world view is further complicated, as much of the trading and settlement occurs outside the exchange. It's best to assume that many jurisdictions are likely involved. The era of company, exchange, and investor all being located in the same jurisdiction is as antiquated at the dial-up modem. And yet many regulators are stuck in the past, seemingly oblivious to this reality.

In the mid-2020s, governments increasingly became involved in what companies could list locally. In some cases, they threatened to delist companies; Chinese companies listed in New York are but one example of this. Once again, the threat woke up risk managers and exposed once hidden vectors of uncertainty.

Delisting is inconvenient for all parties, but a far cry from seizure. For seizure, we need to look deeper down the layers. Let's focus on the registrar and the custodian. Think of the registrar as the "keeper of the books" for who owns what, and the custodian as the "safe-keeper" of the actual assets.

The custodian is usually a regulated entity, but like cash or gold, savvy market participants can choose jurisdiction or self-custody. Moving paper shares in and out of the digital world is a huge headache. Legacy registrars with names like Computershare, Equiniti and Continental have little incentive to modernize. In fairness to registrars, they are a huge attack surface for fraud. Why rob a bank when you can simply convince a registrar to update the ownership record to your name?

In a globalized world, where the register or custodian is domiciled does not matter, as long as they subscribe to the agreed application of law. Conversely, in an internationalized world this matters a lot!

Timing also matters. The legacy infrastructure is slow, and delay introduces systemic risk. As a general rule, fast settlement increases trust; slow settlement reduces trust. In a globalized world, the risks from a settlement delay are small because parties can be trusted to eventually settle to pre-defined rules. In an internationalized world rules can change, and thus quick settlement is an important tool to limit risk exposure. The world's public equity infrastructure, sometimes referred to as "rails" is rapidly modernizing to respond to the needs of capital providers.

Capital is international. Wealth is decentralized. Investors are everywhere. They desire a well-run market for direct access to tomorrow's most innovative companies. There is an unmet need for both growth companies too.

Summary

The "stay-private-forever" era is ending. It is time to let public markets fuel growth again, not just have a parade once a company has made it. The coming chapters are about adding optionality and exposing choices. Founders are now able to choose where and when they go public, in the same way that investors can choose where and when to invest.

In this first chapter, we have examined many of the important aspects that are combining to create this new "Era of the Global IPO." These include:

- Capitalism is inherently global. Talent, customers and capital are distributed; no nation dominates all three.
- Macro pressures are re-accelerating the IPOs playbook. Employee liquidity needs, cap-table cleanups, LP fatigue, harder M&A, PE underperformance, and higher interest rates all push companies toward public markets.
- Technology & market structure are enabling new public paths. Internet, mobile retail investors, AI-driven research, tokenization/blockchain, and better rails lower friction around listing and discovery.
- Globalization is giving way to "internationalization."

Geopolitical risk, sanctions, and asset-seizure precedents have eroded trust in single-jurisdiction systems, raising the importance of multi-jurisdictional listings, custodians, and fast settlement.

- Exchanges and post-trade infrastructure must modernize. Centralized exchange economics, legacy registrars/custodians, and slow settlement create jurisdictional risk. Founders now can choose where and how to list to preserve optionality and access global capital.

The next chapter highlights the many benefits of being public, and also considerations for staying private.

Chapter 2
Why Go Public

"Going public is a way to get the capital to do the things you want to do. It's a way to get the currency to make acquisitions. It's a way to give your employees a sense of ownership."
Marc Benioff, Founder & CEO of Salesforce

Benefits of Being Public

Going public should be viewed as a strategic financing with many long-term benefits, not as "an exit." Going public is not an ending; it is another milestone in the growth of a company. The IPO event will certainly raise the profile of the company, but managers should not be nearsighted by focusing on the short-term benefit of IPO capital and publicity.

The purpose of going public is to be public! To strategically position the business, and to leverage the many benefits that the public markets offer. These include the following:

- Enhanced credibility, visibility and prestige
- Better and lower cost access to capital
- Simplification of the cap table
- Liquidity, flexibility and resilience
- More flexibility in attracting and retaining talent

- Pocket acquisitions (M&A)
- Strategic signaling
- Broader investor feedback
- Governance & control

Credibility, Visibility and Prestige

Amazon is a top-five corporation in the Forbes Global 2000,[1] but back in 1997, Jeff Bezos, the founder of the company, was facing a serious credibility problem. Bezos needed to convince people to use their credit cards on the internet, at a time when ecommerce was in its infancy. In order to solve this problem, he turned to the bankers Frank Quattrone and Bill Gurley, with the aim of taking Amazon public. The act of listing raised the profile of the company, and added credibility to the new "category" of online ecommerce.

The strategy was used again in 2004 by Marc Benioff, founder of Salesforce, the cloud-based software pioneer. Back then, the idea of hosting company's software and data offsite was as "scary" as using a credit card on the internet was in 1997. Benioff used his IPO (and subsequent follow-on offerings) to increase the credibility of both his company and the entire category of cloud-based software.[2]

Indeed, the strategy of using a public listing to convey legitimacy was so successful that Salesforce became one of the world's most valuable companies. Salesforce's strategy is cited as a case study in the seminal book on Category Design: *Play Bigger*, published in 2016, and co-authored by Al Ramadan, Dave Peterson, Christopher Lochhead and Kevin Maney.

Being listed has financial benefits, but can also be beneficial when it comes to publicity and marketing. Being listed can attract media attention, and not just from financial media. Journalists are far more likely to cover any founder, company or service offering when they have a base of public documents on which to base their story.

Going public creates greater brand recognition with consumers, potential acquirers, suppliers, and customers. This applies not only to management and the company, but, crucially, also for the company's products. As one company founder told me, "We started getting inbound calls from customers we did not even know existed before the IPO." Going public can provide a powerful opportunity to establish credibility for your category and company. Yet, credibility is not the only reason to list.

Better Access to Capital

An IPO provides efficient access to substantial permanent capital from a diverse spectrum of investors. More important, being public provides ongoing access to capital—both equity and debt. I like to say to anyone that will listen, "You don't go public to raise money; you go public to be public," in that much of the benefit to the company builds over time as the company executes, and as public market investors get to know the company.

As a founder, think of the fundraising process as a private company, compared to a public company. As one founder described it: "Every 18 months, I need to go figure out how VCs are looking at my industry, and then invest six months closing a fair deal." As a public company, a founder can compress this process into days.

One international investor explained to me how quickly this process can be executed: "The banks and management have a good idea of who is looking to get a larger position, trading is halted, notifications distributed and the whole process is wrapped up, often the same day." Debt providers also often see being public as a reason to move faster and offer better debt terms, knowing that the company has the option of raising equity to pay down debt.

This superior access to capital also spills over to the months and quarters before the IPO. Companies who have announced a near-term intent to go public can expect increased fundraising options, also called "optionality." Companies listing outside the U.S. often refinance existing debt, or capitalize on favorable terms secured in a pre-IPO investment.

Capital can be evergreen, referring to permanent, reinvestable equity capital that a public company raises through its IPO and subsequent offerings. Unlike private equity (PE) or venture capital funds, evergreen capital doesn't need to be returned on a fixed timeline and will often participate in follow-on fund raises.

Capital can also be passive. Some investors aim to match the performance of a market index rather than beat it. They typically invest through index funds, exchange-traded funds (ETFs), or other vehicles that hold a fixed basket of securities in proportion to an index. This is becoming increasingly popular; indeed, about half of all investment capital is passive in the contemporary market.[3] Once public, a company can often have a predictable demand for shares, especially once they are included in an index. Passive funds are mandated to buy and hold stock in proportion to its index weight. This creates ongoing demand as an ever-increasing portion of paycheck is allocated to passive funds—every payroll cycle, more money is seeking a home. This ongoing process is ready to support follow-on equity raises or secondary sales. Passive funds often absorb supply without needing a marketing push.

Public markets offer the deepest pools of capital and, as with the railroads of the 1800s, there are multiple capital-intensive emerging technologies. AI, Energy, Electric Aviation, Climate Tech, Advanced Manufacturing and BioTech will all require capital at a scale only public markets can provide.

Simplification of the Cap Table - Elimination of Preference Stack

As a company takes on more private rounds of capital, its cap table and related preference stack becomes more and more complex. This complexity can scare off international investors.[4] Perhaps even more important, multiple share classes creates a brittleness, owing to possible misalignment among investors. It is common for early investors to push for liquidity so they can demonstrate returns (DPI), whereas later investors are incentivized to keep the company private, thus extending their funds' AUM and related fees.[5] From the founder's perspective, each round creates more preference shares that get paid before they see any wealth, which is not typically in the interest of the founder. By contrast, an IPO moves everyone to a single class of stock (or two classes, if there are supervoting founder shares). The process, sometimes called "cap table clean up," aligns all investors, and lays the groundwork for more investment or pocket acquisitions.

Unifying all investors under a single class of stock also allows investors who no longer share the founder's vision to leave. Imagine what might have happened if Intel had been private in the 1980s when it pivoted from memory to CPUs. The company went on to become one of the most valuable companies in the 1090s, but had it been private in the 1980s it may not have been able to raise the required capital. What new VC wants to invest in a company that is pivoting without the support of their existing VC shareholders? Intel would most likely have died, but instead the investors who originally bought into the "memory vision" were able to sell, and were replaced by investors eager to support the growing CPU market. The public market investors who supported Intel in that shift saw their investment increase in value over 8,700%.[6]

Liquidity, Flexibility and Resilience

Public listing offers partial or full liquidity to existing shareholders, providing a path to easily buy or sell their stakes. This liquidity also attracts new investors. For founders, it allows for asset diversification and partial exit, so they can focus on growing the business. The last thing investors want is an ambitious founder to suddenly become timid because they are concerned about their kids' tuition.

For early-stage VCs, liquidity is critical if you hope to raise additional funds. Limited Partners (LPs) willing to re-invest based on purely paper gains are becoming as rare as a populist politician who respects central bank independence. From a societal perspective, early investors, including venture capital and angel investors, often recycle proceeds into new start-ups, seeding the next wave of innovation.

Attract, Motivate, Reward and Retain Top Talent

Publicly listed companies often find it easier to attract and retain top-tier directors and executives. Once listed, Employee Stock Ownership Plans (ESOPs) and stock options have more tangible value. There has been a dearth of IPOs for so long that many start-ups have had difficulty convincing employees to take less cash compensation in favor of equity.[7] Public companies can have an edge there, not just in compensation tools, but also at the tip of the funnel. Founders are often surprised by the increase in volume and quality of their recruiting funnel post IPO.

Pocket Acquisitions (M&A)

As industries mature there tends to be accretive acquisition opportunities. If acquisitions are part of the strategy, being public will be an advantage. The ability to use quoted shares as liquid M&A currency is a negotiation advantage.[8]

Private-on-private transactions are especially hard in venture capital because a transaction often requires restructuring of the preference stack, a process that almost always diverges the interest of the company from those of various classes of shareholders. Inevitably, the private acquiring firm wants to use common stock because it is at the bottom of the preference stack, while the firm being acquired wants to be paid in cash, or if not, then in "top of the stack" most preferred shares. Often these differences are insurmountable, but a public company has "'script" in the form of stock valued by the market every business day. A public company has the flexibility to use shares, cash or a mix of both for acquisitions.

There are also tax implications when using cash. Never underestimate the "tax bill psychology" of the seller. Stock transactions are often taxed later, when they sell the stock, whereas cash transactions are usually taxed immediately, meaning that the seller can be highly sensitive to taking this hit in taxation, even if they are interested in the transaction. The other big problem with paying cash is that employees are less likely to stick around, as opposed to receiving stock that they are incentivised to help increase in value.

An excellent example of that is the network equipment company Cisco, which went public in February 1990 at a valuation of approximately $224 million.[9] The team then went on to make hundreds of acquisitions, and become one of the most valuable technology companies of the era. Imagine the result if instead of using equity to align all newly acquired employees, their options had converted to cash. Without public stock, turnover would have skyrocketed, and value would have been destroyed. As John Chambers, former CEO of Cisco, frequently emphasized, "Employees are the most valuable asset of a company."[10]

Strategic Signaling

We already discussed how an IPO can help transform a company's image from niche operator to category leader. This is generally true when listing on any major exchange. However, there is an added signaling opportunity when going public in a jurisdiction outside the country of incorporation. It signals the company's transition (or intent to transition) from regional player to global aspirant. This can be especially valuable if growth plans depend on international supply chains or customers. Most of the world's business professionals are not early adopters; they would rather do business with a company they perceive as "big" versus an "upstart" which may be gone tomorrow. Being public is a way to signal you are established and here for the long run. Being public globally signals resilience due to diversification across multiple economies.

Greater Control of the Companies Destiny

As one of my investor mentors explained to me, "If a public investor does not like the management, they swap investments. If a private investor doesn't like the management, they swap management." With proper planning, founders can maintain control of their company, and their job. It is now common for founder-led IPOs to adopt a dual-class structure, with super-voting rights for the founder's shares.[11]

It is also important to note that as a private company, investors usually have a timetable for exit. These investors may push for a sub-optimal sale of the company due to their internal timetables. As a liquid public company, management can focus on building shareholder value, not tailoring strategy to the needs of private fund managers, and their fund-funding cycles.

Broader Investor Feedback

Public companies can receive more diverse feedback than companies that stay private. A public company has a larger and more varied group of investors, each with different perspectives and time horizons. Conversations with long-only funds, hedge funds, international funds and sector specialists provide management with deep insight into market expectations, regional regulatory trends and competitor positioning.

One supportive shareholder once described this additional insight to me as "extra-sensory organs." He explained that a good investor is like a tentacle, out in the world, exploring and relaying back information they think might be useful for the founder. I concur; As a serial founder, I have found that kind of input helpful, especially when navigating markets so different from my home market.

I am not the only founder to benefit from investor feedback. In 2011, Facebook's user growth on desktop was slowing, mobile usage was surging, and the company's app experience lagged badly.[12] Facebook risked losing relevance. Several investors pressed Mark Zuckerberg to prioritize mobile development. Zuckerberg initially resisted "mobile-first" thinking, but eventually agreed to make mobile a core strategic focus.

By 2012, mobile advertising became Facebook's primary revenue driver, once again highlighting the value of investor feedback.[13]

There are many examples of companies changing strategy based on investor feedback. These include Adobe's transition from boxed software to SaaS,[14] Netflix pivoting away from the Qwikster acquisition to refocus on streaming and content,[15] and Microsoft's pivot toward Azure and subscriptions.[16] These transformational strategies might have been missed without a chorus of outside voices.

For a public company, feedback comes in many forms, including in real-time in the form of price and ongoing commentary. I like to say that, "A founder's job is to listen to diverse advice and then figure out what seemingly good advice to ignore." Being public is a good feedback loop if a company has strong leadership.

Governance & Control

Founders often associate IPOs with loss of control, but going public can formalize and institutionalize governance in ways that protect long-term founder vision. One critical element is alignment of the hold period. Most venture funds are 10-year vehicles, and fund managers are under pressure from Limited Partners (LPs) to return capital in that timeframe. This introduces a subtle but profound distortion in decision-making: unnatural forced liquidity timing and misaligned time horizons. Companies feel pressure to sell prematurely, not because it's best for business, but because VCs owe returns to LPs and need to exit to be in a position to raise their next fund.

As one Silicon Valley founder who listed his company in London described it to me: "You're still running your company." He also contrasted this with other exits: "Once you're sold to a strategic, basically you're just incorporated. You know, your company's dead. They might have bought you for an Acqui hire. They might have done it for some other reason, but essentially, your freedom to run your company your way has gone, and then you exit. If instead you sell to PE, then, frankly, at that point, you're just sort of being managed by children with spreadsheets. And, I mean, it's not a fun experience."

A well-designed IPO should be a catalyst for aligning the founder vision with the long-term interests of shareholders.

Benefits Begin Before the IPO

Many benefits of being public begin when a management team *starts* to take IPO readiness seriously. Attracting talent, negotiating acquisitions, and accessing capital all become easier. At our fund, we like to say, "Valuation is driven by optionality, and a credible plan to go public means any other option has to be that much better."

Public Markets Are The Big Leagues

One of the most compelling arguments for going public is there is about 8x the investable capital of private markets. The public market represents a much deeper and more diverse pool of investors.

The Argument for Staying Private

Nonetheless, it's worth noting that being publicly traded isn't for everyone. It comes with additional regulatory compliance, cost, and reporting requirements, as well as increased scrutiny from the public, regulators, media, and investors. Conversely, that increased scrutiny can also help raise standards across multiple areas of a company.

The availability of private capital allows high-potential companies to stay private longer and raise their funding outside of the public market. There are several considerations when evaluating the strategic benefit of being public, including:

- Revenue predictability

- Costs, distraction & scale
- Lower governance requirements
- Secrecy
- Lower regulatory profile
- Weak leadership

Let's examine each.

Revenue Predictability

The public market overvalues predictability and hates surprises. If the core engine of your business is highly unpredictable, or you are still figuring out your business model, finding a small group of specialty private investors has its advantages. The best public companies have a stable core and lots of potential upside. It is equally important that management can articulate both elements of the upside. This is surprisingly rare.

Costs, Distraction & Scale

Public companies, especially companies listed in the U.S., are subject to a thicket of regulation, litigation risk, and additional reporting requirements. Although these costs are generally significantly lower outside the U.S., especially litigation-related expenses, there are still benefits to staying private.[17]

It is important that any company intending to go public plans to have sufficient scale by the time of their IPO. They must have sufficient resources for the cost of being public to be immaterial. For companies listing in the U.S., this tends to be measured in multiple billions of dollars of market capitalization. It therefore follows that for many well-regulated non-US exchanges, appropriate scale tends to kick in when a company's market cap starts to be measured in hundreds of millions.

Lower Governance Requirements

Private companies have more flexibility on governance.

Many would argue that sloppy governance results in lower valuation over the long-term, but there could be strategic reasons not to disclose ownership or inner workings. One example of this is that a private company does not have to disclose related-party transactions. This opacity could benefit the company if key relationships are critical to its competitive advantage.

Secrecy

Sometimes a business is working so well that it is preferable to avoid attracting competition. A good example is ByteDance, which honed its recommendation engine quietly in China, before exporting it via the social platform TikTok. The company downplayed its global ambitions, and kept its algorithms proprietary and opaque.[18] A public listing would have exposed its scale and drawn competitive fire from Meta, Google, and new venture-backed start-ups. The company wisely stayed private, and by the time Western incumbents and their backers had woken up, TikTok was already dominating user attention.

Lower Regulatory Profile

For companies disrupting regulated industries, another reason to stay private is to keep a lower profile. If your technology is going to displace taxi drivers, hotels, family farms or union employees, do you really want to draw attention before establishing a large, vocal base of satisfied customers?

In its early years, Uber operated in legal gray zones, and it was sometimes outright illegal under certain city taxi laws where the company was operational.[19] As a response to this, Uber utilized a "launch first, fight later" tactic to scale demand and driver supply before regulators could respond. As a public company, Uber would have had to disclose regulatory risks in each market, giving opponents ammunition and possibly preventing expansion.[20] By the time the regulatory spotlight was unavoidable, Uber had already become indispensable to riders in dozens of cities.

AirBnB has a similar story. Hotel industry lobbyists hated the competition and *eventually* fought hard to limit consumer choice.[21] Fortunately for AirBnB, hotel lobbyists were late to understand the threat and their job was made much harder by the millions of satisfied clients and hosts AirBnB had already connected. AirBnB and Uber both benefited by staying private, keeping a lower regulatory profile and getting scale before going public.

Weak Leadership

The management of a public company is under constant pressure to balance the short-term demand for growth with strategies that achieve long-term goals. Founders who can't articulate their long-term vision and justify near-term investment should not move into the public market. The annual shareholder letter from Jeff Bezos is an excellent example of how to attract the right public investors. For many years, Bezos clearly articulated why Amazon was deferring profitability as a continuous trade-off for long-term growth.[22] Amazon went on to become one of the most valuable companies in the world, and investors who shared his vision were rewarded with a massive return of over 187,000%.[23]

Private companies are not subject to the intense media and investor-relation demands that begin just in advance of the IPO and continue post-listing. For more circumspect and less confident CEOs, staying private offers an opportunity to stay out of public scrutiny. The public markets are "the major leagues," and quite frankly, some founders' egos, vision, drive and/or intellect are just not up to the task.

Summary

In this chapter we have examined many of the benefits and considerations when exploring a public marker pathway, including:

- Going public is strategic, not an exit—an IPO is a mile-

stone that strengthens long-term positioning and financing.
- Public listing builds credibility and visibility. It legitimizes both the company and its category (e.g., Amazon, Salesforce).
- Public companies access the deepest pools of 'evergreen' capital-efficient, ongoing access to large, diverse, and even passive investor pools.
- IPOs simplify ownership by unifying investors under one class of shares, reducing misalignment, and easing future financings or acquisitions.
- Investor feedback reshapes strategy. Public markets provide real-time signals that have driven major pivots (e.g., Adobe, Netflix, Microsoft).
- Being public creates an intelligence feedback loop.
- IPO benefits start with preparation. Many advantages (talent, M&A optionality, capital) begin as soon as a company takes IPO readiness seriously.

Investors, companies and the public in general have a lot to gain from the re-emergence of the IPO. But many falsehoods and misconceptions have also taken root. We address some of the more common myths and misconceptions in the following chapter.

Chapter 3
Myths & Misconceptions

After four centuries of viewing stock exchanges as local institutions, and two decades in which public markets ceded ground to private capital, misconceptions about the modern IPO have taken hold. Particularly around multi-jurisdictional listings, within the venture industry, and among a new generation of founders.

Recency Bias

The bursting of the dotcom bubble, and the subsequent regulation response, created a generation of investors deathly afraid of premature IPOs. As a consequence, the following generation of founders and venture capitalists never experienced a world where IPOs were both early in a company's life, and frequent in society.

Specialization

The VC world is notoriously specialized, and few of today's operators have any real IPO experience, especially on a global scale. For the industry to evolve, operators need to build global capital market relationships, in the same way past generations of VCs had strong relationships with U.S. East Coast investment banks.

Historic Geographic Bias

For thousands of years, most humans died within 20 miles of where they were born. The digitally-interconnected world has changed a lot, but human brains have not. Human bias is towards the people they meet in their daily life. It's easy to forget the billions of customers, millions of investors, thousands of bankers and hundreds of exchanges outside your local geography.

IPO Bogeyman Narrative

The zero interest rate environment (ZIRP) of the 2010s, especially post-2008, created the perfect conditions for a new narrative to take root: IPOs are a headache, and staying private is smarter.[1]

The first two decades of the 21st Century were characterized by higher regulatory frictions associated with going public.[2] Many of those frictions have been reduced through technology and competition between listing jurisdictions, but the misguided narrative of "Stay private longer; public markets bad" remains.[3]

Some of this wariness was justified, but it is important to note that there were many parties who benefited from pushing, or continuing to push, this narrative. For example, deep-pocketed investors and their portfolio companies. Superior capital access became a competitive moat, and the big players went to great lengths to pull up the drawbridge. This reduced IPO activity, and capital became a weapon. If you were backed by SoftBank, Tiger, or Coatue, you could fund a strategy that burned billions to acquire users, subsidize services, or scale rapidly. If you didn't have this backing, then you were effectively excluded.

Late-stage funds were able to deploy vast amounts of capital, charging management fees far in excess of anything a professional public market investor would be able to deliver. Limited partners (LPs) liked their paper markups and the lack of accountability associated with the volatility of the public markets. Early venture capitalists (VCs) also benefited as extended fund life resulted in a longer stream of fees. These early VCs also were able to monetize their participation rights, as they created fee-generating special purpose vehicles (SPVs) with each new funding round.

Meanwhile, secondary markets like Forge gave the largest unicorns liquidity without going public. Insiders were able to collect transaction economics on secondary shares, far in excess of fees possible in a transparent market. So the IPO became not a milestone, but a kind of boogeyman.

Almost inevitably, this rapidly evolving marketplace has caused confusion, and some of the most common misconceptions we hear from venture capitalists and founders will be discussed in the following section.

Myth 1: You Need To Be Big To Go Public

False: It all depends on where you list. It turns out that greed works, and there are lots of investors on the hunt for exceptional companies. Unfortunately for smaller companies, the U.S. equity markets have evolved into mega-cap markets.[4] Sophisticated investors recognize that a small company listing in the U.S. has structural disadvantages, higher costs and greater litigation exposure relative to remaining private or listing abroad. Smaller companies can list earlier in their growth cycle if they choose an exchange that is appropriate for their size. This smaller company exchange role was once filled by the Nasdaq, who, as they boasted in the early '80s, "Could list a company until they were big enough to list on the NYSE Big Board." Now, the role of connecting smaller growth companies with investors can be fulfilled by exchanges outside the U.S. in the same way companies that have grown too large for the international exchanges can list in the U.S. to connect with the biggest investors.

Attracting long-term institutional investors is critical for a public company. Back in the 1990s, when hundreds of companies went public in the U.S. each year, there was a wide range of active institutional investors.[5] They would roll up their sleeves and do the hard work needed to understand a public offering. But the world has changed. Those U.S. funds got too big to pay attention to small offerings.[6]

Ironically, if you go to these same U.S. institutions as an international issuance, and you talk to a different portfolio manager, suddenly you can attract their attention. But the reason you're talking is because you're viewed, not as a "too small" U.S. listing, but instead as a "sizable" international listing. A $500-million market cap company going public in Australia or London gets a lot of attention from investors. That same issuance, for that *exact same* company in the U.S. would attract no attention.[7]

Long-term price support for smaller companies means less dilution for insiders looking to grow the company and access the capital markets in the future.

Myth 2: Companies Must List In Their Home Country

False: About 20% of all IPOs are cross-border, meaning the headquarters and the exchange are in different jurisdictions, according to Ernst & Young.[8] It is quite common, especially as digital trading and AI-based information analysis becomes increasingly accessible.

Companies can go public outside of their home country for a variety of reasons. Some companies may choose to do this to access a larger pool of capital, as the stock exchange in another country may have more investors and a deeper market than the exchange in their home country. Additionally, going public on a foreign stock exchange can also increase a company's visibility and brand recognition, which can help to attract customers and talent.

You should expect to see more U.S. companies listed abroad as LPs realize they want more transparency and liquidity, and as founders realize an IPO is strategic evergreen capital. In fact, it is capital that unlocks all sorts of opportunities and corporate flexibility.

Another reason for going public on foreign stock exchanges is that the company is not size-appropriate for listing on their home country exchange. For example, U.S. companies should usually not consider listing in the U.S. until their revenue can be measured in hundreds of millions or even billions, yet this figure is more than adequate for most of the world's top exchanges.

Companies may also choose to go public outside of their home country in order to diversify their investor base, and reduce their dependence on domestic investors. However, going public outside of a company's home country can be more complex and costly than going public domestically.[9] The company may need to comply with different regulations and accounting standards, and may also need to have their financial statements audited by a different auditing firm.[10]

Myth 3: The U.S. is Always the Best Market

False: Size matters. There may be no better place to list if a company has a $10-billion+ valuation. The U.S. public markets are the mega-cap envy of the world.[11] The valuations are full. The rules are clear. The speed of the rising secondary capital is unparalleled. The costs are *de minimis* relative to a large market cap. The largest companies enjoy index inclusion, further supporting deep pools of liquidity.

If you are the CEO of a $10-billion+ private company, you can stop reading. Congratulations, this book is not for you. It is for leaders still on the path of becoming a decacorn. And it is for investors who want to identify companies *before* they grow into decacorns.

The grim reality is that the U.S. public markets are horrible for companies smaller than $2-billion market cap.[12] One of the major reasons for this is that going public is hugely expensive relative to company size. And what's even worse for a busy, fast-growing company; the undertaking is long, tedious and hugely distracting. The process robs senior management of their most precious resource: time. Being public at this size is no better. Litigation is common. Liquidity is limited. Another problem is that in the U.S, $2 billion companies are too small to attract much index inclusion or institutional support.[13]

Yet, because of many institutional investors' massive size, smaller Silicon Valley-based companies often get *more* attention if they IPO outside the U.S. The U.S. public markets do a poor job of supporting companies smaller than $2-billion market cap. One investor told me, "Listing a billion-dollar company in the U.S. is a fast path to becoming a $400-million market cap company." You should expect to see more U.S. companies listed abroad as LPs demand more transparency and liquidity, and as founders realize an IPO is strategic evergreen capital.

Myth 4: Valuation Multiples Outside the U.S. Are Inferior

False: Our investment team hears this a lot, but the data does not hold up, because again, size matters. Most people look at U.S. multiples and include the Magnificent 7. Sounds great, and it is if you are listing a $100B+ market cap company. But look at smaller companies and the multiple data starts to look more homogenized. Once you exclude Apple, Microsoft, Alphabet, Amazon, Meta, Nvidia and Tesla, listing location matters less.

The best way to think about multiples is to look at companies with similar revenue, margin and growth. Here, the data is much less conclusive on any specific day, with the key observation being "any specific day." Markets are notoriously efficient over time, and valuation multiple arbitrage tends to disappear over days, weeks or months. Choosing a stock exchange based on the multiples this quarter makes as much sense as choosing a heating system based on this afternoon's weather!

A longer-term view is necessary, and once listed on a top global exchange, your shares are accessible to most institutional investors, regardless of location. A well-run investor relations process matters much more than today's multiples. Over time, story, fundamentals and execution should take precedence over listing venues, as they drive price.

Myth 5: Private Capital is Cheaper, or IPOs Are Just About Funding

False: Let's unpack that. Sometimes the exception does not prove the rule. We all hear about the company that brought in capital at a huge valuation. These stories make for headlines, but the reality is often more nuanced. Journalists and outsiders seldom have details about the impact of the preference stack, the debt equity mix, or how much of the investment was primary vs secondary. For example: If I believe your company is worth $800 million, I am happy to buy $20 million of preferred shares at a $2-billion valuation, provided the company also takes on $200 million of debt from me at 18% interest rate. Another deal structure involves giving the investor 2X liquidation preference and a guaranteed 8% dividend. In yet another scenario, the investor buys $200 million from early investors at a $400 million valuation, then invests another $20 million at $2 billion. In all three cases, the news headline is "Company raises $220 million at $2 billion pre," yet in all three cases the reality is much darker.

Exceptional valuations in the private market do happen. It is important to remember that just because a late-stage private round offers a higher valuation than what a company might fetch in the public markets doesn't mean that the capital is cheaper over the long run. What will that next round of capital cost if the lead investor signals an unwillingness to invest further? What is the cost of the added liquidation preference if the company has a setback? These are important considerations.

It is easy for founders to underestimate how the preference overhang compounds across rounds, and to therefore misjudge the *effective* cost of that capital.[14] In the end, capital raising is only one dimension. Going public creates a currency for acquisitions, improves brand credibility, facilitates employee retention through liquidity, and allows access to lower cost of capital over time.[15]

Myth 6: It's Too Much Reporting To Be Public

False: Again, size matters. Once a company is a decacorn, it has teams to deal with all the administrative frictions. Smaller companies can list where the level of reporting is appropriately sized for the stage of the company.

Another big difference in the U.S. is quarterly reports. Many exchanges only require bi-annual reporting,[16] although a firm may opt for quarterly as a mechanism to deepen relationships with institutions.

In the U.S., quarterly reports have become so prescribed as regulatory reporter reports and regulatory filings that these documents have become very much boilerplate, filled with legalese. They've become less useful in practical terms, but more important and expensive to create and distribute[17]. I recently looked at a regulatory filing, and there were several pages included in the document before it actually explained what the business does! Some describe it as "disclosing so much you disclose nothing." How is this sensible? How is this in the best interest of investors?

It is not just the length of disclosure, it's also the frequency. Quarterly, "batches" of filings result in a legal scrubbing where everything is reviewed by teams of lawyers. This increases costs, but also changes the tone. One portfolio manager described it as "going from reading *Bonfire of the Vanities* to the ingredients label on the back of a cereal box." Other countries use a framework called "continuous disclosure." In their well-run markets if something material happens to a company it is promptly disclosed. No teams of lawyers, obfuscating over piles of paper, just information quickly distributed to the market. This approach is much more in line with the 24-hour trading world we're moving towards.

In 2025 (and previously in 2018) the U.S. president proposed that US-listed public companies should stop being required to file quarterly financial reports with the SEC and instead report twice a year (semiannual reporting). If markets like Canada, London, Australia and Hong Kong are any guide, continuous disclosure seems to reduce regulatory burden.

It is possible that continuous disclosure and optional semi-annual reporting gets implemented in the U.S. For now, U.S. companies looking for a more open, less litigious and easier stock exchange, best look abroad.

Frank, ongoing conversations with the market work. Markets are efficient to the extent that they reflect all available information. When companies continuously disclose, there are fewer surprises, this enables investors to reprice risk and growth prospects in real-time, improving capital allocation and investor participation.

Batching is inefficient. Whether it's industrial parts, toothpaste, software updates, or quarterly reports, grouping work into large batches creates delays and hides problems. A better approach is continuous flow. This principle is central to what later became known as "*lean,*" a philosophy rooted in the teachings of W. Edwards Deming.[18]

Myth 7: An IPO Prospectus Is Too Much Work

False: Litigation and regulation has taken the joy out of reading a U.S. prospectus—dense legalese does not make for fun reading. In 1980, the entire Apple IPO prospectus was 35 pages; by 2025, the average U.S. S-1 Prospectus was about 300 pages.[19] Some modern U.S. prospectuses have pages of legal disclaimers before it even says what the underlying company does.

In other markets, regulators have realized the benefit of prospectuses that are more engaging. For example, a prospectus for an Australian listing reads like a marketing brochure in plain English, with pictures and diagrams. This difference is important because it can engage a larger, more diverse group of investors, and it also means that the drafting process is not dominated by expensive lawyers.

Myth 8: You Need To Restructure Or Re-Incorporate To List Abroad

False: Companies do not need to re-domicile.[20] Often the advice to re-domicile is a sign of an uninformed lawyer or accountant. We sometimes see local bankers trying to sell a listed shell company; for bankers, the profit margins on so-called "RTO transactions" (Reverse Takeover) can be lucrative. The problem is that they deprive management the opportunity of building a proper relationship with investors via a normal "front door" IPO. RTOs often result in inheriting legacy shareholders that will most likely add selling pressure in the future.

That said, if a company expects to restructure for strategic, geopolitical, tax or governance reasons in the longer term, it's best to complete that transformation before moving into the public market. Certain types of restructuring are easier when there are fewer shareholders or may not be possible when public. Some IPO investors view "We'll fix that later" as a red flag.

Myth 9: Going Public Means Losing Control

False: While public companies face greater scrutiny and governance standards, founders often retain significant control, especially with dual-class share structures.[21] By the 2020s, most global exchanges and their regulators had realized they needed dual-class shares to attract the most ambitious, high-potential founders. Institutional investors increasingly respect the importance of a founder's vision, especially in industries with rapid technological disruption.

Myth 10: The Public Markets Are Too Short-Term Focused

False: This is often a scapegoat for poor communication, or lack of strategic clarity. The best public companies (e.g., AMZN, NVDA, TSLA) have clearly articulated, long-term visions, and have thus educated the market accordingly.

Most VCs claim to be "patent capital," but that song changes when their investors are ready for an exit. PE by its nature is designed for relatively quick returns in just a few years. Public capital can ideally serve long-term public benefit. A PE-backed company is optimized for peak profitability in five years, but a publicly-funded company can be designed to enrich for fifty—there are very different timescales involved.

Public Institutions can be very patient, provided that they get a coherent narrative and consistent execution.

Myth 11: Going Public is a Fast Path to Litigation

False: Another big problem in the U.S. is litigation. Since regulatory changes enacted after Enron, U.S. trial attorneys have found a money tree in suing U.S. companies listed in the U.S.[22] Suing foreign companies listing in the U.S. has proven less lucrative. As a consequence, U.S. companies going public in the U.S. should budget hundreds of thousands of dollars just for directors and officers insurance. Many companies get sued. Some studies estimate 20% of all IPOs result in a class action lawsuit.[23] It's a huge distraction for all involved. Shareholders should want their innovative entrepreneurs focusing on changing their industry, not depositions and legal expense management. Litigation is generally value destructive.

Outside the U.S., litigation is rare, which allows companies to focus on value creation. For example, from 2013 to 2023, there were about 3,225 securities class-action lawsuits in the U.S., compared with five in the U.K.![24] Shareholders in U.K.-listed companies benefit because resources are directed at growing the business instead of litigation. Perhaps equally important, a dearth in litigation results in management being more willing to talk with investors! The result is better price discovery and more engaged investors.

Myth 12: IPOs are Exits, an Endgame

False: Going public isn't the finish line. It's just another tool, a way to raise capital, enhance reputation and scale faster. The IPO isn't the end of the story, it's a mile-marker on a much longer road. Too many founders treat it like they've arrived, when really, they're just entering the big leagues. Amazon, Apple, Microsoft, Nvidia and Oracle are good examples—they all built their real value after going public.

Myth 13: Public Companies Can't Innovate

False: Innovation constraints stem from culture, incentives and leadership, not listing status. Amazon, Google, and Apple are paragons of scaled innovation as public companies. Public currency enables greater innovation via talent attraction, R&D scale, and M&A agility.

Myth 14: You Have To Be Profitable To Go Public

False: What you should have is a credible path to profitability, not current GAAP or cash flow profits. Capital markets have long embraced high-growth, high-burn companies (e.g., Salesforce, Snowflake) if the unit economics, TAM, and execution are convincing. Profitability on IPO Day 1 is not required, especially for tech and biotech.[25]

Myth 15: There Is Too Much Volatility In Public Markets

False: Volatility laundering refers to the *illusion* that lower risk is created by holding an asset in a fund that is only priced periodically and with incomplete information. The cohort of private companies is generally smaller, has more debt and also has inferior access to capital.[26] The idea that this cohort would be *less volatile* defies common sense. I call this "head in the sand" investing—just because you can't see the change in value does not mean it has not happened.

Pension boards, endowments, and outsourced chief investment officers prefer the illusion of a smooth ride. Volatility laundering caters to this preference, but as the legendary investor Howard Marks points out, this is a "denominator effect" problem—people believe portfolios are safer because private "marks" look steady, until liquidity crunches force sales at true market prices. Cliff Asness (from AQR) has written extensively about this, arguing that the "myth of low volatility" in private markets is essentially a statistical mirage.[27]

Jeff Bezos addressed this issue directly in his 2000 Amazon shareholder letter, after his stock collapsed in the dotcom bust. Amazon stock was down roughly 80–90% from its previous peak. In this letter, Bezos reminded everyone that the stock price is not the company. He said "So, if the company is better positioned today than it was a year ago, why is the stock price so much lower than it was a year ago?"[28] He went on to explain why Amazon was actually in a better position than it was a year ago, despite a plummeting stock price. Bezos argued that large swings were inevitable for an innovative, high-growth company, and that investors needed to have the temperament to withstand them. Some investors pulled out, but those that stayed in on Amazon benefited handsomely. As the famed investor Benjamin Graham said: "In the short-term, the stock market is a voting machine; in the long-term, it's a weighing machine."

Myth 16: Trading Happens on an Exchange

False: Once upon a time, shares were taken to the floor of an exchange and traded. That world is long gone. Although a share may be authorized for trading or quoted by an exchange, modern trading is much more sophisticated... and global. Consider that years ago you needed a human in a city to make transactions happen, far removed from the age of technology that exists today. Nonetheless, this outdated mental model still impedes the making of money. The reality is that equities (and their derivatives) trade *everywhere*! Darkpools, Electronic Communication Networks (ECNs), crossing networks, over-the-counter, Multilateral Trading Facility

(MTF), peer-to-peer, Alternative Trading Systems (ATS), and so much more.

Telecommunications, technology, protocols and greed make markets liquid. Boards that think only local investors can access local exchanges are missing out on the interconnected nature of modern finance.

Myth 17: There Is No Liquidity Outside The U.S.

False: The proper question is, Compared to what? Compared to a company the size of Exxon, sure. Over 99% of all the world's exchanges can't meet that level of liquidity, but 99.9% of all companies are smaller than Exxon. You need to think of liquidity based on your financial size. Liquidity across markets tends to depend on the specific nature of the company much more than the company's choice of listing venue.

Another mistake is trying to compare liquidity across public markets, when a more relevant comparison is public versus private secondary markets. Again, size matters, as liquidity discount and closing time differ drastically based on company size, but in almost all cases, public liquidity (and block trade discounts, if any) is significantly superior.

Many investors mistakenly look at daily trading volume and then divide the size of their position and assume this is how to look at liquidity. That is wrong for two reasons. First, in a modern era, much of the trading volume occurs off the exchange.[29] Second, and more important in many markets, quality bankers will know who would be a buyer if a large block of shares became available. This is especially true of pensions in countries with young populations—with each payroll cycle more money needs to find a home.

Myth 18: There is No Equity Research Anymore

False: In this area, geography matters a lot. It is true that quality equity research in the U.S. has regressed since the 2000s—

turns out some brilliant regulator thought the markets would be better with less content. Brilliant! I'm looking at you, Eliot Spitzer. He was the N.Y. State Attorney who felt the world would operate better if investors had *less* information about companies, a highly curious notion, particularly in today's Information Age. Of course, research is biased, as it continues to be compiled by subjective humans. Even AI-based research will contain bias. But are investors really better off with less research? Unfortunately, other jurisdictions decided to follow the U.S. lead with the introduction of the MiFid legal framework in Europe,[30] and by extension the U.K.

The good news is that these rules only impact select institutions, both research producers and consumers. Those regulatory-constrained institutions are increasingly less relevant as new banks, jurisdictions and investor types hunt for equity returns. And independent research platforms (e.g., Stratosphere, Value Investors Club, Substack analysts) have stepped up to help fill the intellectual vacuum left by the commoditization of traditional big bank research. In fairness, there are still some outstanding equity research departments inside of banks, they just have become few and far between.

New datasets are also being used to generate new forms of equity research. Satellite imagery, credit card data, and web traffic are all being turned into research products. Let a thousand opinions bloom!

A family office, for example, will happily look at any research, generated anywhere, to better understand a potential investment. Why worry about the regulated exchange of research between top banks and the largest institutions when the market, and associated research products, have moved on?

Furthermore, with AI and global talent sourcing the cost of producing high-quality research. Artificial Intelligence is unlocking whole new ways to identify and analyze equities. In some jurisdictions, a listed company can even hire an analyst to publish equity research.

Myth 19: Good Bankers Won't Pay Attention To Smaller Companies

False: Outside the U.S., there are investment banks that specialize in smaller IPOs.[31] In the U.S., there was an era when the top bankers, people like Frank Quattrone and Mary Meeker, paid close attention to small new IPOs. Super-small companies (at the time) like Intel and Cisco got high levels of service from highly competent people.

Today, it's hard for a banker in the U.S. to make money with small caps, while the very best talent has moved to other parts of the market. Contrast this with the situation internationally, where there are outstanding bankers who would crawl on glass for an issue as small as $50 million. (If you talk to an American banker, few will even get out of bed for a $100 million issuance.) Small IPO bankers exist in the U.S., but they are often not of the same stature as you would find abroad for a comparable-sized IPO.

Myth 20: Indexes Don't Matter Or Are Unattainable

False: This is an enormously dangerous myth. Indexes do matter and they are attainable. Founders should seek to get into an index, as it drastically expands the investor buying base, and over time should improve valuation.[32]

Globally, there has been a big move into "passive," meaning that they don't look at things until the company has been included in an index. This does not support the U.S. IPO process. Most U.S.-traded companies need to be over $9 billion market capitalization to be index-eligible,[33] whereas overseas it is a different story. Many top global indexes, such as the ASX 200 and FTSE 350, are eager to include companies with valuations under $2 billion,[34] and numerous local specialty indexes include companies with market capitalizations as small as a few hundred million. Some have argued that because many stocks are indexed by market capitalization, passive indexing pushes money into the largest firms, regardless of whether the companies are performing well. Like most things in investing, "past performance does not guarantee future performance," but, regardless, companies are smart to have a strategy that supports passive capital. In a world in which about 50% of all investment capital is deployed via passive investment funds,[35] founders and board members are smart to consider size-appropriate listing venues. Venues that support passive capital sooner, rather than later.

Myth 21: Stocks Need To Be Quoted In My Currency

False: Many novice investors believe that when they buy a stock quoted in a foreign currency, they are taking a position in that currency. This notion is superficial and incomplete. The reality is that every equity investment is taking a position in all the currencies that companies use to conduct business. Equity investment is ultimately a claim on future cash flows. For example, a software company that bills clients in USD that has back-office operations in Canadian dollars, but is quoted in pounds sterling, should adjust based on the cash flows of the business.

The currency markets are the most liquid in the world,[36] and companies that clearly explain the currency of their operations may find additional liquidity in the form of currency hedge funds looking for arbitrage opportunities.

For professional investors, the growth and quality of the equity matters much more than the currency used to quote the ticker.[37] Don't worry, modern back offices know how to translate performance into the currency used to pay the portfolio manager their bonus!

Summary

The myths debunked in this chapter tend to center around habits—habits of memory (recency bias), of practice (specialization) and of sight (geographic bias), which are reinforced by economic incentives that have rewarded staying private.

An IPO is a strategic tool, not an exit or an item of finality.

The right market depends on specifics, and is reliant on company size, investor mix, and long-term ambition. Listing outside your home country is frequently rational and preferable, but it's important to understand that reporting regimes and litigation environments differ significantly across jurisdictions. Investors and advisors would be well advised to abandon their discredited *echo-chamber assumptions*, and engage with the full set of options that the modern interconnected global public market offers.

The preceding pages have dismantled the myths of modern markets. Now we turn to history, not out of nostalgia, but to uncover clues. The next chapter explores the history of capital markets to build a framework for anticipating what comes next.

Chapter 4
Historical Perspective

"The farther backward you can look, the farther forward you are likely to see."
Winston Churchill

In this chapter, we provide a historical perspective to better empower the reader to navigate the future. Barring an AI singularity, the nature of human behavior, market dynamics and geopolitical patterns tend to outlast each human generation. For investors, it's a reminder that while exact circumstances may differ, structural forces like greed, fear, innovation, and overreach recur with recognizable signatures.

"History doesn't repeat itself, but it often rhymes."
Mark Twain

The age of stock exchanges around the world varies greatly. Some of the oldest stock exchanges include the Amsterdam Stock Exchange, which was established in 1602, when the Dutch East India Company began issuing shares and trading began on a formalized exchange in Amsterdam,[1] and the London Stock Exchange, which dates back to the late 1700s.[2] The New York Stock Exchange, established in 1792, is another one of the oldest.[3]

On the other hand, there are newer stock exchanges, such as the NASDAQ, which was founded in 1971,[4] and the Shenzhen Stock Exchange, which was established in 1990.[5] The Singapore Exchange Limited (SGX) was established in 1999.[6] There new exchanges—such as The Long Term Stock Exchange (LTSE),[7] Texas Stock Exchange (TXSE).[8] and Global Growth Market,[9] all in planning at the time of this book's publication.

At a high level, the history of stock exchanges can be characterized by the mood and interests of investors. Each era has its own characteristics.

1600s: The Dutch Golden Age & Birth of Public Equities
1700s: British and French Mercantile Empires
1850s: Railroads & Industrialization
1880s: Trusts and Consolidation
1890s: Panics & Gold Standard Tensions
1910s: War Economies & Utilities
1920s: Credit & Tech Consumerism - Roaring Twenties
1950s: European stocks
1960s: Nifty Fifty
1970s: Emerging markets
1980s: Japanese Stocks
1990s: American Technology
2000s: Emerging markets/Commodities
2010s: American Mega Caps
2020s: Globally-listed companies

What remains consistent across history is the presence of dominant investor narratives. Each era is defined by a prevailing consensus—that is until that collective perception fractures, triggering a transition to a new market paradigm. Today, we are entering a new paradigm, as we transition to a more interconnected, abundant and information-aware world. Historically, markets needed to centralize in one location, whereas today the markets are distributed.

Stock exchanges are the ultimate double-sided marketplace. Superior inventory of securities attracts diverse investors, while a deep pool of investors attracts more companies looking for capital. The network-effects lead to centralization of the market.

However, networks have always been constrained by the available technology. In the 1800s, the "technology" was meeting face-to-face, which is why physical buildings played such a critical role. The scope of the market was constrained by travel. Next came the era of the telegraph, and then the telephone. These tools built new networks that were national in culture and language.

Our future is not about phones, any more than it is about physically meeting. The future is about computers, AI and the internet. The network is now global, as is the distribution of wealth. It therefore follows logically that the winning exchange, the one with the winning network-effects, must be global.

Exchanges must specialize on their specific security and then pursue every investor who may have an interest in that security. It is the only way to win the "network effects" race for exchanges: have the largest selection of a certain type of security.

Exchanges tended to centralize over time to achieve the network effects critical to markets. This was always because of the available technology: Face-to- face to telegraph, telegraph to phone, phone to networked computer. But today's technology is different in its availability to be decentralized and distributed.

In the UK, prior to 1973, Sheffield, Leeds, Newcastle, Liverpool, Manchester, Birmingham, Glasgow, Edinburgh and Belfast all had exchanges.[10] In the U.S. a similar story played out—Cleveland, Philadelphia, San Francisco, Detroit and Chicago were all proud of their local offering. These exchanges are all gone today. The nature of markets is to seek the best execution, and the network effects then become the market.

Today, the same thing is happening, but at a global level. The internet, mobile-computing, 24-hour trading, APIs and Artificial Intelligence are connecting formerly fragmented providers of liquidity. Technology is connecting investors and companies globally, in the same way that the telegraph and the telephone drove connections in earlier eras.

The Role of Junior Boards

The United States once had a senior board and a junior board. The New York Stock Exchange was the Big Board, where huge, profitable companies would go to access some of the deepest liquidity pools in the world. There was a junior board too, called NASDAQ, and smaller companies that weren't yet profitable could go there to list.This was a shrewd policy, and the NASDAQ was a wild success. They were self-governed, and designed rules for the benefit of both high-growth companies and investors who wanted direct access.[11]

Household names such as Intel, Adobe, Apple and Oracle all benefited from this private-to-public pipeline. Structural changes in the early 2000s all but ended the IPO opportunity for small cap growth companies in the U.S., not least because of a wave of new regulation. Based on today's U.S. standards (even when inflation-adjusted), household names such as Intel, Oracle, Amazon, Cisco, Adobe Systems and NVidia would have been too small to IPO in the U.S. The U.S. markets became fraught with legal risk, and compliance costs skyrocketed.[12] In short, the distraction factor became too burdensome.

This is reflected in the decline in U.S. IPOs. From 1990 to 2000, there was an average of 406 IPOs in the United States per year.[13] Since 2001, that average has dropped to less than 120.[14] By 2020, private companies were staying private much longer. Time from venture capital investment to monetization lengthened from an average of three years in 2000 to over 10 years by 2020.[15]

The U.S. exchanges had to adapt, and they did. They focused

on servicing the needs of the most active traders, and focused on only the most liquid companies. They also moved to support ETFs, mutual funds and other passive investors.[16]

Elsewhere in the world, things evolved differently. Over the first 20 years of the century, there was increased integration of capital markets. The forces of globalization, industrialization, urbanization and digitization combined with an embrace of market economics to empower a new class of investor. The proliferation of digital communications would only accelerate this interconnectedness. Technology and a desire for profits accelerated the trends toward global, distributed capital markets, while simultaneously creating new paths for liquidity and capital formation.

The corporate disclosure "compliance burden" was size-appropriate, meaning smaller companies did not need teams of lawyers and accounts just to be public. There was a framework for companies and investors to easily communicate.

Tick size also matters. In the '80s and '90s, U.S. Small Cap Equities in the U.S. were traded with a 25¢ or 12.5¢ bid ask spread.[17] The result was that broker-dealers and market makers could profit from listing and trading securities. Today U.S. equities are traded in 1¢ increments and when this is combined with a U.S. minimum listed stock price of $5.00, the result is a transaction cost of less than 0.20%—the lowest of any developed market.[18] The result is little economic incentive for a properly functioning public capital market, and low allocation of public capital to small cap growth companies. One of the reasons that the secondary markets have grown is the pricing inefficiency that allows traders to make money.

Again, capital markets evolved differently in the 21st Century outside the U.S. There was less support for sub-second or fractions of a penny trading.[19] In some markets, securities were often priced under a dollar, meaning that small moves could make money for the market makers. Turns out when well-intentioned regulations like the U.S. "best execution rules" are implemented, market-makers leave and liquidity dries up.

The U.S. markets of the 2010s were outstanding if your average hold period was measured in milliseconds, but if you had long hold periods, especially of smaller companies, it turns out that a seemingly less-efficient market is actually better for you.[20]

Rule 144 and the Securities Act of 1933

No history of equity markets would be complete without mentioning the U.S. Securities Act of 1933. This foundational law demands that virtually all securities offered or sold in the U.S. must be registered with the U.S. Securities and Exchange Commission.[21] There are exemptions for selling abroad via Reg S, and other exemptions for selling to the largest and most-qualified U.S. institutions. Critically the 33 Act was extended by the SEC in 1972, with the adoption of Rule 144, which would prove to have a significant impact on the equity markets.[22]

Rule 144 imposes a six-month to one-year holding period on most U.S. securities acquired before the IPO. For venture capital and insiders, it means a 180-day lock-up when listing in the U.S. For pre-IPO investors, this means not being able to sell during the IPO, and even for a period after a company has gone public. Forced into long holding periods, investors refrain from providing pricing signals immediately before the IPO. The result is mispricing, to the detriment of existing shareholders, and to the benefit of the most active hedge funds, who tend to only hold the security for the first day.[23]

Outside the U.S., markets evolved differently. Investors have incentive to buy immediately before the IPO, providing important signals leading into IPO pricing, and getting investors off the capital table, who might otherwise produce selling pressure once listed. The result is that Day One trading prices align more obviously with the IPO price, which is better for early investors and founders.[24] Another benefit is that institutionally-targeted pre-IPO rounds also act as a pre-marketing opportunity to meet investors who can participate at the IPO or beyond.[25]

By looking back at how exchanges, market structure, and investor incentives evolved—from face-to-face trading floors to telegraphs and telephones, and now to global computer networks and AI—we gain important insight into what comes next. The same structural dynamics that created dominant exchanges in previous centuries are at work today: superior inventory attracts investors, deep pools of capital attract issuers, and network effects amplify winners. What changes are the technologies and the policy choices that either accelerate or blunt those forces.

The next dominant exchange will be the one that marries deep liquidity with truly global distribution and a distributed architecture. The winners will be those who heed the lessons of the past, while building for a future that is digital and interconnected. The practical effect of the evolution of equity markets in recent decades has been a climate in the U.S. that favors extreme liquidity for the very largest of companies, alongside regulatory and microstructure changes that raised the cost of being a public for smaller companies.

Meanwhile, other jurisdictions allowed frameworks to evolve that better supported earlier public access and more natural pre-IPO price discovery. The consequence: fewer IPOs, longer terms as private entities for companies, less transparency and a global opportunity for exchanges that can combine specialization with truly international investor access.

Summary

- Investor behaviors repeat even when technologies change.
- Technology shifted the market from local to regional and now to global; the winning exchanges must be connected cross-borders.
- U.S. regulation, tick sizes and compliance costs contributed to a decline in small-cap IPOs and longer private lifecycles.

- Rule 144 and lock-up/hardening mechanisms altered both pre-IPO and post-IPO price signaling, which was often disadvantageous to early investors.
- Different international approaches can preserve price discovery and capital access for smaller issuers—a potential competitive edge.
- Policymakers and exchange operators should be focused on reserving efficient price discovery, rethinking rules that discourage small listings, and pursuing global distribution to win network effects.

In the next chapter, we will examine how to prepare an IPO offering for the global stage.

Chapter 5
IPO Readiness & Preparation for the Global Stage

Planning your IPO will help you to build a better business. Unfortunately, like so much that needs to be done in a fast-growing company, the best time to start is usually a year ago! The sooner management starts preparing for the public market, the better prepared they will be at IPO. In fact, in some top, well-run international markets, a business can go public as quickly as 12 weeks.[1] But don't allow this timeframe to mislead you; remember that an IPO is a long-term project, not just a financing event, and should never be a hasty process.

In common with any form of capital-raising, an IPO inevitably diverts attention from the delivery of customer-centric value. Also, in common with any fundraising, the best leaders also plan ahead on how the current financing, in this case an IPO, will impact future access to capital.[2] It is best to pace the IPO process so it is not all-consuming. Thinking it through can unlock enormous long-term value. The amount of distraction can vary drastically depending on the jurisdiction and exchange. In later chapters, we will discuss some of the factors in evaluating the listing friction of a given exchange.

Nonetheless, regardless of which exchange a business lists with, a company doesn't go public because the IPO is easy;

they go public because, after you're publicly traded, every future round of financing will be less distracting.

In a fast-growing company, management's time is usually the most constrained and valuable resource. Investing mental bandwidth in preparing your IPO, however, yields strategic benefits, even if the company ultimately pursues an alternative path. Many of the benefits of being public (superior access to talent, lower capital costs, greater strategic optionality, etc.) don't simply "turn on" at IPO.

They accrue and expand as plans become more tangible.

Story, Story, Story

"The best investments are usually simple, easily explainable, and have a compelling story. If you can't tell the story of a company in two minutes, it's probably too complicated."
Bill Ackman—Billionaire Investor

"Never invest in any idea you can't illustrate with a crayon."
Peter Lynch—Manager, Fidelity Magellan Fund from 1977 to 1990

Too many managers worship "the numbers." They brag about a 3% margin shift as if it's the whole story. It's not. Numbers matter, but they're not enough. To build a great public company, you need a story, a damn good story.

That's why most venture-backed companies start with a story, and it must be a story good enough to attract top talent and raise serious VC money. Public market investors, however, are not VCs. The old story won't cut it. The story must evolve. The good news is that if you prepare properly, and start pitching your story to public market investors years before the IPO, your story will be ready by the time that it really counts.

This works well for investors, because if they hear the story years before the IPO, they will be in a privileged position to evaluate the company (and its management). An investor who meets management well before the IPO will know if they have a consistent history of vision and execution.

The investment bank, board and CFO of your company can help with refining your story, but direct feedback from professional institutional investors, well before you move into the public market, will probably prove most valuable in developing your story.

In the era of wind-powered ships, navigators who could unerringly follow the progress of their ships across the charts were said to be "worth their weight in gold".[3] The success of the entire journey depended on their expertise. Similarly, developing your VC story into your public story is also a journey, and no less perilous than those voyages across oceans in bygone days. This whole process can sometimes feel intimidating, but there are professional navigators who can help: specialists in public market investor relations.

Nonetheless, finding a good one can be difficult. In common with many salespeople, they are often better at selling themselves than they are at selling the product. This does not necessarily mean that you need to retain a public markets IR professional full-time for years before an IPO. It does, though, mean that you should evaluate these individuals well in advance of when you will need them.

A good IR professional will probably tell you to define your category and simplify your story. They're probably right.

Public Market Investors Are Not Like Venture Capitalists

A good venture capitalist is a founder's partner. One founder said, "Your problems are their problems; they are along for the journey." This stands in stark contrast to public market investors, who can bail out at the press of a button.

Here's an example: in a private company, if you forecast 60% growth and achieve 59% growth, most VCs would think,

"Great, the company is growing fast, maybe the fastest in its category." Whereas a public market investor is likely to think, "They missed their forecast, maybe I should sell."

We have discussed the importance of storytelling in this chapter, but allow me to contextualize that further. There are more than 40,000 public companies,[4] hundreds of commodities, and dozens of currencies that people invest in. As a public company, you are competing with all of them! This is the major leagues. Your story *must* work.

Another difference between VCs and public market investors is portfolio size. A typical VC manages about a dozen investments in a few specialized industry domains, whereas many public market investors follow hundreds of companies. In short, your story needs to rise above the noise. Complex stories merely add to this noise; to stand out, your elevator pitch must heed the advice attributed to Albert Einstein: "Everything should be made as simple as possible, but not simpler"

Public market investors are busy. They often need to be able to justify their decisions to their colleagues. Many follow the advice of Warren Buffett: "If you can't explain it to a 10-year-old, don't buy it."

There can, and should be, more details for the analyst who wants to dig deeper into the story. The detailed story should align with the simple story, but without the good, simple story, the detailed story won't get an opportunity to be sown into the mind of a public investor.

A venture capitalist's investment framework is shaped by a fundamentally different mindset. As one pension CIO described it: "VCs price deals, investors value deals." VCs price based on forward-looking potential, and tend to be optimists.[5] They are experts in evaluating options that are non-linear, subjective, and have large payouts.

Public market investors are more likely to price based on discounted cash flows, comps, and earnings.[6] Public investors are financial analysts first. Many come from MBAs, hedge funds, or banking. The culture is analytical, conservative, and performance-driven. Public Investors aim for risk-adjusted returns. They focus on beta, alpha, Sharpe ratio, volatility, etc. Valuation is more grounded in financials and multiples, at least in theory. Public market investors are also a much more diverse group. When compared to the millions of global public market investors, Venture Capital is a small and insular cohort.

One founder I spoke with described VCs as "sheep," in that they all seem to want the same thing at the same time. He described his fundraising story process as, "figuring out what was hot in VC Land, and then explaining how my start-up fit that narrative." In contrast, there is every type of investor somewhere in the public markets. The challenge is getting your narrative in front of the investors whose greed matches the company's vision.

However, getting your story in front of the right investors only works if your story stands out. I like to say, "Simple at first glance, but detailed if needed." Management needs to be able to tell a story that holds together under the scrutiny of analytics. Every customer's "emotion" should show up somewhere in the cash flows. Every technological innovation should tie back to an impact on margin.

VCs tend to live in the future, but public market investors will be looking more at past execution. For equity story development, the elements need to both highlight past success and articulate future growth potential. In advance of the IPO, the story needs to be supported by data and historical financial information.

Investors will also be keenly interested in comparing the company's current and expected financial results against a consistent and clear benchmark of its past results. Those benchmarks do not need to be financial, but they do need to be numeric. Meeting with investors well in advance of the IPO will set the stage for them to evaluate the company based on previously defined metrics.

The best investors will keep rigorous notes and watch for moving goalposts, or changing metrics of success, between early presentations and the IPO. This process will continue into life as a public company.

Founder Vision

Vision matters to public investors, particularly institutional ones, because it provides the North Star for a company's long-term trajectory and capital allocation.[7] Vision speaks to a team's capacity to build a durable competitive moat. The founder's vision plays an outsized role in IPO valuations[8] and reduces underpricing.[9] At a venture's inception, the founder holds the entire conception; from opportunity, through customers, to product. Vision shapes the organizational culture and direction. Investors often see this founding insight as irreplaceable.

Public market investors know the empirical evidence—companies run by visionary founder-CEOs outperform those led by non-founders in both stock returns and innovation.[10] One large study showed founder lead companies outperform the rest of the market 310%.[11] If the founder is part of the company's future, it is critical to include his or her origin story in the equity story. Founders should also be ready to discuss how they intend to maintain an equity stake, and also to pursue long-term strategies.

Some of the most successful companies don't focus on the vision for the company, but instead focus on their vision for the category they seek to create.[12] Tesla, Apple, Amazon and Salesforce all emphasized their vision for the future, not how they are incrementally better than the incumbents.

Unit Economics

Top-tier public market investors love to analyze. They'll

debate market-size projections, and they'll accept delayed profits if the logic holds. They'll even stomach the messiness of fast-growth companies with shaky structures, and green managers. But there's one thing they won't touch: broken unit economics. Unit economics describes the revenues and costs associated with a fundamental unit of a business. They answer a simple but critical question: Does each incremental "unit" the company sells create value—or destroy it?

The definition of a unit is not universal. It must be intentionally defined, based on the business and vision. Examples are diverse, and include: customer, transaction, city, store, box, mile-driven, flight or patient encounter. Choosing the wrong unit can distort decision-making. Choosing the right unit clarifies the economics of growth.

The unit should reflect the smallest repeatable economic engine of the business.

Critical to the equity story, the company needs to define what it sees as a unit. Management must show they rigorously measure that unit. Most important, management must have a clear story about unit economics and how they expect those dynamics to change over time. This will make or break the proposition.

Founder Ego & Management

Public market investors will stomach shaky organizational structures and green managers. However, the best investors have learned to stay away from teams that can't identify their own shortcomings. In every fast-growing company, there is always a gap between the team as it exists today, and what will be needed in the future.

"The effective executive builds on strengths—their own strengths, the strengths of superiors, colleagues, subordinates, and on the strengths in the situation, that is, what they can do."
Peter Drucker —Management Guru OG

Effective leadership requires more than recognizing strengths. It demands a clear-eyed assessment of where the team must evolve—a coherent plan. The human development element plan should be part of the equity story.

Other key elements that investors look for:

Business Model Building on unit economics, the equity story must explain how the company makes money, and how its business offering solves an issue for customers.

Improvements & Milestones Ideally, you accomplish something between when you first tell the story and when you next meet that investor. The best stories don't have just great endings, they have great chapters, and great scenes within the chapters. As one investor told me, "They told me what they would do before going public. They did it, and two years later when they went public, I loaded up the truck."

Clear Growth Strategy A clear growth strategy must be part of the equity story. It outlines how the company plans to scale its operations and capitalize on market opportunities. This can involve organic growth, acquisitions, new product development, and/or entering new geographic markets.

Financial Projections and Forecasts Investors expect companies to know how their performance matches up against projections and forecasts. Companies will need to prepare financial forecasts and comparisons against historical performance, which requires a "management muscle" for financial planning and analysis. Investment banks will ask for high-quality forecasts that outline strategy, objectives, and integrated financial projections, and allow for due diligence and other support for the equity story. Longer-term forecasts will enhance investor confidence.

Market Opportunity Total addressable market (TAM) is critical for investors looking to hold long-term. To reach them, the equity story should address the current TAM and present a clear vision for how the TAM will grow over time. Grow through new company capabilities and emerging industry dynamics.

Industry Comparables (Comps) The management of a public company should understand similar public companies. Their equity story needs to be able to explain how the company is different, better or the same as companies with which the investor may be familiar, and have a readily available valuation for side-by-side comparison.

A good way to understand how investors may view comps is to look at who is attending conferences. Most specifically, investment banking conferences connected to the company's peers, or clients. Management will want to understand which companies in a similar universe are attending. Management will want to speak to the bankers and analysts covering those companies. Ideally, management should secure invites for speaking at the conference. These conferences occur around the same date each year so mapping these to a three-, six- and 12-month calendar allows you to block time to participate and meet the investors who are buying shares of similar companies.

Identifying and building relationships with equity research analysts long before the IPO is sometimes called the "shadow roadshow." While the official roadshow targets the Buy-side (investors who buy shares), this process targets the Sell-side (analysts who write the reports those investors read). Being featured in such reports before the IPO is all part of readiness.

Understanding what companies may be viewed as similar helps craft the story and provides insight on how the company may be valued. This could correlate to how the IPO company gets valued. Comp analysis can also serve as a reality check for valuation, especially if the founder is unable to define their unique vision.[13]

Capital Efficiency The best business models can efficiently turn capital into value. If the company has been efficient in the past, you should highlight that. As one public investor told me, "Look what they did with just $100 million. Imagine what they will accomplish with some real money." If there are technological changes, economies of scale, or other factors improving capital efficiency, you should also highlight them.

Need for Follow-on Capital The public markets are much bigger than the private markets.[14] Many public investors are under constant pressure to put more money to work. For some investors, they will only get to know your company if they believe they can invest more over time. If the company's vision may require additional capital over time, you should also highlight this element.

A Reason to be Public The companies with the best IPOs have a reason to be public, and the reason should not be "Current investors are eager to sell!" Companies often go public to fuel growth, and investors prefer for IPO proceeds to be used for expansion, R&D, marketing, capital expenditures, or acquisitions. As with all things in the story, the narrative should match the reality, so management should agree with the strategy and how it integrates with being public.

Use of Funds This is different from a reason to be public, but like any fundraising story, the best story is, "The business is a rocket ship sitting on the pad; investment will be adding rocket fuel." Of course, that story only works when it matches reality. Public market investors must understand how more capital lowers risk, provided that it also matches the reality.

Innovation Companies can achieve better pricing in the public markets by demonstrating growth through research and development (R&D). Here again, vision is a critical element in being trusted to execute an R&D culture of high ROI.[15]

Intellectual Property VCs tend to discount the stand-alone value of IP because IP alone rarely builds a business. In early-stage startups, what matters most is execution, team quality, go-to-market motion, speed of iteration and product-market fit.[16] Note that patents are not in that list. Depending on industry and sophistication, public market investors may put a very different value on IP. Management should re-evaluate how they discussed IP as they transition from private to public market investors.

Some Advanced Elements Of Equity Storytelling:

Connection to Stories Investors Already Understand Institutional investors allocate capital in frameworks such as sectors, themes, benchmarks, and risk buckets. They tend to be busy, and frameworks reduce cognitive friction. Connecting to a known market narrative or comp set reduces the mental lift required to underwrite the story.

"We have three boxes: in, out, and too hard. You don't have to do everything well. At the Olympics, if you run the 100 meters well, you don't have to do the shot put."
Charlie Munger—Legendary Investor

Less mental lift is usually a good thing. Most people who know, or know of Munger and his partner Buffett, acknowledge that they are super-smart, yet even they reject businesses that require too much mental lift to understand.

Geographic Connection Although "local bias" seems to be shrinking[17], some investors still have a bias toward companies where they see a personal geographic connection.[18] Investors are both global and local. If you have operations, reference clients, partnerships, or licenses in a certain geographical location, management must be prepared to weave that into the story. At our fund, we call that "building connective tissue to a market," and not addressing this in advance of an IPO is an opportunity squandered.

In addition, inadequately planning your brand development and media relations can also represent lost opportunities.

Brand Audiences Too often, a fast-growing company focuses on its reputation with prospective customers. Yet this is just a small subset of stakeholders; others include employees, prospective employees, regulators, distributors, and more. Managers should appreciate, and even target, a larger audience before an IPO; otherwise, they will regret it later.

I knew a top scientist who left a company at the insistence of his wife. She did not like the looks her friends gave her due to the bad reputation of the company! It turns out that brand impacts a company in many ways beyond sales.

This is especially true in relation to investors and prospective investors. The best investors like to analyze. They want more data. Their mindset is usually to speak with anyone who has had any interaction with the company. "Any" means *all* touch points. Customer support, packaging, website, product, sales outreach, press, social media, and even the receptionist in the company lobby should be consistent with your equity story. Both experience and messaging should match your equity story.

Pay close attention to any interactions with journalists and social media. As a public company, all employees need to be disciplined about what they say or post. I view all media training, your corporate press process, and social media policy as part of building a great company; all of this should also be part of IPO readiness.

Experiential Brand Building Experiential brand-building creates memorable, real-world experiences that let people feel your brand, not just see it. It's much more than a logo or a tagline. It's a moment. Done right, experiential branding builds trust, loyalty, and love. It's the difference between telling your story and letting people step into it. The best investors will try to experience your business before owning the stock.

Set the pace of media relations so that your marketing activity is not viewed as "conditioning the market" or "gun-jumping." The United States has a strict quiet period prior to the IPO filing, and a 25-day quiet period after the IPO pricing.[19] This restricts companies and underwriters from making public communications that could be seen as "conditioning the market" by the SEC.[20] For example, Google almost had its 2004 IPO delayed because of a *Playboy* magazine interview with its founders, Larry Page and Sergey Brin.[21]

Other jurisdictions, such as the U.K.,[22] Hong Kong,[23] and Singapore[24] have rules or customs that limit promotions immediately before the IPO. But here is the good news: if a company sets a pace of ongoing communications with the world, authorities will generally view those "normal" marketing efforts as not being directed to prospective investors. It is important to establish a communication cadence so you will be able to communicate in accordance with past practice.

Corporate Matters

Regardless of jurisdiction, some matters are easier to structure before going public. This section touches on some of the items that are worth thinking about early in the IPO preparation process. Later in the book, there are more specifics on evaluating the various listing venues. I also recommend discussing these issues with your advisors, as each company is different, rules change, and best practices evolve.

Establish your corporate structural defenses. Many of the most popular defenses, such as a dual-class common stock structure or a staggered board, require shareholder approval,[25] so the best time to institute these measures is while still tightly held (and private).

Other aspects of corporate governance, often embedded in the charter, are also easier to establish while private. You should define a clear policy regarding what requires shareholder approval and when that approval is required. Items could include mergers and acquisitions, follow-on offerings, shelf registrations, and/or potential changes in shareholder rights. Companies will want to pre-clear some shareholder approvals to simplify and focus post-IPO communications.

Restructuring or Change of Domicile If your company requires restructuring, do it well in advance of your IPO. The same applies if you need to change the domicile of your company. Reasons for a change could be a range of factors, including regulation, tax, strategic optionality, or investor perception. If you need to restructure as part of IPO readiness, consult a tax and legal specialist. For tax, look at transactions from the perspective of existing shareholders, employees, future shareholders, and, of course, tax authorities.

Compensation Policy Pay close attention to your executive compensation and overall equity incentive programs. Most exchanges require clear, disclosed compensation frameworks that cover equity incentive plans, stock options, and director pay. Early alignment ensures that you don't face a last-minute compliance scramble across multiple jurisdictions.

Institutional investors scrutinize dilution from equity pools. Establishing your policy early positions your company as a credible, mature steward of public capital. In a cross-border or multi-jurisdictional IPO, multiple shareholder approval thresholds (corporate domicile and local exchange rules) may apply, which potentially require sequencing.

Excessive founder pay, misaligned option grants, and evergreen plans with unlimited dilution are red flags for investors and may depress demand or trigger governance downgrades. Tax treatment of equity grants also varies widely across the globe. Without an early, harmonized plan, employees in different geographies may face inequitable treatment, which could undermine retention.

Board Design A well-run, venture-backed company should already have a solid board composition. As part of IPO readiness, look to make improvements. Do you have the right board members for the next stage of your journey? Do you need to add independent directors? How about establishing new committees (audit, compensation, nominating)? Also, keep in mind that some venture investors may seek to leave the board at IPO, so you should develop a pipeline of "upgrades."

Your choice of listing venue, which will be discussed in detail later, can affect your ideal board structure, but a good rule of thumb is that if you are going to be public, it is best to have at least one board member who has been on a public board.

Financial Discipline and Predictability Every top accounting firm publishes accounting guides about IPO readiness. These guides are very similar, but their utility varies greatly depending on your company's level of sophistication.

Rather than summarize their guides, I recommend reviewing at least one of them and discussing it with a firm partner familiar with the IPO process. I am not saying that you need a top firm to go public. I am saying that you should understand a top firm's perspective. That is how you learn, and they show you what it would be like to work with them. It's win-win.

Regardless of who you work with, start closing books quarterly as soon as practicable. Hiring a top-tier CFO will be extremely helpful in this regard. If you have not already audited the financials, begin producing annual audited financials.

Also, define your metrics and move to a fast month-end close (ideally, less than five business days). One of my mentors, a senior executive at FedEx, taught me that the best metrics always include a mix of three types: activity, financial, and quality. It turns out that 'speed to close' speaks to the quality of your financial operations.

Advisor Selection

There is a wide range of advisors you will want to evaluate and potentially engage as part of the IPO readiness process. Don't worry, I will address their selection later.

Summary

- Treat an IPO as a long-term project, not just a single financing event.
- Meet institutional investors early to get feedback, refine

your pitch and build credibility.

- Remember that public investors are different from VCs; they focus more on past execution, financials and risk-adjusted returns. Emphasize the company's vision for the future.
- Define and prove your unit economics—broken unit economics will undermine investor confidence.
- Put corporate governance and compensation policies in order while still private (board makeup, charter, equity plans, domicile).
- Build financial discipline: audited annuals, fast month-end reporting and high-quality forecasts.
- Control your public communications and brand. Align media, social, and customer touchpoints with your equity story and respect quiet-period rules.
- Assemble the right advisors early (bankers, auditors, legal, IR, tax) and add at least one director with public-company experience.

Preparation touches every part of the business: you need a simple, convincing equity story, clean and fast financial reporting, clear unit economics, and governance and compensation plans that will stand up to public-market scrutiny.

In the next chapter, we will examine considerations when selecting a listing venue, also called "exchange shopping."

Chapter 6
Selecting an Exchange

The top investment banks, legal practices and accounting firms produce guides on how to go public. I don't want to duplicate their good work, and have included a list of many of them in the Appendix. However, all of those guides often miss something central to the high aspirations of a global mindset. These guides tend to be jurisdiction-specific. They mostly assume the company leadership already knows which exchange they plan to list on.

This chapter focuses on identifying exchanges that might be appropriate for a given company's situation, status and growth plan. The goal is to give management and existing shareholders more options, empowering them for future negotiations and strategic planning. This also fits more broadly with the general theme of this book, which is to be open-minded and internationally focused rather than being confined to the limitations of the closest domestic exchange. This book encourages business leaders to think bigger and look beyond the nearest exchange. Just because your ancestors used an exchange in a time of horses, ticker-tapes or blackberries, does not mean that is the right venue.

Intentional About International

At our investment fund, we recommend being intentional about selecting an exchange; after all, the exchange sets the rules for listing and reporting. Technical founders would call it "part of the stack"—in the same way servers, operating systems and development languages are "part of the technical stack."

World-class managers would not use a technology in their stack without thinking it through, and a choice of exchange is no different. No well-run company wakes up and discovers they used an IBM mainframe instead of an Amazon cloud. Every decision requires careful thought, and choosing the right exchange is no exception.

Choosing an exchange is similar to choosing a technical stack in three other ways:

1. Good architecture enables you to do business everywhere
2. The optimal choice can change over time
3. There are always trade-offs

Built to do Business Everywhere

A well-architected stock exchange does more than facilitate trading—it acts as a distribution channel for investor visibility, a platform for compliance signaling and a gateway to global capital pools.[1] It's important to remember that the exchange defines the standards for initial listing, ongoing disclosure, and the mechanics of follow-on offerings. It typically also establishes and publishes the official trading price. Depending on the exchange's structure and jurisdiction, the scope and intensity of oversight will vary under the local regulators. For example, SEC in the U.S.,[2] ASIC in Australia[3] and the FCA in the UK.[4]

The good news is that in a modern, interconnected world, the exchange and their regulators have much less influence on how and where an economic interest in the company is traded. There is a global network of intermediaries, investment vehicles, and derivative structures that ensure a wide range of ways global investors can participate once a company's equity is listed on a top exchange.

Change Over Time

Capital markets, like technology, change over time. Top management monitors these changes, and makes adjustments when appropriate. I have some painful experience in changing technical stack decessions. In the mid-2000s, Roger Erienberg and I launched a company that monitored the internet in real time for hedge-funds. This was early text analytics, the precursor to modern LLMs. Limited by the then-available technology, we set up and maintained hundreds of servers to chew through the data. The system was expensive to maintain and reconfigurations happened slowly. Then an ecommerce company told us they planned to launch a new service they called "cloud." That company was Amazon, and the service became AWS. At the time, the service was unproven and yet to launch.

We decided to not bet the company by moving to this new service. Servers were central to our business, and I did not want to be dependent on a side-project from another company that they could abandon at any time. In hindsight, that was a horrible mistake. Moving to Amazon's cloud would have allowed us to move faster and be much more capital-efficient. The result was a company valued in millions instead of billions. Later entrants in that sector who took advantage of the cloud, such as Dataminr and AlphaSence, went on to become unicorns.

Just as they monitor technological shifts, company leaders must stay attuned to evolving capital markets. Even the most established equity exchanges are undergoing rapid transformation, while a wave of new entrants is accelerating the pace of change. I have found one indicator of a shifting landscape is when outsiders start offering new solutions. In the mid-2000s the idea of "the cloud" did not exist. Servers were purchased from companies like IBM, HP and Dell. Those machines would be hosted in facilities run by companies like Rackspace or Internap. Our start-up had hundreds of machines, and cost us millions. The idea that an online book retailer, Amazon, would win by offering fractional cloud access seemed far-fetched. I missed the technological shift, but you don't need to miss the capital market shift.

Like the incumbents of the mid-2000s (IBM, HP and Dell), the exchange incumbents of the mid-2020s (LSE, NYSE, HKSG, etc) are obvious exchange competitors. But less obvious is the rapid emergence of a whole new set of organizations well positioned to enter the equity exchange marketspace. Some are new equity exchanges like the Long Term Stock Exchange and Texas Exchange in the U.S. Others are exchanges who have expressed an interest in adding equities. Don't be surprised if companies like CoinBase, Robinhood, Galaxy Digital, Binance and Polymarkets start to take IPO volume from traditional exchanges in the first part of the 2030s. Trading and follow-on offerings will happen even sooner.

Today, there are leaders making bad decisions about their choice of exchange that will prevent their companies from becoming unicorns. If I do my job right with this book, that won't be your company.

Trade-offs

As with a technological choice of operating system or software language, there is no perfect choice. There are always trade-offs. Choosing an exchange also comes with trade-offs. Every exchange offers benefits and burdens, you must weigh capital access vs. regulatory load, valuation vs. scrutiny, liquidity vs. control, and other factors. These trade-offs affect institutional interest, future capital raises, and long-term strategic flexibility, as will be discussed in this chapter.

This chapter is designed to help management teams better understand the trade-offs. It is also designed for policy makers and investors who want to understand the market from the company's perspective. As an investor, do you want to invest in a company that has made a poor choice of listing venue? As a policymaker, do you want your exchanges to be uncompetitive? Of course not, so let's dig in.

Size Matters

One of the most important elements of choosing a listing venue is the size of the enterprise. You must choose a venue that is size-appropriate for the scale of your business. As Stephane Boujnah, CEO & Chairman of Euronext, so eloquently said on CNBC's *Squawk Box* in August 2025: "The decision to list is fundamentally a decision of, Do I go to a market where I will be visible, or do I go to a market where I run the risk of being minuscule? Do I go to a market where the all-in cost of operation is bearable, or do I go to a market where the all-in cost of being operated as a listed company is bearable?"

In short, if your profits are just a few million dollars, do you really want a large percentage of the IPO process to go straight to the administration associated with being public? Of course not! In that case, you may want to optimize for an exchange that has size-appropriate compliance overhead, sometimes referred to as "stage-appropriate regulatory framework." The good news is that AI and competition should bring down public reporting and disclosure costs globally, but government regulators *might* not move as fast as capitalism and technology.

Arguably, even more critical when choosing the right-sized venue is ensuring alignment with investor access and expectations.[5] In a large cap-optimized market, such as the NYSE, big institutional investors can't waste their time looking at smaller offerings, because they can't put enough money to work to move their needle on what will be a large portfolio. Most institutions need to buy into an IPO alongside other investors, to manage risk and help ensure they have someone to sell to if they need liquidity.[6] So if a company is "only" raising $150 million, then an institution would seek to keep their portion under 20% ($30 million in this case).

The biggest firms, like BlackRock,[7] Fidelity,[8] State Street[9] and Capital Group[10] manage trillions. For the U.S. managers, $30 million is a gnat on the back of their elephant-sized funds. Ironically, those same funds have managers, usually based abroad, who manage smaller sub-pools of capital. Their compensation is tied to performance in the local market. A $150-million offering on their doorstep is going to get their full attention. Their bonus is at stake so you can count on both fear and greed to be in play.

Appealing to the right portfolio managers or analysts in the global institutions is part of a company's exchange evaluation process, but smaller regional institutions matter too. There are local institutions in the UK,[11] Australia[12] and South Africa[13] that are mandated to look at securities listed on their exchange. These institutions vary in size, but what matters is they will be paying attention if you are listing in their backyard. Many other institutional investors globally look at smaller companies listing outside the U.S.; Singapore institutions are a good example, and their domestic exchange is very global.[14] About 40% of the companies listed on the SGX are from outside the city-state,[15] resulting in a deep pool of professional investors who are accustomed to looking at multi-jurisdictional companies. In my experience, these institutions are often hesitant to examine US-listed small-cap, but don't think twice about looking at companies listed elsewhere (especially Australia, Hong Kong, and Japan).

In short, corporate leaders must ensure that their choice of listing venue is size appropriate.

Comparables

How other companies are trading on an exchange also matters. Comparables (comps) refer to a group of publicly-traded companies that share similar characteristics with a company evaluating an IPO or public listing. These characteristics can include industry sector, business model, revenue scale, growth rates, margin profiles, geography, and customer base.

More from that interview with Stephane Boujnah: "Where are my peers and what are the valuation multiples of my comparable peers?"

Exchange selection (e.g., NYSE vs. Nasdaq vs. LSE vs. HKEX) is not only a function of listing requirements and liquidity, but comparables play a critical strategic role in determining the optimal venue. Here's how:

- **Valuation Optimization** If comps are trading at higher multiples on one exchange, that venue might be preferred to optimize IPO pricing and post-listing valuation.[16]
- **Investor Base Alignment** Exchanges are ecosystems. Local investors familiar with those names will be more receptive to similar companies, creating momentum for building a global investor base.
- **Index Inclusion & Analyst Coverage** Comps help indicate which local indices and analysts will likely follow the stock. Strategic listing near peers improves chances of early index inclusion and coverage.[17]
- **Liquidity and Trading Volume** If comps on a certain exchange have higher liquidity and tighter spreads, this lowers the cost of capital and trading friction for the newly-listed firm.
- **Branding and Perceptions** Firms want to be seen as part of a "cohort of excellence." Being listed on the same exchange as admired comps enhances credibility.

As my grandmother says, "You will be judged by the company you keep." Comps matter. As they say in Turkey: "Bana arkadaşını söyle, sana kim olduğunu söyleyeyim." ("Tell me who your associates are, I'll tell you who you are.")

That said, association is not always the best strategy. Sometimes, it is better to stand out.

Differentiation

Being in a different industry, currency regime, business model, or growth profile than most of the companies listed on an exchange can create distinct strategic advantages. A good example is the Australian Stock Exchange. Years ago, a large portion of its listed companies were tied to the local economic cycle: Hotels, airlines, banks, and real-estate.[18] Local Institutions wanted something different. Local institutional investors had amassed the fourth-largest pool of investable capital. Referred to as Superannuation, Australia's compulsory, employment-based retirement savings system was introduced in 1992.[19] By the mid 2010s, there were billions of dollars looking for diversification.[20]

In 2016, when buy-now-pay-later companies like Afterpay showed up to list, local investors piled into the differentiated growth story. Afterpay had a market capitalization of about AUD $125 million at IPO, August 2016,[21] and was later valued at about USD$29 billion based on a merger offer from Jack Dorsey's publicly-traded Fintech Block, Inc. (formerly known as Square).[22] By being different, Afterpay created immense shareholder value, especially for its founders, Nick Molnar and Anthony Eisen. The company's success became a local comparable; many other BNPL companies later found success listing in Australia.[23]

Connective Tissue and Logistics

If you are going public in a far-away market, it is a lot easier if you are already doing business there. Building long-term relationships with institutional investors takes time; this process is a lot easier if you happen to be in town a few times a year. Only visiting periodically can work to your advantage because your visits have scarcity. As one New York City-based founder told me: "It's actually easier for me to meet investors in Japan than the ones in midtown Manhattan. If I travel 7,000 miles, it's bad manners for them to reschedule."

If you have customers, operations, partnerships or industry events in another country, it's going to be easier to get on the CEO's tight calendar, but it's not just about logistics. Local investors appreciate the familiarity of a business that has employees, media, partnerships or customers that are local. This is especially true if one of those customers or partnerships is a local champion. Doing business with Grab in south-east Asia may not mean much to European investors, but south-east institutions will take note. Lufthansa is just another airline to most U.S. investors, but for German investors it is their flag-carrier.

Having connective tissue to a country or region is one of the many considerations on the multi-factor listing venue decision. The future plans of the company, as it relates to expansion in the region, are also a factor to consider.

Absence of Connective Tissue

A lack of any connective tissue is also a consideration. Good investors may want to understand your "Why here?" Zero connective tissue can be a red flag that management does not value their time, or only cares about money. Chinese companies have gotten a bad reputation for listing abroad purely to access money, and as a consequence, many of those cross-border IPOs have performed poorly.[24]

The Boomerangs

This is in stark contract to companies where part of the founding team or early investor base has local connections. Sometimes called "boomerangs," these companies are seen as returning to their roots.[25] Local investors are able to do extra diligence through backchecks that sometimes rely on relationships dating back to childhood. If you have an early investor, board member or co-founder from a specific market, this might be a consideration in evaluating an exchange.

English Common Law

After the Norman Conquest of 1066, the English monarchy began centralizing and standardizing legal practices.[26] By the 13th Century, this Common Law was applied across the kingdom, distinguishing it from local or feudal laws.[27] As Britain expanded its empire in the 1700s, it exported its legal system to colonies in North America, Caribbean, Asia, Africa, and Oceania.[28] This framework impacts the selection of listing venues to this day.[29] The use of English Common Law in a jurisdiction is a material factor in selecting a stock exchange, because it underpins investor protections, corporate governance standards, and contract enforcement, all of which are critical to capital formation.[30]

Common Law systems emphasize precedent and judicial independence, providing a well-defined legal framework that investors trust.[31] Inherent in this are shareholder rights, like voting rights, disclosure, and fiduciary duties. Rules are often better codified and more reliably enforced under Common Law.[32] If you are incorporated in a Common Law-derived country, such as Hong Kong, Australia, the U.S., Canada or Republic of Ireland, you are going to have greater difficulty adopting an exchange framework that has different roots.[33] Your accountants, lawyers and board will have a heavier lift too.

Venue Optionality for Increased Value Creation

The great news is if you identify a list of potential listing venues, you can pit them against each other to discover the option that is right for your company, your investors and your strategic ambitions. Having more than one option when selecting a listing venue materially improves the decision process, by introducing competitive tension, strategic clarity, and deal leverage.[34] It forces a company to rigorously define what success looks like, not just on day one of the IPO, but in terms of long-term capital access, valuation credibility, governance alignment, and stakeholder resonance.

The Pre-IPO Advantage

Another critical consideration is how and when you can talk with investors. Can management and investors have frank conversations before listing? Conversely, does communication occur only later, with greater expense, through carefully curated legal documents?

Obviously, an exchange where you can easily and inexpensively talk with potential institutional investors before committing to go public is better for efficient capital formation. The popularity of Special Purpose Acquisition Companies (SPACs) in the early 2020s was borne out of the frustration with how and when investors communicated in the U.S.[35] The SPAC allowed management teams to have more abstract and unstructured conversations. There were lots of shortcomings to SPACs, but they illustrated an eagerness for both investors and companies to have a different, more open way to communicate. Communications more like the U.S before Sarbanes Oxley. This type of open communications is still common outside the U.S.

Pre-IPO rounds are a powerful strategic tool that allow companies to raise capital efficiently, while positioning themselves for a successful transition to life as a public company.[36] A pre-IPO is a private funding round, or secondary share sale, that occurs before a company goes public. It allows select investors to buy shares at a negotiated price, usually at discount, to the expected IPO price. Often the discount is fixed, anywhere between 10% and 20%[37] For a fast-growing company, this is both an easy process and inexpensive capital, and the best part is it often results in a higher valuation at IPO.

Outside the U.S., pre-IPOs are very popular for both investors and growth companies. Indeed, for investors there are many advantages in participating in Pre-IPOs:

- Access to high-growth companies at a discount to IPO price, boosting returns.[38]
- Rounds are often invite-only, providing institutional investors with early, scarce access.[39]
- Shorter liquidity timeline, as in many jurisdictions, investors can sell at the IPO or shortly after.[40]
- As an opportunity to get to know the company and management in-advance of the IPO and in advance of their first public earnings call. This is especially true of sovereign wealth funds and global conglomerates, who invest in hopes of building a long-term relationship.[41]

- Shares offer private market exposure to high-performing sectors before public hype.[42]
- Being part of a prominent pre-IPO round enhances reputation and offers influence over future fundraisings.[43]

For companies there are also many advantages in offering a pre-IPO:

- First and foremost, this is an opportunity to pre-market your company to institutional investors. Relationships built during the pre-IPO process can result in important sources of capital at the IPO, or even in following years.[44]
- More cash: The Bridge financing capital from a Pre-IPO financing can be used to accelerate growth, for expansion, acquisitions, or increase operational runway before the IPO. Just having stronger financials (e.g., cash on hand, reduced debt) can also improve the IPO valuation.[45]
- Testing the waters: The process of raising, or failing to raise, a pre-IPO round of financing will give clear indications of investor appetite and price expectations for the company in the public market.[46]
- Signaling: Having credible investors participate in the pre-IPO adds credibility, and can increase demand for the company's shares at IPO.[47]
- Cleaning up the Cap Table: The pre-IPO is an opportunity to get people off the cap table that are likely sellers in the public market, and to get people onto the cap table that are likely to be long-term holders, or ideally long-term buyers of the stock. This reduces selling pressure after the IPO, and provides a tailwind to stock appreciation.[48]
- Dress Rehearsal: Companies and bankers are able to refine their pitches, roadshow materials, and messaging.[49]
- Banker Evaluation: For the company, they get to see the bankers in action. If the chemistry with the banker is not satisfactory, there is still time to reduce or eliminate their role in the IPO.[50]
- Reduce IPO Risk: Securing a round in advance enables a company to be less reliant on favorable IPO window conditions, while simultaneously increasing the team's IPO readiness.[51]

When you look at this list of advantages, pre-IPOs sound great for both company and investor, so why are they not a feature of the U.S.IPO Market? The answer once again is regulation. U.S. investors are bound by Rule 144, which locks in a holding period of six to 12 months.[52] As a U.S. investor, why take the risk of investing in a U.S. pre-IPO, if you will be forced to hold for a year? Generally, U.S.Institutions would prefer to wait for the IPO.

Rule 144 makes it less attractive for U.S. entities to invest right before a potential IPO, because U.S. investors may be unable to sell when the stock becomes liquid. Resale restrictions have consequently had a significant impact on pre-IPO popularity in the U.S.[53] Why buy a stock a few days early only to be rewarded with 180 days of selling restrictions? The good news is that there are plenty of international investors eager to invest in quality companies that plan to list outside the U.S.

Another important point is that non-US, pre-IPO investors often enjoy greater liquidity and fewer resale restrictions than US-based investors. Rule 144 puts U.S. investors at a disadvantage, as international investors can sell during the IPO, or shortly after. As a practical matter, and assuming the company has been consistent on their story, pre-IPO investors often buy more at the IPO.

Pre-IPO participation gives investors bragging rights, as it lowers their average purchase price.[54] Essentially, by participation at the IPO, and holding their Pre-IPO converted shares, they are getting a lower average cost than investors only buying at the IPO. For big institutions, buying pre-IPO and at the IPO has the added benefit of ensuring they can amass a big enough position to matter to their fund. Simply put, a pre-IPO round improves pricing and draws in long-term investors.

For companies to unlock pre-IPO capital, they need to be well down their IPO-readiness journey. Of particular importance is that management needs to have picked a target exchange. Furthermore, the team needs to be able to articulate a clear IPO timeline of less than two years, ideally less than a year. Investors are going to want to see local banker engagement, although the banker involved in the Pre-IPO need not be guaranteed involvement in the IPO.

For early investors parched of liquidity, a pre-IPO can mean seeing cash months before the IPO. For early U.S. shareholders, a pre-IPO round can open liquidity before the IPO instead of 180 days after.

Considering all of these factors, the ability to offer a pre-IPO round is a significant strategic factor when considering listing exchanges. Planning to list on exchanges outside of the U.S. often results in superior optionality around pre-IPO rounds. Pre-IPO rounds often result in better pricing and institutional awareness at IPO.

Two Types of Exchanges

At the highest level, there are two fundamental types of stock exchanges, differentiated by their governance and regulatory structure: government-centric and self-regulated-centric.[55] Government-regulated exchanges operate under direct oversight from a government agency or ministry. The Shanghai Stock Exchange (SSE) and London Stock Exchange Main Board are both examples of Government-regulated exchanges.

Self-regulated exchanges operate with delegated authority to create and enforce their own rules, subject to supervision from a national securities regulator. The SGE in Singapore, ASX in Australia, and the London AIM market are all examples of self-regulated exchanges.

The Nasdaq was once mostly self-regulated. Early in my career, I consulted for the Nasdaq, and got to see the benefit first-hand. To be competitive, Nasdaq had to balance the needs of our investor members, and the companies that issued stock. Everyone had an incentive to keep out bad actors in the same way no wolf-hunting party wants to include someone noisy and careless.

For many decades, Nasdaq's oversight, rule-setting (especially for market makers, quote requirements, etc.), and some enforcement were handled under the National Association of Securities Dealers' (NASD) self-regulatory framework. At the time, Nasdaq itself was not a national securities exchange, in the same sense as NYSE, AMEX.

But much of that autonomy disappeared over time. This began in 1996, with an organizational change that separated the regulatory function into a separate organization.[56] And secondly, and more dramatically, in 2006 when the exchange registered one of its subsidiaries, the Nasdaq Stock Market LLC, as a national securities exchange. As of August 1, 2006, Nasdaq became operational in its capacity as a government-regulated national securities exchange.[57] Around that time, the regulatory division NASD merged with part of the regulatory division of NYSE to become FINRA. The SEC remained the overarching federal regulator, but FINRA became yet another layer of day-to-day rulemaker and enforcer. The result was more regulation, paperwork and costs without the market feedback loop of improving the 'product'. The product being a capital market that serves the 3Is; investor, intermediary and issuer.

Broadly speaking, self-regulated exchanges are often better positioned to balance the needs of all participants, since their success depends less on politics and more on market-driven survival.[58] Regardless of the governing framework, all exchanges need to make a variety of trade-offs to attract investors, intermediaries and issuers.

Main Boards

When thinking of two types of exchanges, there is another lens: main boards vs junior boards. Many countries have a main board and a junior board. The main board is designed for larger, established companies that can meet higher thresholds for financial performance, operating history, and governance, offering them prestige, deeper liquidity, and broader institutional investor access. The junior board is tailored to smaller, earlier-stage, or high-growth companies that don't yet meet the financial, track record, or governance requirements of the main board. For example:

Canada
Main: Toronto Stock Exchange TSX
Junior: TSX Venture Exchange (TSXV)

United Kingdom
Main: London Stock Exchange
Junior: AIM (Alternative Investment Market)

Europe
Main: Euronext Main Market (Amsterdam, Paris, Dublin, etc.)
Junior: Euronext Growth Paris (Dublin, France, Italy, Oslo Portugal)

Singapore
Main: SGX
Junior: Catalist

Hong Kong
Main: HKEX
Junior: GEM (Growth Enterprise Market)

For many years in the U.S., the NYSE was the main board and the Nasdaq was the junior board. In the 1970s and 1980s, part of the pitch for listing on the Nasdaq was, "List here, and uplist to the NYSE once you are bigger."[59] Today, both are geared for very large market cap companies, but also cater to the most active traders and the passive funds that need rebalancing, sometimes daily.

At our fund, the Global Public Offering Fund (GPO), we generally prefer main boards, not only for liquidity, but also for the reputational signaling. We back founder-led, globally scaling companies that we believe can become decacorns in the public market, and we want an exchange that can support the founders' ambitions. All 10 of the world's top-10 exchanges accommodate both rapidly scaling companies, and their global investors seeking returns.

There are also specialty exchanges. At first glance, they may look like junior boards, but they are specialty boards—the National Stock Exchange of Australia (NSX) being a good example. This is not a junior board to the main Australian Securities Exchange; it is increasingly courting companies in mining, energy, and natural resources. Oslo Børs, the Norwegian stock exchange, is known for shipping, while the Canadian Securities Exchange has pursued cannabis and blockchain companies.[60]

Industry-focused exchanges create information density: investors become experts in specific sectors, which improves price discovery. Exchanges that build a concentration of companies in one sector attract specialist analysts, bankers, and investors. In a world where capital is hyper-global and exchange models are driven by powerful network effects, we should expect additional exchanges to pursue industry specialization. Public exchanges must carve out niches and compete globally to stay relevant against the relentless pace of innovation in private markets.

The IPO Pop

Mispricing an IPO, especially underpricing, can result in a significant transfer of value from founders and early investors to new public market investors, typically short-term institutional buyers. That value accrues to hedge funds, mutual funds, and others in the IPO allocation club.

Imagine the frustration of founders and early investors who spend years building a company, only to see much of the value transferred to public market insiders who only participate for a few hours. Renowned VC Bill Gurley, who spent time on Wall Street, described it as, "one of the worst deals in capital markets."

The counter-argument is that a big first-day pop generates headlines, CNBC airtime, and a perception of hot demand. Leaving money on the table is a very expensive way to get attention but does create some exposure. It looks great in the marketing material of a venture fund, but what also looks great is less dilution and sending more cash to your LPs.

Non-US IPOs often exhibit less underpricing (a.k.a. mispricing between the offer price and the first-day close) compared to U.S, IPOs. This is due to increased investor communications before the IPO, more transparent bookbuilding processes, standardized disclosures, and tighter oversight of allocations. International IPOs often rely on local institutional investors (pension funds, sovereign wealth, insurance) with long-term mandates. These investors push for fair pricing, since they're not in the business of flipping IPO allocations for quick profits.

The amount of control you can have as a management team on IPO pricing also varies by market and investment bank. Allowing favored funds to capture first-day gains builds goodwill for the banker, but at a cost to the issuer. Company leaders should be proactive and not simply trust the bankers to look out for the interests of existing shareholders.

The cost of mispricing is further amplified by the potential existence of a greenshoe. A greenshoe option (also called an overallotment option) gives underwriters the right to sell up to 15% more shares than originally planned in the IPO.[61] These options are more or less common, depending on the market and investment bank. If the stock trades below issue price, underwriters might use the option to buy back shares in the open market, supporting the price. More often, if the stock trades above issue price, underwriters exercise the option to sell the extra shares at the IPO price. This increases bank profit and creates additional dilution for existing shareholders. (The term greenshoe in IPOs is named after the Green Shoe Manufacturing Company, now known as Stride Rite

Corporation.[62] It was the first company to include a specific overallotment option in its underwriting agreement when it went public in the 1960s.[63])

In the U.S., greenshoes are as common as underpricings. During the first 241 U.S. IPO of 2025, first-day pops averaged 36%, according to Reuters.[64] My banker friend assures me bankers are not greedy and any correlation is just coincidence. She goes on to point out that, "Greenshoes are fully disclosed and the issuer does receive additional capital," which helps offset the undermarket priced dilution.

Obviously, the size of the IPO, primary vs secondary mix, and the long-term capital needs of the company are factors when assessing the impact of mispricing. Corporate leaders evaluating an exchange should understand the likelihood, level of control and true cost associated with the IPO pop.

Other Considerations

Local specialists can help navigate the ever-changing local landscape of rules, customs and practices; this book will address selecting local guidance in later chapters. In fact, quality and depth of local advisors is in itself a consideration in selecting a listing venue! But, first, let's introduce some other technical considerations:

Ongoing Costs Before selecting an exchange, management should understand the ongoing cost of being public on that venue. AI should be driving down those costs, yet these costs still do differ sharply across exchanges. The process of understanding ongoing costs includes:

- Exchange Fees
- Regulatory & Compliance Costs
- Audit & Accounting (that may be incremental to staying private)
- Legal & Corporate Governance (that may be incremental to staying private)
- Board Compensation (that may be incremental to staying

private)
- Investor Relations (IR) & Communications
- Directors & Officers Liability Insurance ("D&O" may be material in the U.S.)

Opportunity Cost When evaluating a listing venue, management should also consider the opportunity cost associated with delaying or staying private. As Paul Hickey points out in his excellent book *IPO vs VC: 9 Strategic Reasons a $50 Million Small-Cap IPO Beats Venture Capital*: "It would be reasonable to think that you should get public as soon as possible once you understand the benefits and how expensive it is to NOT be a public company."

Ongoing Management Distraction While CFOs usually model the financial costs, the management distraction and cognitive load are often what make or break success post-IPO. Different exchanges impose different levels of reporting, governance, and investor relations burden. The heavier the obligations, the more management must divert time away from strategy, innovation, and execution.

Some exchanges create a permanent public company "treadmill" of earnings calls, investor scrutiny, compliance, and litigation risk. Other venues offer lighter touch regimes, enabling management to stay more focused on running the business. The risk of litigation and the associated distraction is significantly higher in the U.S., which also introduces added frictions on all investor interactions.

Listing Costs Before selecting an exchange, management should evaluate the upfront costs associated with going public in that venue. These costs can materially reduce IPO proceeds and differ significantly by market. The process of understanding listing costs includes the following:

- Underwriting Fees (often the single largest line item, varying by region and size of offering)
- Exchange Admission & Initial Listing Fees
- Legal Advisory Fees (IPO structuring, prospectus draft-

ing, securities law compliance)
- Accounting & Audit Fees (public-company–level audits, restatements, internal control readiness)
- Governance & Board Setup Costs (independent director recruitment, committee formation, policy adoption)
- IPO Marketing & Roadshow Expenses (analyst education, investor presentations, travel, logistics)
- Public Relations & Branding (media, communications strategy, visibility campaigns)
- One-Time D&O Insurance Placement Costs (pricing the first tower is often more expensive than renewals)
- IPO Mispricing and use of Greenshoes

Risk of Pulled IPO Sometimes called a "withdrawn IPO," this happens when a company files, markets, or even prices its offering, but then cancels the listing before shares begin trading—in plain terms, a planned IPO fails to launch. A regulatory framework, and process that surfaces valuation mismatches before the roadshow, reduces the risk (and potential public embarrassments) associated with an abandoned offering.

The concept of "testing the waters" (TTW), privately gauging investor appetite before going fully public, exists almost everywhere, but the terminology, effectiveness and mechanics differ. Some other terms:

- *Pilot Fishing* / Europe, London
- *Investor Education* / Hong Kong, Singapore & Asia
- *Pre-Marketing* / common across Asia-Pacific
- *Pre-sounding* / Nordics
- *Pre-Marketing* / Australia
- *Non-deal Roadshows* / Australia
- *Early Look* / London
- *Testing the Waters* / United States

Understanding the process is important in assessing the risk, but direct interactions with institutional investors are the best way to evaluate your company's specific risk. The sooner this process can begin for the company, and the lower the friction for management, the better.

Timeline to List Refers to the duration it takes from the moment a company decides to go public, until its shares are officially listed and trading on the exchange. This captures the speed, complexity, and predictability of the IPO process. Depending on the exchange, the time can be as short as a few weeks to over a year.

Ease of Follow-On Capital Timeline to list refers to the time required to conduct an IPO, but perhaps more important, especially for leaders who plan ahead, is the ease of follow-on capital. The IPO is just one financing event in the long journey of a generation-defining company; the "ease" includes both the time and cost. With this in mind, many exchanges have frameworks that allow follow-on capital raises to occur quickly, sometimes as quickly as just a single day with proper preparation.[65]

Dual-Class Shares Dual-class share structures allow founders or insiders to issue two (or more) classes of stock. Most exchanges now support dual-class structures, but not all. For those exchanges that don't support dual-class structures, there may be alternatives. For example, block voting agreements are a contractual arrangement in which a group of shareholders agree to vote their shares in unison, usually aligned with founders or management. A dual-class structure can also impact eligibility, as it relates to some indexes or passive investment funds.[66]

Equity Research Although AI is changing where and how equity research is generated, equity research can still be a decisive factor in where a company chooses to list, because the depth, quality, and reach of analyst coverage directly affect valuation, liquidity, and long-term shareholder base composition.

Bankers Local banker quality is often an underappreciated but critical driver of where a company chooses to list. They shape not only the IPO process, but also the company's long-term access to capital and investor base. Good bankers do not just place shares, they provide aftermarket liquidity support, analyst introductions, and follow-on capital raising. It's not just the quality of the bankers, it's also the quality of the bankers who will work with you which defines this. It's near-impossible to get the attention of the best bankers in New York with a "small" $100-million IPO. Supermodel Linda Evangelista once quipped, "We don't wake up for less than $10,000 a day!" Well, bankers are the same way. The good news is that outside the U.S., a $100-million IPO will usually get the attention of the applicable super-bankers.

Shareholder Spread Shareholder spread refers to the distribution of shares among different shareholders, particularly focusing on how many individual shareholders own a company's stock and how concentrated or dispersed that ownership is. This concept is especially important in public markets and IPO contexts, as stock exchanges often require a minimum shareholder spread for listing eligibility.[67]

Tax Treatment Pension funds, sovereign wealth funds and income-focused investors are highly sensitive to after-tax yields. Existing shareholders, founders and employees are highly sensitive to capital gain rules. Tax treatments are always an important lens when considering listing venues.

Controlled Company Status This definition can vary by region or exchange. Some institutional investors apply a "governance discount" to controlled companies, particularly where shareholder rights are weaker. Conversely, some long-term funds (especially those aligned with founder-led businesses) may accept it as part of the value proposition. It matters because exchanges grant such companies exemptions from certain corporate governance requirements, which would otherwise apply to widely held firms.

Free Float Requirements These rules specify the minimum percentage of a company's shares that must be held by public investors (not insiders or controlling shareholders) for the stock to remain listed on an exchange.

Lock-up Periods A lock-up period is a contractual restriction preventing company insiders (founders, executives, early investors, employees) from selling their shares for a set time after the IPO. The goal of lockups is to prevent a flood of insider shares, depressing the stock right after listing. Rules vary by exchange and situation. Venues with longer or stricter lock-ups reduce supply shocks, but may frustrate insiders and VCs eager to monetize. More flexible regimes can attract high-growth issuers seeking early liquidity for stakeholders. Exchanges and underwriters differ in how rigidly they enforce lock-up norms, and companies therefore may select venues where bankers and regulators allow tailored lock-up structures, such as staggered releases.

Size, Age or Profitability Requirements These are some of the most fundamental constraints when a company is evaluating where to go public. These criteria determine who can list, and under what conditions. For example, once upon a time the NYSE and HKSE did not allow unprofitable companies to list, but this changed. Indeed, the popularity of the Nasdaq in the '80s and '90s was partially driven by the fact they allowed unprofitable companies to list. In 2018, HKEX implemented reforms that permitted listings of biotech companies that did not meet the main board profit tests.[68] The NYSE and Nasdaq listing requirements are very similar, both allowing unprofitable companies to go public.

Disclosure Periods Disclosure periods refer to the frequency and timing of financial and corporate reporting that a listed company must provide once public. These generally fall into, annual, bi-annual, quarterly and continuous. Many jurisdictions don't require quarterly reports reducing reporting burden. Instead, many jurisdictions use continuous disclosure obligations, meaning if something material happens then it needs to be quickly disclosed to the market. This approach is preferable for many institutional investors, and results in a more transparent and up-to-date market. For management teams, it means less "frantic fire drill at the end of the quarter" and more "timely disclosure when something big happens."

Pre-emption Rights Pre-emption rights (sometimes called subscription rights) are a legal protection for existing shareholders, handing them the first opportunity to buy new shares before a company issues them to outsiders. Rules related to pre-emption rights can vary by exchange, but they are effectively a tug-of-war between shareholder protection and capital-raising flexibility. If management wants maximum flexibility to issue shares quickly (PIPEs, private placements, strategic placements), pre-emption is less advantageous. If attracting long-term, institutional investors who demand anti-dilution protection then pre-emption could be advantageous.

Trading Hours There is a global trend towards 24-hour trading, yet trading hours can still have a meaningful impact on an issuer's choice of listing venue because they shape liquidity, investor access, and alignment with the company's strategic geography. Liquidity clusters will tend to occur when the company's target shareholders are awake and active. Exchanges in Europe and the Middle East often benefit from partial overlap with both Asia and the U.S., creating a broader window of cross-border liquidity.[69]

ESG and Climate-related Rules ESG and climate-related disclosure rules have become a frontline factor in choosing stock exchanges, because they directly affect compliance burden, investor access, and valuation premiums. Keep an eye on the emerging Texas Stock Exchange (TXSE), as it aims to differentiate the exchange by reducing regulatory burden and costs tied up in compliance with ESG/DEI rules. Conversely, if you believe your company is especially strong as it relates to ESG, you may want to consider markets such as the Deutsche Börse or Euronex, where investors have demonstrated a desire to heavily weigh those factors in their investment decision-making.

Maintaining Listing Requirements There are ongoing rules and standards that a company must be compliant with after it goes public on a stock exchange. These are distinct from initial listing requirements (the hurdles you need to clear to

IPO). They represent the minimum standards to remain listed and avoid suspension, fines, or delisting.

Delisting A board, founder or shareholders may want to delist for many reasons; markets change and it is important to maintain the option to go private. But some exchanges are like the old cockroach commercial: "You can check in, but you can't check out." Before selecting an exchange, be sure to understand what type of shareholder consent (and notification period) is required to leave an exchange.

You may notice that liquidity is not a criteria for selecting an exchange. That is because liquidity is ultimately a function of how effectively management leverages the exchange to cultivate sustained investor interest. It depends on their ability to maintain a base of current shareholders eager to increase their holdings, while simultaneously building a pipeline of prospective investors looking for an entry point. Liquidity is not measured by looking at the daily trading volume of a given company, it is instead measured by the ability of the company management (or existing shareholders) to pick up the phone and place a big block of stock in the market.

Selecting an appropriate venue is part of achieving liquidity, but you don't just throw your stock over an IPO wall and hope investors pick it up on the other side. The process of going public and being public also requires intentionality. The later chapters discuss those stages.

Summary

- **Be Intentional** Treat the choice of exchange like a technology "stack" decision - deliberate, architecture-driven, and changeable over time.

- **Exchanges as Infrastructure** A good exchange has distribution, compliance signaling, and gateway to global capital, trading may occur elsewhere.

- **Tradeoffs Matter** Every exchange carries trade-offs; understand these before deciding.

- **Size & Investor Alignment** Pick a venue appropriate to company scale - large-cap markets attract huge institutions; smaller or regional markets may offer better coverage and fit.

- **Comparables & Alignment** Where peers trade affects valuation, analyst coverage, index inclusion and investor receptivity; sometimes standing out is strategically better.

- **Connective Tissue** Local business presence, founders/ investors with market ties (aka "boomerangs"), and on-the-ground relationships materially improve investor reception; lack of ties can raise red flags.

- **Legal Regime** Common-law jurisdictions offer investor protections and easier alignment for companies incorporated under similar systems - legal fit influences complexity and cost.

- **Pre-IPO Strategy:** Pre-IPOs can signal demand, provide capital, clean cap tables and improve IPO pricing - U.S. Rule 144 limits their attractiveness for U.S. investors, making non-US venues comparatively more flexible.

- **Exchange Types & Boards** Understand government-regulated vs. self-regulated exchanges and main boards vs. junior/specialty boards; industry-focused venues can create information density and better price discovery.

- **IPO Mechanics & Risks** Be mindful of underpricing ("IPO pop"), greenshoe dilution, allocation practices, and the issuer's control over pricing - different markets handle these differently.

- **Practical Costs & Maintenance** Evaluate upfront and ongoing costs, timeline to list, follow-on capital ease, reporting cadence, dual-class rules, free-float, lock-ups, tax treatment, ESG rules, delisting requirements and managerial distraction.

Choosing where to list is a strategic decision, not something to be left to chance or domestic habit. The right exchange affects visibility, investor mix, valuation, regulatory burden and long-term access to capital. Exchanges differ and bring trade-offs between liquidity, control, cost and scrutiny.

Management should build a shortlist of suitable venues, pit them against one another, and weigh upfront and ongoing costs, timeline, ability to pre-market to investors, and the likely post-IPO investor base. Good local advisers, realistic timelines and honest assessment of management distraction are essential: the aim is to pick the venue that best supports the company's growth path and long-term capital strategy, not just the one that seems most prestigious.

In the next chapter, we will dive deeply into the public listing process.

Chapter 7
The IPO Process

"Where you list isn't necessarily where you trade anymore."
Adena Friedman—Nasdaq CEO

The IPO is the gateway to being a public company, but markets are now interconnected, and capital is global, meaning that the best investors for you could be located anywhere![1] The IPO process is broadly similar across global exchanges, but each market has its nuances around regulation, disclosure, and listing requirements. A company's experience will be significantly impacted by their selection of exchange, the nature of their business, and the quality of their bankers. Later in the book, we discuss vendor "bake-offs" and selecting bankers.

In subsequent chapters, we will also discuss the various vendors and investors involved in the transition to the public market. Advisors such as accountants, bankers and law firms should all be able to go into more detail given the specifics. But first: a high-level overview of the process for those less familiar.

Depending on the exchange, the process can be as short as 16 weeks. Other exchanges can take over a year.[2] Of course, the quality of the various advisors and general IPO readiness of the company will impact the length of the process. Core mechanics (filing, marketing, bookbuilding, listing) are universal.[3]

Filing (Regulatory Disclosure & Eligibility)

This phase includes drafting registration documents, which includes audited financials, business overview, risks, and governance disclosures. These documents are submitted to the applicable exchange and regulators, draft filings are reviewed, commented on, and revised (multiple rounds common). For many jurisdictions, a "man on the street" prospectus contains much of the key information.[4] In other jurisdictions, the filing documents are steep in legal jargon and disclaimers.

Companies may want to involve bankers in multiple jurisdictions as part of the IPO.[5] We talk more about selecting bankers later in the book, but having representation in multiple jurisdictions will help in building a diverse base of long-term investors. They are more likely to have solid regional relationships, and It may be necessary to tailor the offering document for marketing in specific languages or jurisdictions. The exchange will conduct eligibility checks (i.e. financial history, market cap, shareholder spread, governance compliance, etc.) before accepting the company for listing, sometimes called "admission."

Marketing (Roadshow & Investor Education)

The first step of marketing will see the underwriters provide early read-throughs to institutional investors ("pilot fishing" in Europe; "testing the waters" in the U.S.).[6] Analysts publish pre-deal research reports. Pre-deal research is common globally, except in the U.S., where regulations from the early 2000s restrict research until after the IPO![7]

The next step is the roadshow. The management team (CEO/CFO, sometimes COO/CTO) conducts one to two weeks of presentations. There are a mix of lunches, dinners, large presentations, and 1-on-1s with top funds. Company leaders should expect bankers to provide background on the funds in advance of all meetings, but should anticipate that some unexpected "targets of opportunity" may pop up during the process.

Hopefully, by the time of the roadshow, management has already started building a relationship and reputation among some long-term investors. The roadshow is the part of an IPO where companies expand existing relationships, begin new relationships, and further shape investor perception.

Obviously, the best leadership teams prepare and rehearse. Founders may have given the pitch a thousand times, but this is different. Public investors are not venture capitalists or the media. Get professional feedback and be prepared to tailor the pitch by the background of investors. Investor feedback is collected in real-time, and the story articulation is refined throughout the roadshow. Yet management and bankers also need to maintain narrative discipline on the key elements of the story.

It is also worth noting that since COVID in 2019, video conferencing has become increasingly common, and acceptable.[8] Companies should look at this as an opportunity to expand the roadshow to a broader, more diverse and more distributed set of institutions.

The goal is to drive demand for the equity and set up long-term aftermarket performance. Once a company is public it will be easy to speak with existing investors, but it will be harder to reach future investors. As one CEO said: "It's easy to reach my existing investors—they are owners and always want to know what is happening. The harder part is getting in front of new investors; being public makes the effort a little easier."

The roadshow is not just about an IPO; like pre-IPO rounds, it is an opportunity to start a relationship with future investors.

Pro tip: Under-promise and over-deliver. Credibility on IPO day drives long-term multiples.[9] Public market investors don't just buy the shares, they buy the management team's word. If you promise too much and miss a little, credibility is damaged, and the stock can trade at a discount for longer than anyone wants. Alternatively, companies that consistently beat expectations earn a "credibility premium" and enjoy evergreen access to additional capital if needed.

Bookbuilding (Order Collection & Pricing)

The bookbuilding phase is where the IPO is truly assembled. Orders are collected, demand is gauged, and the final price is set. The quality of this step determines allocation, aftermarket stability, and long-term shareholder base.

The first part of the bookbuilding process is order collection. During the roadshow, underwriters solicit bids from institutional investors, and then the investors indicate price and size preferences (Indications of Interest—IOIs).

Next, IOIs are tiered by quality and prioritized. Tier 1 = long-only and anchors; Tier 2 = hedge funds; Tier 3 = fast money.[10]

Throughout the phase, underwriters monitor demand vs. price range. If oversubscribed, price guidance moves upward; if weak, range can be cut. The feedback loop needs to be between investors, underwriters, and management.

Next, the Final IPO price is generally set the night before listing.[11]

Finally comes allocation. This is where the inside baseball of IPOs really comes out. The bookbuilding process looks straightforward on the surface; collect orders, set prices. But in reality it's an exercise in psychology, investor relations, and strategic allocation. For managers, open debate is guaranteed to improve your understanding of your future shareholders. It is important to prioritize sticky, long-term holders over speculative buyers. The quality of feedback and chemistry during the process is also a consideration.

Listing (Trading & Stabilization)

This phase is the IPO's public debut, the culmination of months of preparation. This is when shares begin trading, stabilization mechanisms kick in, and the company transitions from a private entity to a public one. When this is done right, it sets the tone for aftermarket credibility and long-term valuation.

This is the day leadership "rings the bell." Different exchanges use different systems to establish the first trade price, but the stock shifts to open-market trading. Liquidity, volatility, and price discovery are now driven by investors.

Market makers and underwriters may also coordinate post-IPO support to balance supply and demand.[12] This "stabilization" can last for as long as 30 days, and you can expect the use of a greenshoe option (15% overallotment) to buy back shares if the stock trades weakly, or exercising the option is advantageous for the banker. In practice, most greenshoes are exercised not because the stock is weak, but because demand is strong.[13]

A Wedding Party is Not a Marriage

The key is getting the stock into the hands of long-term supportive shareholders. As we read a few chapters back, a senior executive at the Dubai Exchange said, "Confusing an IPO with being public, is like confusing a good wedding party with a successful marriage." In other words, an IPO is just an event in a company's life; a Global IPO is about building evergreen relationships with investors who want to support your vision. The IPO is not about oversubscription headlines, it's about the quality and stability of the share registry.

What is Dual Tracking?

Often the process of filing will trigger inquiries from a new set of strategic Investors or acquirers.[14] But it turns out that lots of global strategic investors don't proactively build relationships with start-ups—their banker and board relationships tend to be local. Potentially even more important, their strategic needs and objectives may be confidential, reducing the chance of the companies connecting. This all changes once a company files to go public. The increased profile increases, and the private company gets noticed, as many corporate acquisition teams monitor pending IPOs. Existing public market shareholders are also more likely to bring the private company to the attention of a potential acquirer.

More potential acquirers will become aware of the company as a result of an IPO than could ever be identified by a banker running a simple M&A process. It is not uncommon for a company to be acquired shortly in advance of a pending IPO. If unexpected, you can assume the terms were attractive. If it happens on purpose, with the proactive involvement of bankers, it is called "dual tracking."[15]

Listing increases M&A optionality, but completing an IPO also can support M&A. I once angel invested in a company that went public on the Nasdaq. The CEO told me he felt the acquirer, Adobe, would have never bought the company had it not been for the transparency of being a public company—underlining the value of an IPO as part of the path to an exit.

Credible, which IPO'd at a $300-million market cap on the ASX in December of 2017, is another good example. The company was bought by Fox in August 2019 for $585 million.[16]

Alternative Listing Approaches

This book focuses on traditional IPOs, but this section discusses alternate listing approaches, such as SPACs, RTOs, and Direct Listings. Our investment fund prefers shareholder marketing opportunities associated with a "Front Door Listing." That said, there are other ways to become a publicly listed company. When I hear alternate approaches, I am reminded of the Warren Buffett 1987 shareholder letter: "I call this the 'cigar butt' approach to investing. A cigar butt found on the street that has only one puff left in it may not offer much of a smoke, but the 'bargain purchase' will make that puff all profit."

Very few of us are fans of cigar butts! His metaphor was about cheap companies, but I believe it often applies to cheap listing approaches—just because an approach is inexpensive does not mean it is good value.

Reverse Merger (RTOs) Reverse mergers, also called reverse takeovers, have been around for decades as an alternative to IPOs. Often, they involve a company that once had operations and is now a publicly listed shell. SPACs are a subset of RTOs, but are generally set up with the specific purpose of a reverse merging.[17]

The initial cost, speed and certainty appeals to some corporate managers. However, one of the risks is "dirty shells"—when a shell company has hidden liabilities (lawsuits, bad shareholders, accounting issues), the merged company inherits them. The other risk is that the shell's existing shareholders will likely be selling their shares, driving down price, the first chance they get.

Bankers, and existing shell owners (which in some markets may be affiliated) will pitch the 'easyness' of the process. Best to be skeptical, RTOs are not financing or marketing events. Reverse mergers only create a listing, companies often need a PIPE (private investment in public equity) alongside the RTO to raise fresh capital. RTOs contrast sharply with front door IPOs which are a fundraising event that also includes a listing and more importantly, an investor marketing event.

SPAC (Special Purpose Acquisition Company) Essentially a blank-check shell company created for the sole purpose of taking a private company public through a merger.

The SPAC organizer, or Sponsor, typically gets around 20% of the merged company. The pitch to the company looking to list is the process is easier, and some of the money in the SPAC will be available to fund growth, but there is a catch—usually the existing SPAC investors can redeem the cash.

SPACs have existed for decades but became very popular in the U.S. the 2020-2021, when a record breaking 600+ were launched.[18] By 2022–2023, most traded below IPO price as redemption rates hit 80–90% and PIPEs dried up.[19]

The popularity of SPACs shows the frustration with the U.S. IPO process. Basically, the U.S. process had become so broken companies were willing to try something new. But how was it broken?

Well, the U.S. basically has two IPO problems:

1. For a smaller company, it was hard to go public.
2. As a smaller company, it was hard to get institutional interest once public.[20]

First, the process of going public had changed in the early 2010s. Serbanes-Oxly, and a raft of regulations, had created a process that was satisfying to both investors and company leaders. The investor discussions had become tedious, as everything seemed to require layers of layers. It was arduous and laborious, and the result was that listing timeframe elongated, while costs ballooned.

How bad was it? It was so bad that founders were willing to give up 20% of their company simply to get public![21] SPACs did a good job at addressing the first problem. The process was simpler—communications with investors were more open, while outcomes were more predictable. But SPACs did not address the second problem. In fact, they did the exact opposite.

Let's put that second problem into context. By the early 2010s, many U.S. Institutions had become quite large. In the '80s and '90s they would eagerly look at small IPOs, but by 2010 they could not be bothered with small IPOs. To be successful as a listed company in the U.S., you need to build relationships with smaller long-term oriented institutional investors. There are many of them on a global basis, but SPACs are not marketed to long-term investors. There is no IPO Roadshow, the marketing is for fast money. These are often investors who are investing before they even know what company is going to be acquired! These investors will most likely dump all of the shares the first chance they get.

Companies that list via a SPAC are denied the huge opportunity to market to investors that are associated with a well-run IPO, long term investors. And, even worse, they find themselves listed with all the wrong investors, needing to go find a new set of longer term investors, without the benefit of the introductions associated with a traditional IPO. A de-SPACed company's price will suffer till they find suitable investors. Finding the right investors can take years.

Direct Listing Here a company lists existing shares on an exchange without raising new capital.[22] Shares just start trading. Big names such as Spotify, Slack, and Coinbase all used this approach, and it might be appropriate if the company is not seeking additional capital and does not feel the need to market to new investors. It is a mechanical dumping of shares on an exchange without a banker-lead institutional road show.

One important result is the company is now listed and has much greater financial flexibility. M&A, credibility, capital raises and employee compensation should all benefit. This flexibility also extends to shareholders who now have a market to sell shares.

Direct listings save underwriting fees and avoid IPO underpricing, but they raise no new capital, while missing the opportunity to raise the profile of the company, and kick off new relationships with long-term investors.

Form 10 Filing A way for a private company to become a public reporting company with the SEC, but without being listed on an exchange.[23] Essentially, a company is signing up for all the paperwork associated with being public. It's sometimes called a "backdoor" or "quiet" IPO. There is no capital raised. There is no roadshow or underwriter. There are more ongoing filings including (10-Ks, 10-Qs, 8-Ks). The company also needs to now comply with Sarbanes-Oxley and other various proxy rules.

Why Do Form 10? Generally, Form 10 can become necessary if a company has too many U.S. Shareholders, or if they want to lay the foundation for a future public offering. Certain transactions (like spin-offs) may need to file a Form 10 to register securities being distributed to shareholders, especially if the shareholders are not all qualified investors. Company management may also want to support shareholders who are conducting transactions OTC, or in private secondary exchanges.

OTC (Over-The-Counter) This is often misunderstood. For some companies, it's a deliberate alternative to the full IPO path; for others, it's more of a stepping stone for uplisting, for others it is used as a complement to a primary listing outside the U.S.

Listing on OTCQX/OTCQB (U.S.) or equivalent OTC venues avoids the heavy compliance burden of the NYSE or Nasdaq.[24] Companies don't need to file a full SEC registration/prospectus. Ongoing annual costs are significantly lower partly due the the lack of Sarbanes-Oxley compliance. In some cases, shares can even be listed by a third party, without the involvement of the company. As an example, foreign-listed companies often list OTC American Depositary Receipts (ADRs) as a way to give U.S. investors easier access, without going through a U.S. IPO.

OTC listings save underwriting fees and avoid IPO underpricing, but they raise no new capital, while missing the opportunity to raise the profile of the company, and initiate new relationships with long-term investors. Use of the OTC usually only makes sense as part of a global listing and trading strategy.

A 144A Offering can be used in the U.S. to complement an offshore IPO.[25] It is a way for a company to raise capital from large U.S. institutional investors through a private placement, bypassing the complexities and costs of a full SEC registration. This is basically a "global" IPO that is not-available to the U.S. Retail Investor. Big Institutions that can be classified as "Qualified Institutional Buyers" (QIBs) read a tailored prospectus.

So a 144A offering lets a company go public outside the U.S. while simultaneously "privately" targeting a specific subset of U.S. institutional investors. A 144A Offering creates a mechanism to target U.S. institutional investors, who are only based in the U.S with a private offering.

U.S. Regulation S U.S. Companies going public on an exchange outside the U.S. can also target U.S. Institutions that have an International investing entity.[26] Founders and company leaders of U.S. companies should work with their attorney and international bankers to understand the rule. The key is targeting the managers where there is a reasonable expectation they are managing funds in non-US domiciled investment vehicles.

A good Investment Bank based in Europe, UK, or Asia should have relationships with the right 'international' investor, physically sitting outside the U.S or even in the U.S. Yes, funds technically domiciled in places as far away as Cayman Islands, Singapore and Dubai are often managed from places as close as Greenwich Connecticut, New York, New York, and San Francisco, California.

International Tranched IPO The term has different meanings for bankers sitting in different regions, but the best way to think of it is: have a portion of your IPO tailored to different regions.

A tranche is a slug of stock you plan to make available for a set of investors. A tranche may require specific:

- Regionally licensed banker (also called distribution channel)
- Regional paperwork/filings (ie; 144, Formulário de Referência, or Reg S)
- Bankers with local relationships
- Translation of prospectus into another language

Ideally the different tranches compete for allocation, and regions that have limited participation at time of IPO, may become important sources of capital or liquidity as the company grows.

Tokenized Equity Offering Once a company equity is publicly tradable, there are international services that can issue an equity token fully backed one-to-one by stock held at a regulated custodian—essentially, the digital representation of traditional shares of a company. Ownership, transfer, and sometimes even settlement of those shares, can happen via tokens rather than through legacy clearing systems. You can think of this as wrapping a stock in a blockchain-based format. Apple, Microsoft, Coinbase Nvidia and Intel are all examples of equities where crypto-savvy non-US investors can buy tokens backed by the stock.[27] The organization issuing the token may or may not have any association with the company. Some companies may want to tokenize shares as a brand signal, positioning themselves as tech-forward, investor-friendly or aligned with blockchain adoption.[28] Other companies may want to tokenize to diversify their investor base and attract new 24-hr liquidity pools.

Think of tokenized equity as similar to stablecoins, except instead of being backed 100% by currency or government bonds, the tokens are backed 100% by equity shares. As a global wallet infrastructure gets built out for stablecoins, investors will discover that same infrastructure can be used for investing.

By the mid-2020s there was a large and fast growing global cohort of investors trading all things tokenized.[29] These include both short-term speculators who provide liquidity and seek to benefit from short-term market inefficiencies, as well as long term investors looking for quality assets. Long-term crypto-centric investors may require they hold assets in tokenized form so they can use it as collateral for smart contracts. Crypto-centric investors include both human and AI based participants. Sometimes called autonomous agents or algorithmic agents, these AI-based market participants are likely to prefer tokenized assets because they enable programmable, permissionless execution with embedded compliance, faster settlement cycles, and granular data access that aligns with autonomous decision-making protocols.

Cross-Listing A company can list on multiple exchanges at the same time during its IPO. More common: a company IPOs in one market (its "primary listing"), then later cross-lists elsewhere. This avoids the complexity of doing everything at once, and enables the company to establish itself first.

Shares are usually fungible across markets, in that an investor could buy them in one country and sell them in another. Dual Listing and Cross Listing are often used interchangeably in casual discussion, however in some markets they can take on different technical meanings. For example, Unilever operated for decades as two legal entities: Unilever N.V. (Netherlands) and Unilever Plc (UK), with coordinated operations and identical economic rights. Not a cross-listing, a locally defined duel-listing.

Cross-listing can increase trading volume by making shares available in multiple time zones. For example, Toyota and Samsung trade both in their home markets and in the U.S. Brand positioning is one reason to cross-list but liquidity is another. Some academic research shows cross-listed firms often enjoy a liquidity premium and broader analyst coverage.

In some jurisdictions, local investors have regulatory constraints related to buying in foreign markets; in this case a cross-listing can be helpful when seeking to unlock specific regulated capital pools. Cross-listing can also impact index eligibility, which can drive new pools of passive fund flows.

If a company announces a longer term plan to cross-list as part of a well designed IPO, the promise of cross-listing can be used as a method to strengthen regional marketing. For example, a London IPO that promises to cross-list in the Middle East shortly after going public may be more likely to attract Middle East investors, who understand the long-term demand for the equity in the region.

Summary

- An IPO is an event, not the end: the real goal is to build a stable, long-term shareholder base, not just an oversubscribed launch.
- There are multiple ways to go public, and the optimal approach depends on the specific long-term strategy of the company.
- Core mechanics are universal: filing (disclosure & eligibility), marketing/roadshow, bookbuilding (order collection & pricing), and listing/stabilization.
- Exchange selection should align with the company's target investors and strategy.
- Quality of advisers and bankers materially affects timing, allocation, and long-term investor mix. Choose them carefully.
- Roadshows are marketing and relationship-building exercises: narrative discipline and preparation win trust; under-promise and over-deliver.
- Bookbuilding is strategic: prioritize 'sticky' long-only investors and anchors over short-term, speculative money.
- Allocation matters: who gets shares shapes aftermarket stability and long-term multiples; treat it as investor-relations work, not just math.
- Tokenized routes are becoming valid options for inves-

tors, often helping to expand liquidity.
- SPACs/RTOs can deliver speed and certainty, but often bring the wrong investor base or legacy liabilities.
- Direct listings save fees, but forego fundraising and marketing.

The roadshow and pre-IPO marketing are critical opportunities to build durable relationships and shape investor perception. Narrative discipline and the simple principle of under-promise and over-deliver can determine the long-term credibility of an IPO and business. Timelines can vary, but the goal is always the same—attract sticky, long-term capital.

In the next chapter, we will examine some of the key players in the public market, and how they impact the IPO field.

Global IPO

Chapter 8
Knowing the Players to Understand the Game

"Show me the incentive and I will show you the outcome."
Charlie Munger—Legendary Investor

Berkshire Hathaway's longtime Vice-Chairman Charlie Munger believed incentives drive nearly all business and human decisions, and often more powerfully than most people are willing to admit.[1] And yet, despite the immense volume of IPO guides published by banks, exchanges, accountants and lawyers, our team was unable to find a document that looked at the process through the lens of incentives.[2]

I believe this chapter is the only IPO process documentation written through the lens of incentives, which matters because incentives drive outcomes.[3] It will summarize the key factors, but let us state up front that greed, fear, ego, and peer pressure all play vital roles.[4]

It's important to note that companies don't go public alone—it takes a team.[5] This chapter is a no-nonsense guide for how to choose, wrangle, and manage vendors. Just as critical, it unpacks the cast of characters prowling the public markets—investors on the hunt, and what makes them bite.

As discussed earlier, an IPO is like a wedding party, but should not be confused with a marriage. Taking the metaphor further, a wedding party has its support crew—planners, caterers, bar tenders and musicians. For company management, an IPO is an important step in a long-term relationship with public market investors, but for many of the participants, this is just a transaction.

Who is Organizing Your IPO Party?

Your IPO "party" is going to have lots of advisors—investment banks, lawyers, accountants, investment relations specialists. In theory, they are looking out for you in the same way a wedding planner should be helping you with your wedding party. They may be friendly, but they are not your friends! They all have their motives, which we will explore later, but they are focused on the IPO event. Many advisors are no more focused on the success of the event than a wedding planner is focused on the long-term success of a marriage. They see a one-time transaction and only care about what's in it for them. The best advisors treat the event not as a small transaction but, instead, as a reputational proofpoint (leauge tables) or the possible beginning of a long and lucrative relationship.

Company leadership should view the IPO as an opportunity to begin or extend investor relationships. When this is conducted effectively, the relationships that result can last for many years. Management needs to have a longer-term view. Perhaps the IPO event is the ultimate marshmallow test?[6] As one visionary founder said: "It's not about who is going to invest at the IPO; it's about who is going to invest years from now, when one of those investors sells."

Just like for a wedding party, management has a lot of say about who attends and who to spend time with during the party.

The Lead Banker is often referred to as the "lead left" in a syndicate of bankers supporting an IPO.[7] ("Lead left" refers to their name placement on the cover of the prospectus.)

They are arguably the most influential external players in a global IPO—part-quarterback, part-diplomat and part-rainmaker—so their selection can have significant implications on valuation, execution quality, long-term shareholder base, and post-IPO performance.[8]

Once your intention to go public becomes known, it is common for board members to "know a guy," but this is not the best way to select a banker.[9] The selection process should be a formal bake-off based on relationships developed over time. We will talk more about the selection process later, but the importance of chemistry with the team should not be underestimated.

Bankers get fees, and being the economically motivated animals they are, most will try to convince you to work with them exclusively.[10] They will explain that they can do everything and should not have "anyone else on the cover." Don't fall for it! There are a few reasons why you should be resistant to this notion. Firstly, bankers get busy and you can't guarantee that you will get their full attention during the IPO. Markets are always changing, and the best bankers often get pulled into more lucrative transactions. An IPO is too important to entrust to one institution. I've watched smaller firms outperform giants by recruiting sharper teams, implementing greater urgency, and demonstrating an unrelenting drive to win.

Second, no single bank, no matter how prestigious, can cover every angle of a successful IPO.[11] Every bank has a region, sector, reputation or relationship that gives them an advantage with those investors. If you want to be successful, you want to have a lead banker and joint bookrunners.

Joint Bookrunners These banks help build the order book and meet with investors, but don't lead the deal, and will typically appear on the "right side" of the prospectus cover.[12] As a general rule, joint bookrunners receive smaller economics and have less influence over pricing and allocation.[13]

Joint bookrunners matter immensely in a global IPO because they enable the issuer to tap into diverse capital pools, execute across jurisdictions, and optimize for both pricing and long-term shareholder quality. In a cross-border offering, where market access, regulation, and investor appetite vary widely, the right bookrunners multiply the reach and credibility of the offering.

Regional institutional investors often choose to make purchases through local banks they trust and have long-term relationships with.[14] Another issue that is critically important is that bookrunners are competing with the lead bank and each other, because bankers are paid by how much they place as part of the book build.[15] The optimal outcome for a bank is to do as little work as possible, while placing the most important bank clients, but joint bookrunners introduce healthy competition into that process. The management team should let the bankers' greed benefit existing shareholders. Perhaps even more important is having more investors at the table during the book build, as this enables management to choose the "best" shareholders, usually the investors they believe are likely to hold for a long time, and who will buy more shares when they become available.

More bookrunners is not necessarily better. Just as in venture capital with "party rounds," where no one shows leadership or real commitment, syndicates can be *too* big. If too big the banks are not motivated, as their share of the economics is too small. Too many egos can also be a problem. The bookrunners, also called brokers, have been known to have egos, every time you add one you run the risk of interpersonal rivalry. Industry veterans call this a "pissing contest," where egos and bravado get in the way of a successful raise. Syndicate membership should have complimentary strengths not duplicative.

Equity Research Analysts In global IPOs, where diverse investor bases, multi-jurisdictional listings, and asymmetric information are common, strategic research coverage is a huge advantage.[16] Equity research plays a pivotal role in the success of a global IPO, before, during and especially after the offering.

Outside the U.S., analysts host investor calls, attend conferences, and run non-deal roadshows (NDRs) where they talk about your company.[17] In the U.S., SEC rules and FINRA regulations create a strict separation between investment banking and research functions.[18] U.S. equity research analysts do not publish pre-IPO reports or participate in formal investor education before the IPO.

When selecting jurisdictions and banks, access to equity research analysts is a core part of the selection process.

"Getting Spitzered" became shorthand in finance for being subject to regulatory restrictions imposed by the 2003 Global Research Analyst Settlement—a settlement spearheaded by then-New York Attorney General Eliot Spitzer.[19] As a consequence of this legislation, large banks have a "Chinese Wall" separating banking from research.

However, many international banks are "non-Spitzered," meaning their research analysts are more involved in the listing process.[20] Boutique advisory firms, or firms without large trading operations, can also lean into research.

A company's syndicate of bankers should include "non-Spitzered" banks because management and research are allowed to have a healthy interaction.[21] This approach allows equity research to play a greater role in shaping and amplifying the narrative.

Critically important, and often underappreciated, analysts not only help share the narrative with potential investors, they also play a critical role in training other members of your IPO team, including sales.

Sales The sales team at your investment bank is the human link between your company and the global buy-side, translating the story into conviction, and conviction into capital.

While bankers build the deal, and research shapes the narrative, sales is who gets the money in the door.

In a cross-border IPO listing, the right regional sales teams are essential to navigate local capital markets, culture, and investor psychology, helping bridge the gap between the issuing company and unfamiliar local markets. They can also help coordinate with legal, investor-relations and syndicate teams to ensure disclosures and marketing comply with local rules, while also smoothing cultural frictions that can affect trust and demand.

An IPO sales team at an investment bank is motivated by a mix of individual incentives, institutional dynamics, and client relationship priorities. Salespeople are ultimately driven by revenue, and IPOs are major fee events. They typically earn credit for orders from their clients that are allocated and priced.[22]

This is important because high-performing IPOs can boost the sales bankers year-end comp, especially if their book performed well relative to others on the desk.[23] Having said that, it is important to remember that for the sales team, many of these relationships are long-term. Sales will typically do a much better job promoting your security if they understand and believe in the company's potential.

Long-term sales want to build profitable relationships with clients, which are investors. In this sense, your security is simply a product or commodity. This might mean bankers are incentivized to place your stock with an institution that will simply flip it.[24] A bank's most profitable institutional clients often are active traders and use leverage. This is great for a bank, but those bank clients are much less likely to be long-term company shareholders. Yet another reason company management needs to be diligent during the book build process.

In selecting a bank, management teams should meet some of the sales team. Important tip here—don't be afraid to ask for constructive feedback. A good sales team should be already thinking about the pros and cons of your narrative, and can therefore provide critical insight.

Trading On IPO day, the trading desk is essentially running the cockpit of your stock's first flight.[25] They sit at the center of a live feedback loop with syndicate, sales, and exchanges, ensuring that the stock opens smoothly, trades with confidence, and sets the right tone for the aftermarket.

Traders are the bank's eyes and ears in the market.[26] They know which funds are holding or flipping, and can feed that intelligence back to management, while giving insights into who's buying, selling or shorting in the early days. This feedback helps company management plan follow-on offerings and manage shareholder relationships.

Without strong trading support, you risk a weak open, excess volatility, and long-term reputational damage.[27] With the right trading desk, you instead get a stock that's liquid, stable, and attractive to new investors over time.

Market Makers are trading firms or exchange-designated participants that commit to quoting both buy and sell prices (a two-sided market) for a security on a continuous basis.[28] They care about continuous liquidity, not about how good your IPO looks.

Market makers may have different names in some markets. (For example, "designated sponsors" in Germany and "liquidity providers" in Hong Kong).[29] But regardless of the title, the role remains the same, providing short-term liquidity through the buying and selling of securities.

In a global IPO, the market makers are like the plumbing: you don't always notice them, but without them, the debut (and aftermarket) would be chaos.[30] They aren't deal marketers, like bankers or salespeople, and they don't defend the stock like the lead-left trading desk, but they are critical for liquidity and credibility.

Most issuers don't think about market makers until very late in the process, which is problematic. Thinking about it before selecting a bank and exchange should influence the selection of both. There are two factors that ensure you have market makers for your IPO:

- Exchange rules (structural requirement)
- Syndicate arrangements (banker-driven support)[31]

Many exchanges require at least one sponsor bank to also act as a market maker.[32] In some markets, these are selected from a menu of licensed specialists. This selection may be driven by the company, or mandated by the exchange, depending on venue. In other words, some exchanges guarantee there will be a market maker, but the quality, scale, and incentives can vary by exchange.

The lead-left's trading desk (and often other joint bookrunners) effectively acts as an informal market maker in the aftermarket.[33] The desk will step in with stabilization bids, and should also ensure that block trades don't destabilize the market. In fact, not only do they not act as a destabilizing force, they also ideally provide liquidity backstop during the fragile first weeks.

In global IPOs, issuers often request that banks engage strong third-party market makers to supplement exchange-assigned ones. Company management should discuss with their bankers to understand what is appropriate in their specific situation.

Market makers should not be viewed as some kind of public utility; they're very much for-profit trading firms.[34] They aren't motivated by your IPO's story, in the same way as sales or research are. They're motivated by economics, market share and incentives set by exchanges or issuers.

The business model of market makers is capturing the bid–ask spread. Buying slightly below market, and selling slightly above, and do this thousands of times per day, at scale.[35]

They make money on volume and velocity, not on directional bets. One highly successful market maker described the process to me as "picking up nickels." He explained: "We just pick up nickels all day in front of the market steamroller; the whole key is to know when to expand the spread so we don't get crushed by sudden volatility." Much of this work is performed by algorithms, but in a 24-hour, global market, it is common to see a mix of human and machine market-making activity, with flesh-and-blood and algorithmic traders acting in tandem.[36]

Legal & Compliance These teams operate inside the banks. They're not out pitching to investors or stabilizing your stock—they are the people who keep the entire process within regulatory guardrails, which is especially complex when you're listing across multiple jurisdictions.[37] They oversee the due diligence process, ensuring management, auditors, and lawyers produce full, accurate disclosure.[38] They also review and approve all investor marketing materials, such as roadshow decks, test-the-waters presentations, and analyst reports.

There are also local variations. What is considered legal marketing in Hong Kong may be a violation in the U.S.[39] A disclosure may be required in Europe but unpermissible in the Middle East. A regional institutional investor may therefore be unable to review equity research that is permissible, and freely available, to the general public.

Legal & compliance will help ensure that your material is tailored by jurisdiction, and also that it contains the appropriate local disclaimers. Liability is shared, and if disclosures are wrong then both the issuer and the banks may incur expense or reputational harm. For global offerings, you sometimes see a prospectus with a menu of disclaimers, each applicable only to a specific country.[40]

In a global IPO, the bank's legal team is constantly coordinating with the company's management, external counsel, auditors, and other advisors to make sure that the whole process holds together. It is important to remember that the bank's legal & compliance team does not work for the company—they work for the bank. They are motivated to avoid embarrassment and reputational risk for the bank, while the company will have their own, separate attorneys, doing the same for them.

Banker Bake-off

An IPO banker "bake-off" is a formal selection process in which a private company evaluates competing investment banks to determine who will underwrite and lead its upcoming initial public offering (IPO). It's a structured, high-stakes event in which banks pitch their qualifications, proposed strategy, valuation views and execution plan.

It's a "beauty contest" with strategic implications. The outcome determines not only who gets the IPO fees, but also how the company's public market debut is positioned, valued, and perceived.

Generally, it is best to select a listing venue, and then have a bake-off, but the selection process can be conducted in parallel. Every exchange is happy to recommend bankers to include in a company bake-off.

The primary goal of an IPO banker bake-off is to select the syndicate leaders who will price and distribute the IPO. The bake-off will also help with other goals, such as:

- Giving management a sense of how public investors will view the business
- Helping align internal vs external valuation assumptions (often a gap exists)
- Shaping expectations for the board and existing shareholders
- Providing a market map as to how investors view the competitors, sector and business model
- Clarifying market positioning by forcing consensus on the most compelling equity story and how to present it

- Stress-testing readiness by surfacing gaps in disclosure, KPIs, governance, or financials that need attention before filing
- Identifying IPO adjacent transaction opportunities such as M&A, debt, pre-IPO rounds or secondary sell downs
- Generating feedback on risk factors and valuation drivers that can shape pre-marketing materials and investor education

A well-run bake-off creates competitive tension among the banks, often leading to better economics (e.g. lower fees, stronger commitments, better allocations). Given that the IPO process can take many months, an IPO issuer may want or need to pursue a private offering in advance of the IPO. This can increase cash and credibility going into the IPO. A pre-IPO financing, run by a bank, can act as a final "test" before final selection of the lead bank.

Most capital markets outside the U.S. support convertible pre-IPO rounds. A pre-IPO round provides flexibility to issuers in evaluating market interest before incurring the costs associated with an IPO. Private financing can be a good first engagement when evaluating the lead banker. If a bank can successfully perform the pre-IPO, or other private round, the action should give confidence to company leadership.[41]

It's okay to have the banker prove themself with a paid engagement before hiring them as lead banker. A pre-IPO round also provides a valuable opportunity to refine your messaging, and build lasting relationships with leading global institutional investors, which can be highly valuable.

Attorneys Companies with the scale to explore an IPO already have at least one law firm. "Why can't we just use our existing global counsel for the IPO?" they might wonder. On paper, it makes sense: many large companies already have a global outside law firm (Goodwin, Skadden, Latham, Cleary, Freshfields, Clifford Chance, etc.) handling corporate or regulatory matters. In reality, there may be regional firms much more experienced in listing on a given exchange. A review of recent prospectuses should be all that is needed to understand which firms are worthy of consideration.

In every IPO, there are two main legal teams: issuer's counsel, who represents the company, and underwriters' counsel Legal & Compliance, who represent the banks.[42] Your usual law firm may be too close to you to credibly act for underwriters, and vice versa. Conflicts of interest may force the issuer to hire different firms.

If you have already read the chapter on IPO readiness and the chapter on selecting an exchange, you know that the company will have already worked with the lawyers to address a wide range of corporate matters. But IPOs are different beasts, with different legal team selection criteria:

- Gaps in coverage (especially cross-border)
- Conflicts of interest with banks.
- Slower execution if the firm isn't IPO-native.
- Credibility issues with a segment of investors

The IPO attorney's role is to translate a company's reality into a legally defensible, regulator-approved investment story that can be sold worldwide. This may require specialized regional expertise, regional reputation, or simply availability.

If your counsel isn't recognized for its top-tier IPO work in all jurisdictions you plan to approach investors, or your law firm has a conflict with any of the banks, exploring additional counsel for your IPO process is prudent. The process of interviewing other law firms will provide a second opinion. If their perspective does not match other market participants, dig deeper.

Auditors and Accountants don't just sign off on the numbers, they are the credibility bridge between a private company's financial story and the public capital markets. Without their work, the deal can't get through regulators, underwriters won't underwrite, and investors won't buy.

During the IPO process, auditors and accountants will work with lawyers and bankers to ensure that financial disclosures in the prospectus are accurate and consistent. Anywhere underwriters are taking on liability for disclosure, they demand auditors' comfort letters to protect themselves. It is important to note that details can vary by jurisdiction and exchange.

One common mistake companies make in preparing for a Global IPO is underestimating accounting lead times.[43] Audit readiness takes time. Many private companies operate with financials that are good enough for venture investors, but not for regulators or global institutions. Underestimating accounting lead times is further complicated by the potential need to accommodate different (or multiple) accounting standards.

Indeed, accounting standards are the "language" of financial global markets but, unfortunately, the language has local dialects. U.S. GAAP and IFRS are the two big ones, but both GAAP and IFRS have equivalent regional substandards.[44] For the most part the standards are similar, but your accounting firms will need to understand the subtle "*accents*"[45] in order to remain compliant.

Many exchanges will accept both GAAP and IFRS, but the exact governance of your filings should be discussed with the entire IPO team. Investors want comparability, transparency and trust. AI and Technology is making it easier for investors to compare across "accents," nevertheless, well-designed reporting will only help valuation. Cost, time, regulations and investor expectations all play a role in reporting optimization.

Both IFRS and U.S. GAAP are high-quality standards, but they diverge in several areas that hit tech companies especially hard, namely revenue, R&D, stock comp, and intangibles. Anyone on a company management team that will be interacting with global investors should understand how the company's approach to accounting impacts these four areas.

What used to be the "Big Eight" of global auditing firms

collapsed into today's "Big Four" (PwC, Deloitte, EY, KPMG).[46] As an alumni of what was at the time the "Big 6," I see the benefit of a respected brand—their hiring standards and employee training remain exceptional. For smaller or earlier-stage companies looking at an IPO, the Big Four carry enormous weight in the global capital markets. As successful public companies grow, they will see their audit and reporting needs grow concurrently. Big Four firms have the staffing depth to support expanding needs and occasional unexpected rapid responses, which makes them well suited for these periods of rapid growth.

However, they aren't always the right fit for every issuer. This is particularly true for smaller companies that will place more of an emphasis on cost. Big Four audits are expensive, often multiples of mid-tier firms, and fees balloon during IPO readiness (restatements, comfort letters, advising).[47] Ongoing annual costs as a public company will be greater, and investors often would rather see those fees directed into earnings.

Another consideration is that a small company may not be a priority for a big firm. For small-cap IPOs, you risk getting a junior team with limited partner attention, as the Big Four firms allocate senior resources to marquee clients (mega-IPOs, Fortune 500). One approach is to keep your big firm, but find a local office that may have both more attractive fees, and will be willing to dedicate more senior resources to the IPO.

Regardless of price or engagement-team seniority, there still may be reasons to look beyond the Big Four. All four of these giant firms tend to be bureaucratic and rigid in their decision-making process, often requiring multiple approvals. In short, they don't have to take risks! Founder-led, entrepreneurial businesses may find "Big Four" teams overly corporate and risk-averse. IPO timelines are compressed, smaller firms may move faster and be more hands-on. The right boutique firms partner can provide strategic hands-on guidance, especially on IPO structuring, valuation models, or investor messaging.

Accounting firms, like law firms and banks, are only as strong as the team they put on your engagement. For U.S baseball fans, I say, "You're not hiring the jersey, you're hiring the hitters," which translates everywhere else as, "You don't hire the club crest, you hire the starting eleven. It comes down to who's on the pitch." Turns out, idioms, like accounting standards, have their regional differences.

Tax Advisors focus on tax implications for the company, employees, management, existing investors and future investors. Opportunities are missed because companies often think "our accountants handle tax" when, in fact, tax advisors in an IPO context do a very different job.

A good tax advisor will focus on future structure and optimization. As part of the IPO readiness phase, they will advise on where and how to domicile. As part of the IPO, they will advise on where to hold and list shares. They also help solve for jurisdictional complexity, investor tax exposure, and governance, and attempt to predict the future—shaping the IPO to maximize efficiency, valuation and M&A flexibility.

Accountants sign off on the past; tax advisors design for the future. The distinction becomes especially important in cross-border IPOs, where the wrong structure can impact valuation, regulatory approval, or create huge tax headaches for existing shareholders, including the management team.[48] Companies and Investors have huge flexibility on where, how and if they conduct business. Capital controls, ownership requirements, tax treaties and tax policy are all considerations.

Operations in jurisdictions with opaque or arbitrary tax regimes should be minimized. Investors will demand higher risk premiums for companies that have too much of their operations in those countries. Recently, unfortunately, even some of the largest economies have been arbitrary and capricious. The global trend of ballooning government debt has not helped. International investors are trained to look for "concentration risk." Smart business leaders diversify team, technology, revenue and investor base across jurisdictions. Tax advisors provide input into the broader risk management and scaling processes.

Compensation Consultants are independent advisors who specialize in executive pay, equity compensation and incentive structures. They are important, especially in global or cross-border listings where compensation rules, investor expectations and tax regimes may collide.

Compensation is a narrative issue as much as a financial one. Compensation policy isn't just about attracting and retaining talent. In the public markets it's tied to index inclusion, passive investor flows and long-term shareholder alignment. Sophisticated investors will accept big numbers for management compensation, but only if linked to performance.

Consultants help avoid negative headlines, such as "Founder cashes out, employees diluted" or "CEO pays out of line with peers." Compensation structures may want to be modified to attract a new group of investors, improve retention, or lay the groundwork for further international expansion. Management does not need to navigate compensation on their own, advisors can consult on lock-up periods and support employee equity communications.

Most IPO prospectuses require detailed disclosure of executive pay, option plans, and equity ownership. Consultants help ensure these disclosures stand up to regulators and shareholder expectations.

Compensation consultants matter in global IPOs because they bridge private-company equity culture with public-market governance and investor expectations. They design executive pay and employee equity plans that are tax-efficient, regulator-compliant, and culturally acceptable to a wide range of global investors.

Proxi Advisors Specialized governance consultants who help companies anticipate, shape and survive the proxy-advisor ecosystem, especially ISS and Glass Lewis.

Index providers and passive investors often follow proxy advisor recommendations on governance, including executive pay. If a company's comp policies score badly, proxy advisors may recommend "against" votes on directors, which can spook institutions and delay index inclusion. Active investors can sell if they dislike your governance, whereas passive funds can't sell; they're locked in as long as you're in the index. A good compensation advisor will consider the perspective of both index providers and proxy advisors, and provide you with critical insight

Specialist Advisors For many investors, compensation and ESG are inseparable. Some regulators see it the same way. For some investors, compensation is the heart of governance; to others, performance-based pay signals whether leadership is truly aligned with the company's environmental and social commitments. Like many specialty advisors, ESG consultants can weigh in on a range of items beyond compensation including strategy, risk, disclosure, operations and supply chain.

The use of advisors is often driven by the specific industry. Regulatory experts, actuaries, geologists, scientists or medical consultants may be relevant. As one banker pointed out, "The closer a risk is to killing the IPO, the more likely a specialist gets hired."

Successful IPOs are less about hiring "more advisors" and more about hiring the right narrow experts to reduce the one or two risks the public market will not forgive.

Investor Relations "IR" consultants are where finance meets storytelling. They bridge the gap between the company's numbers and the capital market's expectations.

A good investor relations professional will:

- **Help Position the Equity Story** Translate strategy, financials, and vision into a narrative investors can model and believe.

- **Investor Targeting** Identify which funds (long-only, hedge funds, sovereign wealth funds) should be in the book.
- **Roadshow Prep** Anticipate and prepare management for tough questions.
- **Ensure consistent messaging** Help coordinate with legal, finance and compliance to ensure consistent messaging in filings, earnings calls, and roadshows.

IR should build and maintain an investor Q&A playbook. It's not just about feeding the CEO and CFO 'lines." The playbook is about ensuring that management is ready for anything that investors, analysts, or even regulators might throw at them.

Before, during and after the IPO, IR will be cultivating relationships with sell-side analysts, institutional investors, and key market participants. IR will also think about passive investors & index providers to ensure long-term visibility and inclusion. Think of IR as the ambassador between the company and the market. The sign of a good IR team is when a company does a followup offering, or a big shareholder decides to sell, and the shares get sopped up quickly by the market.

Public market investors tend to favor in-house IR leadership, viewing it as more transparent and closely aligned with the company's operations. Unlike private investors, public equity investors have distinct expectations around disclosure, cadence, and engagement. Companies transitioning to the public markets may find that existing IR resources, often built for private capital relationships, are not fully equipped to meet the demands of public market communications. Responsibilities, roles or personnel changes may be necessary.

Some investors say they'd rather hear directly from the CEO or CFO, but those same investors ultimately want leadership focused on running the company. That's where IR earns its value—whether in-house, external, or a hybrid, a strong IR function frees management to lead, while ensuring investors get the insight and access required to be a fractional owner.

External IR professionals also bring a broader perspective. Operating across multiple clients means they can aggregate insight into how the buy-side is thinking, informing all their engagement. One company's narrative success helps them refine playbooks for others, and vice versa.

During an IPO, an external IR firm may be especially well-positioned to add value. Good external IR firms have run dozens of IPOs, so they are more likely to know what questions investors will ask (and how to answer them). They can staff-up quickly to handle prospectus drafting, roadshow prep, or analyst teach-ins support. They are also outsiders so they can provide a more objective investor's-eye view, meaning that, as an example, they are more likely to push back on over-optimistic messaging. They have an objective outlook that sometimes an insider may not possess.

Specialist IR firms can be valuable for targeting specific investors or regions, which should be considered for participation on the IR team. Take Australia, for example; it has the world's fourth-largest pool of investable capital thanks to its mandatory retirement savings system, known as Superannuation. Regional IR experts know how to tailor a story to resonate with these long-term investors. A company's IR team, in aggregate, needs to understand regional investor cultures (U.S. hedge funds vs European long-only vs Asian sovereign wealth funds).[49]

Banks, accountants and stock exchanges may all have opinions about what makes a great IR professional, but what I care most about is the perspective of public market investors.[50] One big public market investor told me, "In my experience, the best IR professionals have come from the buy-side. They know what it means to buy and own a stock." The best IR professionals believe in the company vision and want to have skin in the game. I tend to favor IR firms or individuals willing to have some of their compensation in stock.[51]

The best practice in global IPOs: pair an external IR advisory firm for the transaction with an internal IR lead that takes over post-listing.[52]

Financial PR & Media Advisors They help shape the corporate narrative, manage perception, and ensure regulatory alignment throughout the lifecycle of a global IPO.[53] Their role spans three key phases: pre-IPO, IPO execution, and post-IPO.

Financial media is different from traditional media, and regional media is different from industry-specific media. Each has their own twists and motives. Often, the media relations team supporting customer growth is ill-prepared for financial media. It is important that your general media and financial media efforts are coordinated, not least because investors may also be customers, and customers indeed may be investors. A prospective customer researching your product may see what the financial press is saying, and investors researching your background will certainly take an interest in what is being said in the non-financial press.

The specifics of their role vary significantly by jurisdiction due to differences in regulatory regimes, media landscapes, and cultural attitudes toward publicity and capital markets.[54] For example, in Hong Kong financial media typically convey enthusiasm, media blitzes and aggressive statements. In contrast, German regulators have stricter disclosure requirements, and expect the tone in public to be more conservative and risk-averse. This is important because a company's financial PR vendor selection is impacted by the choice of exchange and marketing jurisdictions.

Cyber-Security Specialist In a fast-growing company, cyber-security is always competing with other priorities. Preparation for an IPO is a great time to be proactive.[55] Most well-run companies have in-house security capabilities, but it's unfortunately very hard to "grade your own paper." Best practice is to have a third-party do a red-team penetration test before the IPO roadshow.[56]

You may not have encountered the term "red team test" before, so here's a quick explanation. Public companies are prime cyber targets. A data breach could have a material impact on reputation, volatility or valuation. Bad actors don't need a stock to go up or down to profit, they can profit by using options and creating volatility. A red-team test simulates real-world attacks to identify vulnerabilities in systems, networks, and people before public exposure. It ensures that defenses are battle-tested under realistic threat scenarios, not just checklist audits.

Leadership must be ready to prove cybersecurity, data privacy, and compliance readiness (GDPR in Europe, CCPA in California, ever changing cybersecurity rules in other jurisdictions).[57] Investors and regulators increasingly ask about IT resilience, and there have been many high-profile IT breaches in recent years.

Regulators & Exchanges Any discussion about IPOs would be incomplete without discussing regulators & exchanges. In some jurisdiction the exchange is the applicable regulator, in others the regulators are separate. At some point in the IPO process, the company's team will interact with regulators. I recommend prioritizing regulatory transparency by being proactive rather than reactive.

The speed at which regulators move at can vary widely by jurisdiction. There are many jurisdictions where answers from regulators come in hours or days, while others may have longer or more unpredictable timeframes. The choice of marketing and listing venues should be impacted by the quality of the regulator at the time of listing.

Unfortunately, regulations are constantly changing. Don't assume less-stringent regimes are easier in the long run. Light-touch regimes can reverse sharply under political or macro pressure, and bad regulation can be revoked. Increasingly, jurisdictions are pushing for their regulations to be enforced elsewhere. For example, the EU is pushing sustainability disclosure (CSRD) with extraterritorial effects, while China is pushing for pre-approval for overseas listings of companies doing business in China, even when the owners and corporate headquarters are outside China. The days when a company's chief council could meet with a lobbyist to understand the changing regulatory landscape are gone. Well-run companies use AI empowered data services like FiscalNote or Quorum to stay one step ahead, such is the fast-moving nature of the contemporary landscape.[58]

Issuers and IPO investors will move to exchanges where regulations are appropriate.[59] Expect fierce competition among jurisdictions as technological and geopolitical factors rapidly expand choices for both innovators and their profit seeking financial backers.

Internal Resources A global IPO is not just a financial transaction, it's a company-wide mobilization. Each function has a defined role, but global IPOs open up new opportunities to leverage the team. In general, the CEO fronts the roadshow and investor meetings. But the team presenting may change depending on the audience. Some investors will value time with technical or sales leaders, others will care most about the CFO.

In conversations with U.S. institutional investors, the CFO and General Counsel have an opportunity to shine, while the founder(s)—even when not the CEO—can also play a key role. Investors are sensitive that, in aggregate, companies with strong founder involvement outperform others,[60] particularly in industries being disrupted by technology.[61]

Another consideration is the role of the Chairman, if they are not also the CEO. In several markets outside the U.S., it is not uncommon for the Chairman to lead many of the meetings with investors. If the Chairman's message is synchronized with the CEO and the leadership team, there may be opportunities to increase investor engagement.

Board members are a different story. Their public comments can become problematic during the roadshow or prospectus period, or IPO day. The board should not be upstaging management or changing the narrative. Sometimes companies need to do damage control. Board members, like all members of the team, need to make sure all communications are through the company's designated channels.

As a general rule, our fund recommends budgeting for one additional financial headcount for IPO preparation and ongoing life as a public company. This applies to companies listing outside the U.S. Larger, more complex or U.S.-listed companies may require more staffing. Sometimes that one headcount is an incrementally shared workload across the finance department.[62]

IPO Project Manager Most banks, law firms and accountants claim they can manage your IPO. The problem is each looks at the transaction through the lens of their profession.[63] In markets where smaller IPOs are still common, there tends to be a range of IPO advisors specializing in keeping the IPO process moving forward. The IPO Project Manager needs to push internal workflows, oversee data room integrity and coordinate a range of vendors. Prospectus writing will brings critical matters. When an IPO Project Manager does their job right, they shoulder a lot of responsibilities, freeing up management.

When there are delays, it's all too common for the bankers to blame the accountants, the accountant to then blame the lawyers, and the lawyers to blame the regulators.[64] The IPO Project Manager steps in and sorts out[65] this mess; an IPO Project Manager results in accountability, giving the CEO one "neck to wring."

IPO Project Managers are unpopular with lead banks because they increase accountability. Project Managers may also be unpopular because early in the bank selection process they may create competition between banks, driving down banker fees. There is not enough transparency in the IPO process to ever know if the added cost of a Project Manager is offset by lower banker fees. An IPO Project Manager will be happy to tell you the benefits, and a banker will be happy to explain why they are not necessary. I suspect the right IPO Project Managers pay for themselves in reduced banker fees and improved valuation.

When listing globally, IPO project management is about orchestration, not just administration. You're balancing the strategic vision of the founders and CFO with a fragmented mosaic of local regulators, customs, and investor norms. It's a bit like producing a global film with multiple directors: the key is tight script control and flawless coordination. An IPO Manager helps ensure that the demands of the IPO process do not distract management or dilute operating performance in the critical period leading up to the first post-IPO earnings call.

Ultimately, it's up to company leadership to decide whether to engage an IPO Project Manager. Chemistry with the team and reference checks are both important. I recommend meeting with a few IPO Project Managers before selecting a bank. The conversations will be instructive. A top IPO Project Manager will be able to articulate their value. If they can't, the choice is easy.

Summary

In summary, there are some key takeaways from this chapter:

- **Incentives first** Start with Charlie Munger's insight: incentives (greed, fear, ego, peer pressure) largely determine outcomes.
- **You don't go public alone.** IPOs are team events with many vendors and advisors, each driven by their own motives and focused primarily on the IPO moment.
- **Pick the right lead and partners.** The lead banker ("lead left") is the deal's quarterback - choose them via a formal bake-off; use joint bookrunners to widen reach, create healthy competition, and avoid single-point failures.

- **Use equity research strategically.** Research amplifies the story. Note U.S. regulatory limits, "spitzered" issues; non-spitzered or international research coverage can be a competitive advantage overseas.

- **Trading and aftermarket intelligence matter.** Trading desks help manage the open, stabilize the market, and feed back who's holding vs flipping - vital for post-IPO planning.

- **Lawyers and auditors translate credibility.** Issuer/underwriter counsel and auditors make the story legally defensible and financially credible.

- **Specialists shape long-term structure.** Tax advisors design future corporate and shareholder structures; compensation consultants align pay, governance, and investor perceptions—both affect valuation and index/passive flows.

- **IR, PR, project management & cyber** IR crafts the investor narrative and builds relationships; financial PR manages perception across markets; an IPO project manager enforces accountability; pre-roadshow red-team cyber tests reduce material risk.

- **Pre-IPO rounds** can be an efficient way to raise capital and test the team of advisors in advance of an IPO.

In short, you should ensure that you hire the right actors, insist on transparency, and think beyond the deal day. If you get the alignment of incentives right, you won't just survive debut day, you'll have set up the company to thrive in public markets.

Good bankers, lawyers, auditors, market makers, and IR teams make the listing possible, but great ones help your company build a durable shareholder base and a smoother aftermarket life.

The next chapter talks about the various types of investors, how to prioritize and most important how to attract the *right* investors.

Chapter 9
Attracting the Right Investors

"You never get a second chance to make a first impression."
Will Rogers—American Humorist

The best company leaders build relationships with public market investors before the IPO, possibly via a pre-IPO investment round, or through a non-US testing of the waters. Regardless, for any well-run IPO, many of the institutions will still be learning about the company for the first time. It is important to get in front of the right investors, and ideally include them in the company's IPO book build.

Adobe went public in 1986, the bankers "on the cover" included Hambrecht & Quist and Morgan Stanley[1]. Oracle listed in 1986 and included Merrill Lynch & Co. and Alex Brown & Sons as underwriters, raising just over $31 million[2]. In 2004, Salesforce went public with Morgan Stanley, Deutsche Bank Securities Inc., Wachovia Capital Markets, LLC and William Blair & Company, L.L.C., raising about $110 million.[3]

Why did they have multiple banks involved? To get exposure to a diverse group of investors—different regions, investment strategies and risk profiles. The same is true for a modern global IPO. Companies need a mix of bankers who can attract different regions, investment strategies and risk profiles. Businesses that fail to do this are missing a world of opportunity.

As an interesting aside, Adobe, Oracle and Salesforce would be deemed too small to list at time of their listing in the U.S. had the bankers applied the standards of 2020.[4]

Smaller companies can still go public earlier in their life, but instead of having a country-specific underwriting team, they need a global banking team. This chapter will highlight some of the investors who may be worth targeting. Understanding the target investors should help in selecting investment bankers, but be skeptical. Every bank will claim that they have global reach, but this is seldom true for smaller IPOs. The appropriate underwriting team for your IPO is likely a mix of regional and global banks.

The most obviously global banks are often geographically siloed. Furthermore, the incentives of an individual bank may vary by region. This can work for a company, or against it. As an example of this, one top-10 investment bank based in New York would rarely even look at a $100 million IPO out of their U.S. office, and in the unlikely event that they did, the bank would only give such a company its most junior resources. But take that same transaction to Australia or London, and you will have the full attention of the bankers. A growth company can raise $100 million in an IPO with a top banker on the cover... just not in the U.S.

Another good example would be a top-10 global investment bank based in Switzerland. The bankers outside the U.S. would be more than happy to run a $100-million IPO of a high-growth Silicon Valley company, but internal policy dictates that this opportunity will be passed to their U.S. team, whom has no experience or economic incentive to list abroad.

In response to this, company leadership needs to be proactive and not just delegate to the bankers. When a company goes public, especially in a global offering, cap table design becomes a strategic exercise. Proper planning directly impacts post-IPO performance, governance resilience, and long-term valuation.[5]

The public cap table is more than just a record of ownership; it's a foundation for growth, a base for resilience and a signal to markets about the long-term potential of the team.[6] Building investor demand is like playing chess—deliberate, multi-dimensional, and (hopefully) fun. The right moves can lay the foundation for future options, defense and success. The investors you invite onto your cap table aren't passive—they bring behaviors, incentives and expectations.[7] As in chess, each move (investor allocation) affects the state of the board, from future fundraising, through shareholder activism, to index eligibility. You must play both offense and defense, as public markets are dynamic. The capital stack must be built to support growth (offense) while protecting against volatility, hostile actors, or misaligned governance pressures (defense).

In designing your investor base, you're always playing several games at once:

- Future Flexibility for Capital Access
- Corporate Culture & Governance
- Long-term Valuation
- Liquidity and Shareholder Base Management
- Strategic Alignment

Investor selection and targeting shapes company behavior and outcomes. Investors don't just provide capital, they influence incentives, decision-making cadence, and even the culture of the company post-IPO. Investors who understand the long arc of innovation and scale, rather than just short-term earnings, can be true evangelists, not just financial passengers.

I have an example of this from my family. My aunt was a stock and product evangelist. As a child, I remember her telling the whole family about Steve Case and AOL. No amount of money could have paid her to promote the company at our Thanksgiving dinner, but as a shareholder in AOL, she could not resist. A good product combined with an enthusiastic investor base was a tailwind for the company. Her $10,000 investment went on to be worth $1.7M when AOL merged with Time Warner.

It worked for AOL, but as with so many things in business, there is no single optimal strategy. All investor base mixes have tradeoffs. In general, we encourage the companies we invest in to focus on institutional investors, of which there are many when you think of your IPO as a global undertaking.

Diversity Builds Resilience

Company leaders should aim for diversity across investor types, strategies, time horizons and geography. On the flip side, watch for over-concentration in a small number of funds or geographies, which may impair liquidity or create correlated outflows in stress scenarios. Try to include funds from markets you intend to expand into, as they will provide you useful feedback and regional insights. Good leaders communicate with the investment community, why not target investors that can help inform long-term strategy?

Years ago, I was building a multinational business. My international shareholders were concerned about the technical risk. I added some Silicon Valley investors to the cap table, and immediately the global investors opened their wallets. A year later, we needed more investment—my U.S. investors were hesitant because they were unsure of the market demand outside the U.S. This time, it was the global investors who moved fastest and drove up valuation. Without shareholder diversity, I would have spent more time fundraising, for an outcome where I owned less of the company post-funding.

Anchor and Cornerstone Investors

Anchor investors, sometimes called "cornerstone investors," are institutional investors who commit capital to an IPO before it is fully marketed, committing to purchasing a fixed amount of shares before the IPO bookbuild begins.[8] This practice is common outside the U.S.[9] Their participation is typically publicly disclosed in the prospectus, and announced to the market as part of the IPO marketing.[10] These investors are usually subject to a lock-up period (often three to six months) and typically are not involved in the governance of the company.

Sometimes "anchor" is used to describe an investor who is well-regarded and indicated early interest or demand for IPO shares before or during the bookbuild, often through soft orders. Yet the participation is not contractual and not publicly disclosed pre-IPO—terminology and specifics can vary by region.

Companies with dual-class shares or concentrated founder control need to proactively court well-known governance-focused investors to counterbalance perception risk.[11] Reputable long-term holders such as Capital Group, AustralianSuper, Ontario Teachers' Pension Plan (OTPP), Temasek Holdings and Abu Dhabi Investment Authority (ADIA) add credibility.

Why It Matters to Companies Cornerstones add credibility, reduce risk and build momentum. Securing a cornerstone (often sovereigns, pensions, or family offices) who commits capital before the bookbuild provides validation and ballast. Their presence signals confidence, discourages short-term churn and gives new investors confidence that there will be someone to buy if they need to sell.

Long-Only Institutional Investors

These are global or regional asset managers with mandates to invest in public equities. Examples include Fidelity International, Capital Group, Aberdeen Standard, First Sentier, Nikko AM, AustralianSuper, Baillie Gifford, Jupiter, Schroders, M&G,, Amundi, Legal & General and BlackRock.

It is important to target the portfolio manager whose coverage includes the exchange where you are listing. The fidelity manager in the U.S. is unlikely to care about any $100-million offering, including a U.S. company going public in Europe, but the European portfolio manager will pay attention.

Long-only investors generally care about the management team, fundamentals, long-term TAM (Total Addressable Market), unit economics, and governance quality.

Long-only investors build credibility and can support the company in future follow-on offerings.

Sovereign Wealth Funds

Sovereign wealth funds (SWFs) are among the most influential long-term investors in global capital markets.[12] In the context of an IPO, particularly for companies with operations in Asia, EMEA, and frontier markets, they serve not just as capital providers but also as strategic validators that can transform the perception and stability of a deal. Sovereign wealth funds have deep pools of patient capital and strategic interests. Examples include Temasek, GIC (Singapore), Khazanah (Malaysia), QIC and Future Fund (Australia), EPF (Malaysia), Korea Investment Corp (Korea), KfW Group (Germany), ADIA (Abu Dhabi) and PIF (Saudi Arabia).

They tend to focus on strategic alignment, regional growth, ESG alignment and governance structures.

Why It Matters To Companies This capital is generally long-term capital; they also have an overweighted positive reputation among other sovereigns and regional investors. The right sovereign fund can also play an oversized role in helping a high-growth company expand in a particular region, either by reputation or thorough direct introductions.

Strategic Investors

Strategic investors (eg., corporations or supply chain partners) are rarely featured in the IPO allocation in the U.S., but are not uncommon outside the U.S. In Asia, the Middle East, and parts of Europe, it is far more typical to include a strategic investor as part of an IPO, often in a cornerstone or anchor capacity.[13] For investors in Asia and the Middle East, strategic participation is often welcomed or even expected as part of the IPO process.

Strategic participation can add regional credibility, deepen distribution partnerships, or reduce perceived geopolitical risks. Corporate leaders should consider including strategic investors such as corporate partners, ecosystem enablers, or customers. However, this should only be done if their involvement strengthens long-term execution or ecosystem lock-in. Company leaders should be aware that strategic investment is not always value-maximizing on the public cap table. Strategic investors can scare off potential partners and investors, and they may also limit future M&A flexibility (both real and perceived).

ARM Holdings, 2023 Nasdaq IPO is an interesting case study. ARM allocated IPO shares to Apple, NVIDIA, Samsung, Intel, TSMC, and AMD.[14] The result was that investors understood ARM was part of a larger partner ecosystem.

Why It Matters To Companies When a leading corporate player, often a potential partner, supplier or customer, invests in an IPO, it acts as a third-party endorsement of your business model, tech stack or market thesis. For example, If Siemens takes a stake in an industrial IoT company IPO, it tells the market that the tech-ecosystem is credible and commercially viable. In 2000, Hewlett Packard invested into one of the companies I founded, and for many years the association proved helpful in opening doors. Association can boost product pricing power and enhance institutional confidence, while derisking perception around execution.

Pre-IPO Funds

Pre-IPO funds are investment vehicles that deploy capital into companies in the final 6–18 months before they go public. Their involvement bridges the private-public valuation gap, signals institutional quality, and helps both pre-market and de-risk the listing.

They're much more common outside the U.S., due to structural and regulatory differences. The U.S. SEC Rule 144 basically discourages pre-IPO participation for U.S. listings.[15] However, U.S. and non-US companies listing outside the U.S. should strongly consider pre-IPO Investment.[16] A well-structured pre-IPO investment round should result in better pricing at IPO and less overall dilution for founders and existing investors.[17] They can also lay the foundation for select existing investors to get off the cap table (sell) before the IPO, thus reducing selling pressure on the day of (or after) the IPO.

Pre-IPO funds are particularly prevalent in Europe, Asia and the Middle East. Examples include Regal (Australia), Edelweiss (India), UNITED Pre.IPO.Capital (Europe), KraneShares (global), Square Peg (Australia), Bpifrance (Europe), Baillie Gifford (UK). There is a wide range and ever changing group of smaller or lesser-known "pre-IPO funds" including pockets of funds in some Canadian pensions.

The existence of pre-IPO funds is a major structural advantage for top exchanges outside the U.S. A pre-IPO round can act as a dress rehearsal for company management and bankers alike, resulting in either a better IPO debut, or the short-circuiting of the IPO plans early, well before the cost and distraction of a listing.

Pre-IPO investors are not investors committing to a Private Investment in Public Equity (PIPE); these are investors who invest cash months before the IPO. Their investment often converts at a negotiated discount to the IPO price (usually 10-25%).[18] The investment typically converts to freely tradable common stock on the day of the IPO.

Outside the U.S., these investors are not constrained by long lock-up periods, so their shares can contribute to the float of the company, thus limiting the dilution at IPO, while simultaneously freeing up shares that can attract new investors, or trigger index eligibility.

Pre-IPO Investors want to see a clear line-of-sight to IPO. Company leaders seeking pre-IPO investment should be able to talk competently about their anticipated choices of bankers, auditors, legal counsel and exchange.

Some pre-IPO investors will invest 18 to 24 months before a target IPO date, but the number of potential investors balloons when a time-bound plan to go public drops below 12 months. Pre-IPO investors are often more concerned about a path to liquidity than valuation, as they are generally negotiating a discount to an IPO price. Because of a competitive pre-IPO marketing process IPO prices are usually fairly priced in markets outside the U.S.

Pre-IPO investors will want to see many of the same elements as public market investors, so they are ideal for testing IPO readiness. They want to understand the company's leadership, vision, margin trajectory, scalable unit economics, addressable market and competitive moat. They want to understand how, by the time of the planned IPO, the company will grow the organization, have institutional-grade financial controls, clean historical financials, a level of predictable revenue, and appropriate governance.

Why It Matters To Companies For a fast-growing global company, pre-IPO investment is relatively inexpensive capital. It is an excellent way to prepare for a listing, yet is simple and can often be completed quickly. Pre-IPO investment signals to public market investors that a reputable institution already has analyzed the company.

Cross-Over Investors

Cross-over investors are strategically important participants in a global IPO, especially for high-growth companies making the leap from private to public markets. Their involvement is often a signal of quality, institutional validation and long-term potential. When investment is structured correctly, the right cross-over investors can help lay the foundation for a successful global IPO by, as a skin-in-the-game minority shareholder, helping navigate the listing process. Cross-over investors can also buy out investors who are no longer aligned with the company's long-term vision, or that have structural reasons to sell once the company lists. When investment is structured correctly, a cross-over investment round can ensure the company is hardwired for a smooth transition into the public markets.

However, company leaders should be careful to understand the motives of investors and have familiarity with multi-jurisdictional IPOs. Some self-described cross-over investors look to invest several times before an IPO. Some cross-over investors will expect a company to wait till they are valued at tens of billions of dollars before considering an IPO.[19] A cross-over investment round, when structured correctly, should convert to common at the IPO; this means if the cross-over investor values the company too high at investment, or incorporates onerous preferences, they will be strongly incented to delay an IPO. An IPO would likely expose the error in their valuation decision.

Cross-over investors are global. Examples include Baillie Gifford (UK), Durable Capital, (UK/US), Temasek / GIC (Singapore), Mubadala / QIA (UAE, Qatar), and SoftBank Vision Fund (Japan/UK). In the U.S., notable examples include T. Rowe Price, Fidelity, Wellington Management, Capital Group, Coatue Management, Tiger Global and Altimeter Capital.

The fund I co-founded, the Global Public Offering Fund, is a cross-over fund. We look to invest in founder-lead, globally scaling, technology-enabled companies we believe will make exceptional public companies. Ideally, these should be generation-defining companies. We seek to invest in companies before they become unicorns, so at valuations below $1 billion. As shareholders and board members, we help management accelerate international expansion and IPO readiness. We are big believers in the benefit of being public, for the right type of growth company, so we expect to see our companies to be IPO-ready within 36 months of our investment.

In our experience, being IPO-ready results in more optionality as it relates to attracting talent, negotiating acquisitions and accessing capital of all types.

Some cross-over investors, especially those with deep sectoral or regional expertise, act as catalysts for attracting other investors. Their reputation for due diligence and capital allocation serve as implicit endorsements of the company's trajectory. Their participation should de-risk the IPO in the eyes of some for the broader institutional investor universe.

Crossover funds generally hold post-IPO, rather than flipping as with some IPO participants, or selling as soon as possible like some venture capital firms. Some cross-over funds build positions over time, providing a floor of institutional support.

Why It Matters To Companies Cross-over funds often offer board-level or strategic input in private rounds. They help refine your IPO narrative, disclosures, KPIs, and risk factors. Their bias for going public may better align with ambitious founders, in contrast to other investors who may be incented to keep private or sell to private equity. Industry-focused cross-over investors can enhance credibility with global investors in the applicable sector. Global or regional cross-over funds can enhance visibility and access to public market investors in new geographies.

Passive Investors

It may seem odd to discuss courting passive investors, but careful planning can lay the foundation for passive investment. Where you list and how you structure your IPO can have a big impact on eligibility for access to passive pools.

Passive investment funds were first popularized by Vanguard

founder Jack Bogle at the end of the last century; by the mid-2020s, they are estimated to account for almost half the money invested in the public markets.[20] Passive funds are popular because they offer low-cost, transparent and broadly diversified exposure to markets, making them an efficient vehicle for long-term capital appreciation. Fund managers, on average, only perform average. So if you expect average, a fund with lower fees has an advantage. Oh, the tyranny of math!

Passive investment has become one of the most powerful structural forces in public markets, fundamentally altering capital flows, price discovery, corporate governance and IPO strategy. Passive funds have no ability to price an IPO, so they are generally useless during the book-building process. Their rise in the first two decades of the 21st Century has reshaped how companies go public, how they are traded, and how they are held post-listing. The good news is that globally listing companies can lay the groundwork for passive capital.

When listing in the U.S., most smaller companies do not qualify for any indexes beyond the Russell 3000. They miss out on most passive capital, in contrast to the markets largest companies, such as Meta, Nvidia, Apple and Google, who can expect to see buyers as savers automatically allocate more capital every pay cycle.[21]

Companies listing outside the U.S., including U.S. companies listing cross-border, are often index-eligible much earlier in their life as a public company. The U.S. Indexes, like the U.S. exchanges cater to large companies. Company leaders and their advisors need to understand how their IPO bookbuild impacts index eligibility. For example, free-float, governance, trading volume and diversity of shareholders can impact eligibility for a given index.

Indexes are important because of the data feed that drives ownership for passive investment vehicles, such as ETFs, Segmented Management Accounts (SMAs) and Mutual Funds.[22] Passive funds buy based on index flows, not valuation, so they can be a predictable buyer of shares.[23] They also rebalance based on predictable timeframes such as end of the trading day or quarter.quarter. This predictable rebalancing attracts a wide range of speculators, market makers and other short-term traders that can increase overall stock liquidity.

In the short-term, excessive passive investment can dampen traditional price discovery mechanisms, but short-term mispricing cuts both ways. In short, it can work to the benefit or detriment of long-term stakeholders. Unfortunately, there is another dark side to passive investors. They tend to be absentee owners, delegating voting decisions to centralized stewardship teams at massive asset managers like BlackRock, Vanguard and State Street. These teams often operate with limited company-specific insight, and often vote according to broad ESG or governance frameworks. They tend not to have a nuanced understanding of business context.

As a result, excessive passive ownership can weaken the approval of critical shareholder resolutions on issues such as executive compensation, mergers and acquisitions, climate policy, and board composition. If company leaders are not deliberate in their cap table design, they can be excessively influenced by a handful of gatekeepers. Firms can be managing trillions of dollars, and yet not engaged, not active, subject to political influence, and ultimately not behaving like skin-in-the-game owners.

Why It Matters To Companies Passive capital can be a valuable source of permanent capital. As its footprint expands, boards and investors must remain vigilant against the creeping disengagement and concentration of control passive investment can bring. A robust, balanced investor base remains the cornerstone of resilient public company stewardship.

Wealth Advisors and High Net Worth (HNW)

Outside the U.S., wealth advisors and high-net-worth (HNW) investors can play an important role building your IPO order book and attracting long-term patient capital.

In the U.S., the proliferation of low-cost index funds, low-cost internet trading, industry consolidation and a thicket of regulation has all but removed the Registered Investment Advisor (RIA) from IPO involvement. Conversely, in the 1990s, U.S wealth managers, such as Smith Barney, PaineWebber, Dean Witter, Kidder, Peabody, Alex. Brown, Hambrecht & Quist and Donaldson, Lufkin & Jenrette (DLJ), were all actively involved in IPOs.

Those firms are now part of massive organizations that have lots of other products to offer, and massive compliance departments that instinctively recoil at the idea of showing enthusiasm towards a new issue. These companies seem to have chosen to optimize IPO participation for their most lucrative clients; hedge funds that use leverage to sell short and/or produce a lot of trading volume.

Outside the U.S., it is a very different story. The business model of wealth managers has endured, as have their trusted relationships with high net worth clients. There is a wide range of regional wealth management firms that are eager to be involved in an IPO. DBS Private Bank (Singapore), UOB Kay Hian (Singapore), OCBC Private Banking (Singapore/Malaysia) BNI Wealth (Indonesia) and Kasikorn Private Banking (Thailand) Ord Minnett (Australia), Bell Potter (Australia) Shaw & Partners (Australia), Morgans Financial (Australia) and FirstCape (New Zealand) are just a few examples in South East Asia.

In Europe and the UK there are many HNW wealth managers including: Rothschild & Co (UK / Europe), Mediobanca (Italy), Van Lanschot Kempen (Netherlands), Brewin Dolphin (Ireland), Pictet Group (Switzerland) and Julius Baer (Switzerland), to name but a few.

The Middle East has dozens of wealth managers catering to the needs of both the needs of local HNW investors, and HNW investors from other regions who have chosen to manage their wealth from the region. There are also many mid-sized wealth advisors such as Quintet Private Bank, Cannacord, and Raymond James who service HNW in multiple countries. Even mega wealth managers like UBS, HSBC, Citi and J.P Morgan are likely to get involved with an IPO provided their HNW clients *and* the listing venue is far from the U.S.

Company leaders looking to build a diverse and global investor base should consider the role of wealth managers, and their HNW clients. HNW, especially from Australia and Southeast Asia can play a prominent role in a successful IPO.

Why It Matters To Companies They provide public float depth, support price in volatile conditions and connect the company to investors whose wealth is expected to grow.

Family Offices

Family offices are private investment firms that manage the wealth, investments, and financial affairs of ultra-high-net-worth (UHNW) individuals or families, typically with assets exceeding $100 million. They operate as highly personalized supranational entities and are structured to preserve and grow family capital across generations. Their role in global finance is growing and traditional investment banks are struggling to keep pace.

In 2024, the accounting firm Deloitte estimated that there were about 8,030 single family offices globally, and this figure should reach about 10,700 by 2030. Globally, these investors are expected to exceed $10 trillion of wealth some time in 2030.[24] In short, globalization has been good for family offices!

Family offices can be a valuable addition to a company's investor base. Unfortunately, many IPO bankers have not kept pace. Family offices are often long-term holders who remain under the radar of the trading desks that bankers rely on to find IPO buyers. Family offices can also be secretive about their investment strategy and preferences.

Nevertheless, a good investment bank should be able to help identify relevant family offices, before, during and after the IPO. Asia, the Middle East, and Latin American family offices (FOs) have seen explosive growth in first-generation wealth and cross-border family offices. New wealth is often entrepreneurial and tech-native, with a higher appetite for growth and innovation-focused deals.

Why It Matters To Companies As shareholders, family offices can provide valuable insights in navigating local customs, regulations or partnerships, especially in rapidly developing economies. Family offices also tend to have made their money in industry, so they might have industry expertise that enables them to assign a premium valuation to the company, spotting an opportunity missed by pure financial investors. Furthermore, family offices do not face quarterly redemption pressures or institutional mandates. This enables them to hold through volatility, offering a level of price stability and alignment with long-term founders.

Hedge Funds

Hedge funds tend to be very active market participants. They play a nuanced but important role in the IPO process, especially in the pricing, momentum, and aftermarket performance of newly listed companies.[25] Unlike family offices, your bankers will have lots of relationships with hedge funds. The involvement of hedge funds can provide both liquidity and credibility, but can also introduce volatility and short-termism, making their participation a double-edged sword for issuers.

Hedge funds are often sophisticated, data-driven investors who participate in IPO bookbuilds with real-time valuation feedback. Their participation helps underwriters set pricing, especially when comps are unclear (e.g., disruptors, fintech).

The role of hedge funds in IPOs varies significantly across listing venues, due to differences in market structure, regulatory regimes, investor culture, and IPO sizing norms. Their influence is most pronounced in the U.S., emerging in Europe and more constrained or controlled in Asia-Pacific. When cornerstone investors are abundant and credible, the need for hedge fund participation tends to be reduced, but not necessarily eliminated. Generally, investors with a timeframe that aligns with management are best, and many hedge funds are looking for shorter-term returns.

Hedge funds often use options, leverage, derivatives or momentum-driven strategies, which can exacerbate price swings during earnings or lock-up expirations.[26] By default, hedge funds aren't long-term holders, so their presence doesn't always signal long-term confidence the way cross-over or long-only investors do.

Company leaders need to consider that hedge funds might crowd out more strategic or sticky capital, reducing the IPO's share ability that is needed to attract a more resilient, long-term oriented shareholder base.

Why It Matters To Companies Hedge funds use leverage to place significant early orders, triggering demand signals that draw in other institutional investors. They are sophisticated, so they can do the hard work of analyzing and valuing a company. Investment banks and other market participants generally care what hedge funds think, so the right fund can drive new equity coverage, raise awareness, or attract follow-on interest.

Hedge funds bring pricing intelligence and trading velocity to IPOs, but they are not relationship investors. Their involvement should be strategically weighted, not avoided outright, but balanced carefully against long-term holders, family offices and cross-over funds.

The Shorts

Short funds take short positions in a company with the hope of being able to buy the shares at a lower price in the future. That means they are incentivized to convince other market participants, customers and regulators that the company they have shorted is no good. No board of directors or company management team wants shorts involved in their business, but shorts play an important role and are here to stay as part of a properly functioning global market.

Activist short-sellers take a short position in a publicly traded company and publicly challenge the company's fundamentals, governance or disclosures in order to catalyze a decline in the share price.

Unlike passive short-sellers, who simply bet against a stock quietly, activist short-sellers are proactive and often highly public, releasing detailed reports, engaging the media or even pressing for regulatory investigations.

Activist short-sellers (e.g., Muddy Waters, Hindenburg Research) have uncovered fraud, misstatements or unsustainable business models before regulators or auditors saw anything unsavory.[27] In aggregate, short-sellers help with short-term order execution and overall market confidence. Every time a WireCard or Enron is exposed, the integrity of the market is improved.

Shorting involves borrowing shares, so funds should be incurring real interest expenses. Markets outside the U.S., where share borrowing is more expensive, are less likely to have deep shorting activity.[28] Markets that use continuous disclosure, as opposed to quarterly reporting, are also less likely to have a deep pool of shorters because there is no near-term event to trigger a stock drop, so shorts are forced to hold their short for a longer time, incurring more borrowing costs, while they also attract increased risk, as a company may have a positive announcement at any time.[29] A tight-float, or well known cornerstone investor, can also scare off the shorts.

"They can get in your head."
Public Market CEO

A short strategy often centers on misrepresentation, hype or governance failure, not just valuation. A vocal short can do reputational damage that feels personal, especially to founder-CEOs. (Weak or thin-skinned leaders should call their grandmother—Grandma will always be supportive!) Short noise can cause loyal executives, board members and employees to question leadership or growth assumptions. Teams can waste excessive time on damage control, preparing rebuttals, analyzing accusations, and managing staff morale, instead of investing time in productive activities.

Having said that, you might think there is no reason to waste your time as a management team meeting with funds whose primary business model is shorting stocks. However, every short position is a future buy order. As equity advisory firm TKDY says, "Short-sellers are often a company's most committed future buyers." They suggest to the companies they represent: *Don't shy away from shorts. Treat them like any other investor.* They just have the ability to express their cynicism of a company or a sector (or express their misunderstanding of an equity story) in a different way than long-only funds. However, unlike long funds with no position and ambivalence, they are more likely than not to have to buy in the future. So, they are a category of investor to be engaged with.

Why It Matters To Companies Corporate leaders must be able to articulate why short sellers are wrong about their company. Leadership needs to be measured in its response. Most importantly, management needs to have a great company and build a robust enough shareholder base to drown out the noise of short sellers.

ESG and Impact-Driven Funds

Globally, there are funds whose investment decision is either driven by or heavily influenced by criteria beyond simple economic returns. Europe especially has a pool of institutional investors who allocate capital via what is called Article 8 or 9 SFDR-compliant vehicles. The definition of ESG—Environmental, Social and Governance—is as diverse as the stakeholders interpreting it. Impact criteria differs by geography, industry, ideology, and evolving regulatory frameworks. Investment criteria frequently encompass factors such as sustainability metrics, greenhouse gas (GHG) reduction targets, board diversity, and ethical standards within the supply chain.

There are significant pools of capital looking for investments that meet their criteria. Companies should understand how their existing operations may make them eligible for investment. Bankers should be helpful in this process. Fund examples include RobecoSAM, Pictet, Candriam, and BNP Paribas Asset Management.

Companies should also be skeptical about altering their operations just to meet the needs of one specific investor, especially if the administrative overhead is substantial. However, understanding the concerns and metrics of impact investors often results in both stronger management and better operations.

Why It Matters To Companies Impact investors can unlock premium pricing if you are aligned with their impact narratives (e.g., clean energy, circular economy, healthcare access). Understanding the perspective of impact investors can provide a new lens for managing the company and communicating with employees and other stakeholders. Good leaders want to understand and shape the impact their organizations have on society; the right impact investor can provide positive support.

Sector Specialists

Sector specialists are institutional investors, either funds or individual portfolio managers, with deep domain expertise in specific industries (e.g., healthcare, fintech, energy, software). In a global IPO, they can play a disproportionately influential role in pricing, credibility, and long-term support, especially in complex or non-consensus sectors.

If a company clearly fits into a particular sector, management should prioritize sector specialists as part of the IPO process. If a company is disrupting a sector, or has a concentration of customers in a sector, management should also seek to get in front of sector specialists. Even if they do not invest they are likely to provide valuable market insights to management.

Why It Matters To Companies Sector specialists are the "smart money" in their vertical. Their presence in a global IPO isn't just capital, it's a signal to the market that insiders in the field believe in the company's story, valuation, and roadmap.

Retail

Retail investors play varying roles in IPOs across global markets, depending on market structure, regulatory design, cultural norms, and platform access. In some jurisdictions, retail is structurally required and integrated into the IPO process. In others, retail is largely excluded until post-listing.

Retail access is going through a sea-change driven by demographics, smartphone proliferation and a slew of related global trends. This book addresses retail participation in greater depth in later chapters, but, generally speaking, management is best served by focusing on the many institutional investors globally who are eager to participate in new issues. In markets where a level of retail participation is mandated, the local exchange or banker can include a platform or specialist who can ensure adequate retail participation.

For U.S. companies listing outside the U.S., management should ensure that U.S. retail is barred from direct investment participation.[30] In response to this, I would recommend consulting your international banker and attorneys. Too many U.S. retail investors for U.S.-domiciled companies can trigger onerous SEC regulatory expenses, opening the company and its board up to liability and litigation.[31] Too much retail participation can also scare off institutions because retail can be irrational—professional long-term investors want to understand the game, and may not appreciate unanticipated volatility.

Why It Matters To Companies There is one scenario in which retail IPO participation is both desirable and advantageous. This is when a consumer-facing company has or wants a loyal and engaged customer base, or strong brand identity—essentially, companies whose business model benefits from a large community of aligned stakeholders.

The key is to convert customers into shareholders, and/or shareholders into customers. This strategy drives both capital formation and long-term brand engagement. Retail investors can act as brand evangelists, amplifying word-of-mouth and social visibility. Owners are more likely to be engaged customers, deepening loyalty and reducing churn.

Employees

In a global IPO, employees play a multi-dimensional role; as internal stakeholders, brand ambassadors and in many cases, direct shareholders. Company leaders should not overlook their treatment and alignment during the IPO process. Their involvement (or exclusion) can significantly affect culture, reputation, morale, retention, and post-listing performance.

Why It Matters To Companies A well-designed employee participation strategy isn't just an HR initiative, it signals to capital markets that talent retention is part of the strategy. A well-designed employee participation program can be tax efficient for employees, attract lower compensation costs for companies, align incentives with investors, and improve retention.

Existing Investors

At the highest level, existing investors fall into two categories: Group 1—Investors who want to hold and maybe even buy more, and Group 2—inventors who want to, or are required to sell as soon as possible. Managers who don't understand which group each of their existing investors sit within risk suboptimal valuations or poor post-listing performance.

Let's start with Group 1. An existing investor who is not invited to participate in the IPO may feel insulted, especially after the stock performs well. There may be a myriad of reasons management might prefer a new investor, including shareholder diversification, personal chemistry or the value that an increment investor is expected to bring. That said, the existing investors helped get the company to where it is and leadership needs to be careful that existing insiders are not snubbed in the IPO process. An existing investor participating in an IPO is a huge positive signal to new investors, who will be less familiar with the company. If the public market is having trouble properly valuing the company, existing investors can help provide some of the capital, giving new investors more time to truly understand the company.

Group 2 is looking for liquidity. Often, their reason to sell is not based on their assessment of the company's value at IPO, but instead is driven by their fund structure. VCs and PEs have promised their investors liquidity within a specific holding period, while angel investors often seek to recirculate that capital to new angel investment, or to diversify and "take some money off the table."

In the U.S., Group 2 is generally locked until 180 days after the IPO, creating predictable selling pressure and often driving down valuations. Outside the U.S., there is often more flexibility. In some cases shares can become tradeable as part of the IPO process. In many non-US markets, there are multiple opportunities to buy out existing shareholders in the months and days leading up to the IPO. The reason for this liquidity is:

- Increased availability of pre-ipo and cornerstone investors
- Institutional investors, such as pension, who want meaningful stakes
- More transparent testing the waters process - greater information exchange

- More flexible lock-up rules for shares purchased in the lead up to the IPO

As a rule of thumb, management should seek to get sellers (Group 2) off the cap table before the IPO. Leadership should seek to move shears away from sellers, and toward investors that are likely to buy more long-term and/or add other value to the company's strategy or IPO process.

Why It Matters To Companies Existing investors' decisions around IPO participation can materially influence how public investors perceive the quality and durability of the offering. Leaders who identify sellers should make a solid effort to get them off the cap table before the IPO. If the sellers plan to sell at the IPO, management needs to be able to articulate the structural reason they are liquidating shares. An IPO is an opportunity for a company to shift ownership to shareholders who want to support the company's vision and strategy.

Other Considerations When Designing an Investor Base

Company management and their boards should focus on building investor relationships that persist and compound beyond the IPO. Through this long-term lens, the emphasis should be on attracting investors who bring more than money; networks, expertise, patience. Well-run companies—Building a Base That Believes, Buys, and Stays—are creating a flywheel to shareholder composition.

Navigating Cultural Differences

Company management needs to learn how to navigate cultural differences among geographically diverse investors. These differences shape expectations around communication style, time horizons, governance norms, risk tolerance, trust-building and decision-making processes. A one-size-fits-all pitch, or IR approach, almost always underperforms when deployed globally.

Seasonality Considerations

Seasonality in international markets will impact timing or investor outreach, roadshows, IPO execution, and follow-on offerings and ongoing IR activity. Investors in other parts of the world may be eager to invest in a company while other investors are "away on holiday."

Institutional investors across geographies follow distinct vacation calendars, religious holidays, fiscal year cycles, and regional event schedules that impact their availability, attention, and risk appetite. Ignoring these dynamics can lead to low engagement, suboptimal bookbuilding, or dead-on-arrival investor marketing. For example, investors in the Southern Hemisphere may be on summer vacation in January. Companies and their bankers need to plan accordingly.

"No" Means "Not Now"

Companies that build relationships with investors in far-flung locations should not be discouraged if they don't invest in the IPO. Leaders should remember that relationship-building is a marathon, not a sprint. These investors are more likely to become investors in the future now they are more familiar with the team.

Research Sets Expectations

Outside the U.S., equity research has more involvement in the IPO process. They often dedicate meaningful time to understanding the company, its business model and the growth potential. One obvious result is less underpricing on IPO day, but a less appreciated benefit is research can share opinions that would be inappropriate coming from the company. If management sets expectations too high, investors may shun the company for a very long time. Management should be humble—let the independent analysts talk about anything that is uncertain. Better for analysts to be perceived as naive than for management to be considered shifty.

Take Ownership of Cap Table Design

As one successful founder said, "Bankers think the deals are their deal, for quick profit for their best hedge fund clients." Company management is always time-starved, but they should not be tempted to over-delegate identifying, understanding and courting investors. They must understand the IPO book building and be proactive in screening investor participation and allocation. Just because an investor is good for the bank does not mean it is the right investor for the company. Overall, building the right investor base is important and should be viewed as an element of a broader overall strategy.

Summary

- Build investor relationships before the IPO: engage institutions early (pre-IPO rounds, testing-the-waters) so many investors aren't meeting you for the first time on day one.
- Pick a mix of bankers (regional + global), not a single global banner. Different banks reach different regions, strategies and investor profiles.
- Treat cap-table design as strategic: public ownership impacts governance, index eligibility, future fundraising and defensive resilience. Management must own this process, not just delegate to bankers.
- Anchor / cornerstone investors provide validation and ballast, reducing churn and signalling confidence to other investors.
- Ensure that you know the various investor types and their trade-offs, while recognizing the market-structure players.
- Don't overlook family offices, wealth managers and HNW (especially outside the U.S.) they can supply patient capital, local knowledge and retail-style support in certain jurisdictions.
- Sector specialists matter: domain experts signal smart money, materially influencing pricing and long-term support for complex or niche businesses.
- Be deliberate about existing investors: identify who wants

to hold vs who needs liquidity, try to get sellers off the cap table pre-IPO, and use incumbents' participation as a positive signal.

- Plan for regional differences & seasonality: communication style, holiday calendars, reporting norms and governance expectations vary by geography.
- Long view: build a diverse, value-adding investor base. Independent research should set expectations, while it's important to prioritize relationships that "believe, buy and stay," and treat the IPO as the start of ongoing investor stewardship.

In the next chapter, we will examine the impact of mobile platforms, such as smartphones, on the market.

Chapter 10
Smartphone-Fueled Animal Spirits

The smartphone is an overarching element of what is a greater basket of self-reinforcing and interconnected technologies that have fundamentally changed the financial markets. The smartphone-empowered investor is having profound implications for IPOs.[1] The modern stock market is no longer merely a venue for capital allocation and price discovery; it has instead become a global theater for speculation, entertainment, and even self-identity.

In the decade before COVID-19, and even more so after, a wave of intertwined forces rewired the market's architecture, psychology, and tempo.[2] Breakthroughs in access and liquidity didn't just tweak the system, they transformed the global capital landscape in all these ways:

- Inclusive smartphone access & superapps
- Speculation as entertainment & investing as a sport
- Prediction markets and event-outcome contracts
- Options
- Meme stock
- Social media
- Generative AI
- Crypto

What began as innovations in access and liquidity have evolved into a cultural and technological phenomenon where lines between investing, gambling and gaming have blurred beyond recognition.

These interconnected and self-reinforcing elements, combined with social and demographic factors, drive the "degenerate economy." The term was popularized by investor Howard Lindzon to describe a cultural-financial regime where speculation becomes entertainment, investing is gamified and market behavior is driven more by narrative, memes, and participation than traditional fundamentals or intrinsic value.[3] Here are a few more of his thoughts on the matter:

> *"The degenerate economy continues to ramp ... the arms dealers (Nvidia/semiconductors, Apple, Google, brokerages, crypto, social networks) have embedded it and interest rates don't matter to it."*[4]
>
> *"I can't escape the 'degenerate economy'—even in Venice (Italy)... People are finally starting to see that 'speculation is entertainment' and I believe a massively large lifestyle trend."*[5]
>
> *"We are in a degenerate economy where the best way to learn is to play. You don't need credentials, you need curiosity and fast reflexes."*[6]

Hundreds of millions of people all over the world now have instant, frictionless access to the capital markets, entertainment, and knowledge.[7] The smartphone didn't just democratize access; it compressed decision-making, emotional reactions, and market exposure into the intimate, routine spaces of everyday life. But why does it matter?

There is a class of investor that believes stock investing is an occupation that should be limited to select professionals. The thinking is that fundamentals drive valuation, Discount Cash Flows (DCF) models reflect intrinsic worth, Net Asset Valuations are accurate, and markets are efficient. But, in fact, the situation is way more complicated than that. The emotion of the masses matters, and even more so in the age of the smartphone.

Investor George Soros eloquently explains in his theory of Reflexology that expectations altered reality.[8] A company expected to do well has better access to talent and capital, thus increasing the likelihood of the company doing well:
"I believe that market prices are always wrong in the sense that they present a biased view of the future. But distortion works in both directions.... The fundamentals themselves are influenced by the participants' perceptions."

I am a disciple of Benjamin Graham, so I must admit that it took me some time to appreciate the "self-fulfilling prophecy" element of markets. But the evidence is undisputable—momentum, sentiment and speculation are part of the investment landscape. Long-term investors who ignore the signal from short-term speculators run the risk of failing to recognize when reflexive feedback loops are distorting price enough to influence fundamentals themselves.

Nowhere is this more critical than the days just before and just after the IPO. In general, as a board member and mentor to our portfolio companies, I encourage leadership to focus on institutional investors. If management sets their net globally, there are an awful lot of big fish. Institutions can write substantial checks when a company is ready to raise more capital, and institutions can also sop up large blocks of shares when other institutions need to sell. That said, during the IPO, a massive crowd of investors can be especially valuable.

The proper pricing of a new issue is inherently complex. The perfect complexity for the wisdom of a large and diverse crowd. Mispricing of IPO shares is a friction that transfers wealth from founders and early shareholders to bankers and public market insiders. I recently witnessed a NY IPO for a UK company that was growing in Latin America...and guess who was an important day one stock buyer? Korean smartphone-empowered retail investors![9] Turns out that inclusive access via smartphones benefits both investors and new issuers.

Information is also at a premium during the IPO process. Here again there is a critical role for broad participation. Smartphone-empowered investors and speculators don't just consume information, they also produce it. Customer testimonials, snarky comments, industry insights, pictures of cats, and general commentary all combined, creating new signal out of the noise.

Be under no illusion: great insights are not limited to institutional investors. As legendary investor Peter Lynch points out, individual investors observe trends in their daily lives, in the products they use, stores they visit, and services they rely on. They can sometimes spot trends before professionals pick up on them. This "on-the-ground insight" is sometimes referred to as "street lag." Lynch argues that this perspective provides individuals with an informational advantage: "Actually, there are two kinds of investor's edges: the on-the-job edge, in which you have a working relationship with an industry...and the consumer's edge, with which you can capitalize on your experiences in restaurants, airports, and shopping malls."[10]

Lynch goes on to describe other retail advantages that could be especially important during an IPO process. He argues that professional managers often face constraints that limit their ability to act.

Large funds cannot move meaningfully into many small or micro-cap stocks without impacting price or liquidity. This is especially true for the portfolio managers of U.S. funds. They are simply too big to participate in smaller IPOs.

Institutional investors may also be constrained by diversification mandates: many funds must hold many names and avoid concentration, again limiting their participation as they may not have the time to get to know a small company. Fund managers may also be influenced by bonus compensation cycles, causing them to be reluctant to take contrarian bets in the near term, even if they believe they are correct in the long-term. Lynch believed that because individuals aren't under the same institutional constraints, they can remain patient, concentrate bets, and take advantage of inefficiencies that institutions ignore.

Too much retail participation may scare off some institutional investors, but the new reality is that retail access is now a permanent fixture of the IPO and follow-on issuance market.

Smartphone SuperApps

Historically, financial and digital experiences lived in silos. Brokerage apps were built for trade execution and account management, while banking apps handled payments and credit cards. Crypto platforms focused solely on digital asset trading, and gaming, gambling, entertainment, and social media each operated in their own distinct lanes.

Today, those lines are rapidly blurring. The modern SuperApp is collapsing these boundaries, merging trading, speculation, payments, gaming mechanics, social interaction, and even entertainment into a single, always-on platform. The implications are profound for companies looking to use the public markets to accelerate growth, flexibility and resilience.

Today's SuperApps (like Robinhood, Futu, eToro, Binance, and Revolut) are interactive platforms where:

- Predictions and price movement are content
- Trades are stories
- Portfolios are identity
- Trading costs are minimal or free
- Engagement metrics (not just returns) define relevance

This underpins the "speculation as entertainment" shift. Gamified design, real-time alerts, swiping, and social badges now replicate the dopamine loops of TikTok or mobile gaming. TikTok and Robinhood are well-known, but they are just two relatively regional examples. There are hundreds of rapidly evolving apps all vying for attention. This is a global trend; Groww in India, Alipay in China, Spiking in Southeast Asia, Trade Republic in Europe to name but a few.

Apps of all types are increasingly integrated with domestic payment rails and e-wallets. There seems to be nothing slowing the blurring of lines between entertainment, payment, debit, credit, currency, crypto, savings, investment and speculation. Payments-first apps are evolving into multi-functional financial hubs. Other apps are evolving to include payments. The proliferation of modern APIs and AI-assisted software development means they are adding new products all the time, including global IPOs.

Prediction Markets

Prediction markets such as Kalshi, Polymarket and Manifold are accelerating this trend.[11] Prediction markets are financial instruments where users can buy and sell contracts based on the outcome of future events, and they have proven popular with smartphone users. Unlike options or stocks, prediction markets are easy to understand; either something happens or it doesn't. Prediction markets are thus fast-moving—users can see their views play out in real time, adjust positions, and compare with the crowd. Their real-time, 24-hour interactivity boosts session time, repeat visits, and user retention; all core engagement drivers for any smart app.

Also important to note is that the markets themselves are content and signal. Want to know the likelihood of a new tariff? Need to hedge against regime change? Wondering about recession risk? Prediction markets can help.

In the age of webcams and social media, it seems anyone can be a pundit. Like noses, everyone seems to have an opinion. But prediction markets cut through the noise. They deliver real-time signals from crowds of people with skin in the game, not just attention-seeking "expert" opinions. It's not just opinion, it's *conviction*, measured in dollars, not decibels.

"It is not the critic who counts... but the man who is actually in the arena."
Theodore Roosevelt— U.S. President (1901–1909)

Prediction markets provide a real-time opinion from a crowd of people with skin in the game. More important, from an IPO perspective, the integration of prediction markets into super-apps acts as an onboarding mechanism for what may eventually become a new type of risk-savvy investor.

Options

Historically, options were the domain of hedge funds and institutional desks. They were complex, margin-intensive, and buried in terminals. But today, options have exploded in popularity. Retail traders can dominate volumes, particularly in short-dated contracts, such as Zero-Day-to-Expiration (0DTE).[12]

SuperApps like Robinhood, WeBull, SoFi, Futu and Upstox offer one-tap options interfaces. Options have gone from exotic to mainstream. There are four big elements adding to the popularity:

- Unlocking Leverage—High payoff with low capital which attracts small and tactical traders
- Speed—Aligns with mobile-first, real-time decision cycles
- Speculation—Ideal for getting a dopamine hit, especially on binary and intraday events
- Simplicity—Pre-built strategies, slick designs (UI/UX) to simplify execution.

The implications are that options can inject volatility and scare off short sellers. There can be unexpected swings when retail crowds pile into the same trade. The result is gamma feedback loops, where a self-reinforcing cycle of price movement is driven not by fundamentals, but by option-induced hedging activity.[13] Institutions need to buy so they have the shares if the option is exercised. Institutional desks like JP-Morgan and QDS now model retail-driven short-dated options flow as a market force.

Options play a role in the resurrection of the IPO market. SuperApps with options functionality are onboarding a younger, mobile-native cohort into the capital markets, not just in domestic markets but globally.

When options begin trading on a newly listed stock, often in the weeks post-IPO, speculative flows kick in. Options allow traders to express directional views with leverage, which can:

- Accelerate narrative
- Lead to price moves that reinforce visibility
- Attract media and analyst coverage sooner

For issuers, volatility, when it's upward, attracts attention and demand for secondary offerings, PIPEs, or strategic partnerships.

The presence of liquid options markets makes IPOs more attractive to hedge funds, market makers, and structured product desks. Institutional Investors can:

- Hedge against lock-up expiration risk
- Structure long/short trades
- Write calls to enhance yield

The existence of a robust option market can encourage more aggressive institutional participation in the IPO because they can manage risk more flexibly. A stock that is "supported by options speculation" often sees a higher-than-expected float velocity, which helps issuers in follow-on rounds or insider monetizations.

Meme Stocks

The original meme stock was GameStop. In 2021, the company was struggling to survive and major investors were betting against the video game retailer. Investor Keith Gill, better known as "Roaring Kitty," rallied other investors to join him in buying up thousands of GameStop shares, changing the trajectory of the stock.[14]

Meme stock dynamics have proven that retail investors, when coordinated through social platforms, can move prices with scale, speed, and conviction once unthinkable. IPOs, especially consumer-facing, tech, or culturally resonant ones are therefore fertile ground for meme potential.

Meme stocks demonstrate that attention is monetizable in equity markets. Ironically, meme dynamics can attract institutional capital, especially from funds that trade volatility, sentiment, or event-driven strategies. Increased social investing narratives can result in more equity research coverage, increased option activity and general public company awareness. Bankers tell me, IPOs with meme potential now trade at a "visibility premium."

The emergence of meme stocks has redefined the IPO playbook for some companies. It's no longer enough to have fundamentals and projections. IPO issuers and underwriters must now consider narrative velocity, social resonance, and attention architecture.

Social Media

In the 1980s and '90s, the U.S. had a robust IPO market. It also had a network of regional brokerages that "called" their retail clients—called as in *used a phone*!

The "Four Horsemen"—Robertson Stephens, Hambrecht & Quist (H&Q), Montgomery Securities, and Alex Brown & Sons—had huge networks of wealthy customers. Piper Jaffray, Raymond James and Legg Mason also supported IPOs. Online trading, consolidation and regulation destroyed the regional broker as a disseminator of the IPO information. The phone and prolific research reports are gone in leading the IPO conversation.

Social media has risen to fill, and, in many cases, replace, the traditional role of the retail broker by delivering what brokers once provided: access to information, investment ideas, narrative framing, and even trade execution paths.[15] Social media is a vast new resource for information and insights, 24 hours a day, in every language, and in a range of formats. Video, audio, graphics, charts, short text, and long text are all readily available.

Social media provides ideas, sentiment, and community, often faster, more accessibly, and more culturally aligned than traditional brokers ever could. "Micro-influencers," traders with a few thousand followers, now move volume with a tweet.

Sentiment now trades like a factor, alongside momentum, value, and quality. Buy-side risk models increasingly integrate social sentiment feeds. Overall, social media has caused a reduction in information asymmetry. Democratized information has empowered the market.

Again, there are implications for companies planning their IPO. Traditionally, IPO demand was driven by:

- Institutional investor roadshows
- Broker-dealer client pitching
- Controlled narrative
- Selective media coverage

Now, social media front-runs and can amplify IPO hype, weeks before the first pitch deck lands. Online threads analyze filings and spin narratives. TikTok influencers break down IPO buzz in short-form explainers. Twitter/X traders circulate screenshots, valuation snippets, or retail allocations. Retail demand now builds organically, sometimes outpacing institutional outreach.

For SuperApps, IPO access becomes a point of engagement and community pride. New retail-focused IPO platforms use social media to generate waiting lists, build buzz, and tell the equity story to the wider global investment community.

Crypto & Equity Tokenization

The boundary between digitally native assets like Bitcoin and traditional real-world assets such as cash and equities is rapidly dissolving. For many international SuperApp users, this convergence can't come soon enough.

Crypto is compressing the distance between transactional plumbing and user-facing interfaces, pushing SuperApps not just as multipurpose consumer apps (ride-sharing, finance, messaging) but as financial operating systems where trading, payments, social, lending, staking, and tokenization live side-by-side.

Crypto adds "stickiness" vectors: native yield, token rewards, liquidity mining, social tokens, governance participation. These features are powerful hooks within SuperApps—users don't just transact, they participate, speculate, and engage with the platform's internal economy, and this, in turn, changes the economics of retention and growth.

Crypto innovations (like flash loans, automated market makers, tokenized margin) define new liquidity tools. Some of these bleed into equity markets—especially via equity derivatives, ETFs and alternative trading venues.

Leverage

In the 1930s, in the wake of the U.S. stock market crash, the U.S. implemented restrictions on the ability to use leverage to buy stocks. Margin borrowing was generally limited to about 50% of the value of a portfolio reducing the risk of a self-reinforcing margin call market crash. For decades the impact of active retail was muted because of limited access to margin credit. Here again, technology and globalization have rewired the capital market.

Fractionalized derivatives, leveraged tokens, perpetual swaps, and margin trading are now available natively within smartapps. There are now even ETFs offering 5X exposure to indexes or individual stocks.[16] Investors, especially in Asia, LATAM, and parts of Africa, can access a wide range of complex leverage products.

As a result, small-dollar smartphone investors now punch above their weight in volume, often driving price discovery and movements.

Summary

- Smartphone SuperApps have democratized access and compressed decision cycles, merging trading, payments, social interaction and fintech into always-on hubs that turn portfolios into extensions of identity.
- Speculation has become entertainment: gamified UX, engagement metrics, and short dopamine-driven feedback loops make trading feel like sport or content, not just capital allocation.
- Social media and influencer networks have eroded information asymmetry, amplifying narratives quickly; sentiment now behaves like a tradable factor alongside momentum and value.
- The retail options boom supplies cheap leverage and speed, creating feedback loops that can drive pricing independent of fundamentals.
- Prediction markets act as a real-time barometer of risk and crowd conviction.
- Meme-stock dynamics prove that coordinated retail attention can move markets at scale, creating a visibility premium that changes how issuers and bankers think about IPO demand.
- Crypto and tokenization introduce new retention hooks and novel liquidity mechanics that increasingly bleed into equity market structures.
- For IPOs, the playbook has changed: pricing, allocation and liquidity engineering must account for narrative velocity, retail onboarding pathways and derivative flows.
- Founders, boards and underwriters must marry institutional discipline with cultural and attention design.

In short, the smartphone-era has banded, and is further banding together technology, culture, and capital into a single, self-reinforcing ecosystem. The presence of millions of empowered investors, especially during the IPO pricing process will improve IPO pricing, outcomes, and velocity.

Global IPO

Chapter 11
Coming to America - The Double Standard

Companies that view the public market as a global ecosystem can use the benefits of being public to reduce risk and accelerate their growth into decacorn or even a hectocorn (over $100 billion) status.

For many U.S. companies, the smartest move is to list abroad. It lets them avoid the bloated, expensive machinery of a U.S. listing. Going overseas also cuts litigation risk by limiting exposure to a narrow group of heavyweight "qualified" U.S. investors.

Ironically, foreign companies get a sweeter deal in the U.S. They can access both American investors and U.S. exchanges without facing the same regulatory gauntlet. It's a double standard. And it favors outsiders.

As Deloitte points out, "The SEC provides a number of accommodations to foreign private issuers to encourage them to list in the U.S. while reducing the ongoing cost and distraction of complying with certain U.S. reporting and governance requirements, such as the exemption from the U.S. proxy rules and Section 16 insider reporting."[1]

U.S. companies have significant ongoing expenses, estimated

to average about 4% of market value.[2] This reduces earnings and, thus, valuations. U.S. companies also face regulatory and litigation headwinds that impede open communication. International companies by contrast may find the U.S. more hospitable because of the regulator's desire to attract international listings.

In the U.S. markets there is a high density of growth-oriented institutional investors willing to pay for future potential rather than just current dividends.[3] Beyond the initial listing, U.S. markets allow for follow-on offerings, in which a company can raise an additional $500M in a single afternoon, providing capital velocity that is unmatched globally.[4] This option is supported by deep liquidity pools, ready to fill in as the company scales, ensuring that even massive stock sales don't trigger extreme price volatility.[5] Furthermore, in the U.S., there are thousands of analysts who specialize in extremely niche sub-sectors, increasing the likelihood that a complex foreign tech is valued correctly.[6] Like most top exchanges, the Nasdaq and NYSE have a reputation for being global, fulfilling their role as a "seal of approval" that validates a company's governance and transparency to the rest of the world.[7]

Foreign Private Issuer (FPI)

A company that has more than 50% of its voting power, director, officers and operations outside the U.S.[8] can avoid most of the listing headwinds faced by U.S. companies. Foreign companies, especially "Emerging Growth Companies" (EGCs), have much more listing and disclosure flexibility. To be an EGC, an issuer must have raised less than $700M and have under $1.07 billion in annual revenue. The flexibility around disclosure includes:

- Annual, or Bi-annual Reporting vs. Quarterly Reporting
- Option to use IFRS Instead of U.S. GAAP
- No Proxy Requirements (Schedule 14A)
- Exemption from Regulation FD (Fair Disclosure)
- Exemption from U.S. Proxy Rules for Shareholder Meetings
- Executive Compensation Disclosures

- Exemption from Certain Sarbanes-Oxley Requirements
- Option to use some home-country governance practices
- Flexibility in Regulation S-D Offerings (more leeway under Regulation S and Rule 144A for raising private capital outside the U.S., often concurrent with U.S. listings.
- Ongoing Disclosure (6-K vs. 8-K)
- Shortened Ownership Disclosure (Schedule 13D/G Thresholds)
- No Say-on-Pay or Advisory Votes (unlike U.S. firms under Dodd-Frank).
- Exemptions from some NYSE/NASDAQ Governance Rules
- Flexibility in structuring tender offers and going-private transactions
- Fewer Requirements for Auditor Rotation or PCAOB Inspections
- Simpler Deregistration and Exit from U.S. Reporting

One significant advantage afforded to FPIs is the relief from ongoing Form 8-K current reporting and the absence of mandated quarterly reports. FPI may be subject to the semiannual reporting requirements of the Nasdaq and NYSE. It is unclear what the rules will be at the LTSE and Texas Exchange when they become operational.

FPIs have another big benefit: less litigation risk.[9] FPIs listing in the U.S. enjoy a legal shield from one of Wall Street's sharpest weapons: the shareholder class action lawsuit. In Legal, Actuarial and Policy circles the phenomenon is called the "Cheng Gap," named after Beiting Cheng, a Harvard researcher who studied securities litigation for foreign firms listed on U.S. exchanges.

Fewer lawsuits means less management distraction, but it also saves ongoing expenses by driving down directors and officers insurance (D&O) costs. It is not unusual for U.S. companies to spend $250,000 to $650,000 per year on D&O insurance in their first few years after listing.[10]

In the U.S., there are trial attorneys who make a very good

living suing listed companies. A well-designed FPI IPO can further reduce the risk of becoming a litigation target by using approaches unavailable to U.S. firms. FPIs can take steps to impact venue selection, arbitration, information discovery or other procedural barriers. The more cost for litigators and the more uncertainty of outcome, the less likely the company will find itself in litigation. And even if there is a successful lawsuit against a company, foreign courts may not recognize U.S. judgments and punitive damages may be unenforceable.

For U.S. firms, the likelihood of litigation combined with the rigidity of disclosures is an impediment to open communications with investors. When a growth company is impeded in communicating its vision and roadmap, investors assume the worst. Valuations suffer. The litigation and disclosure morass encountered by smaller U.S. companies has an impact on both the IPO and ongoing valuation.

According to the Efficient Market Hypothesis, markets depend on the free flow of information, but the increased paperwork and litigation risk seems to lower efficiency for smaller U.S. issuers. Perhaps more open communications would make it easier for stock analysts, instead of just the highly-structured legalistic 10-Qs, required of U.S. companies.

FPIs are a perfect natural experiment. For foreign listers, there is evidence they are more effective in "Testing the Waters" to educate U.S. investors before an IPO. Mispricing at IPO tends to be smaller for FPIs, causing less dilution for early shareholders. In the years after their IPO, foreign companies appear to continue to benefit from lower costs and more open communications, as stock performance is often superior to that of their domestic peers.[11]

A Well Worn Path

The journey of a foreign company to the U.S. stock market is often described as a transition from being a "local hero" to a "global institution." In 2026, the data showed this trend is accelerating: in the first quarter of 2025 alone, 58% of all

U.S. IPOs were launched by foreign issuers.[12]

Large companies, those with 10B+ of market cap, are attracted to the deep liquidity pools offered by the U.S. exchanges. Examples include:

- Alibaba (China): 2014 $168B IPO valuation
- JD.com (China): 2014 $26B IPO valuation
- Spotify (Sweden): 2018 $26B direct listing valuation
- PagSeguro (Brazil): 2018 $8B IPO valuation
- Coupang (South Korea): 2021 $60B IPO valuation
- NuBank (Brazil): 2021 $41B IPO valuation
- Grab (Singapore): 2021 $40B valuation via SPAC
- Arm Holdings (UK): 2023 $54B IPO valuation

But it's not just large companies.

When MercadoLibre ("The Amazon of Latin America") went public on the Nasdaq in 2007, it was a relatively niche e-commerce site focused on Latin America, with an IPO Valuation of about $800 Million. Leveraging the credibility and financial flexibility of the public market, MercadoLibre grew 12,800%, valued at over $100B by 2026. As MercadoLibre's Founder Marcos Galperin said at a Stanford talk in 2019, "The U.S. listing gives you a lot of institutional framework that in Latin America is very hard to find... it gives you a long-term horizon that is otherwise impossible when your local economy is changing every six months."

MercadoLibre is just one of many smaller non-US companies that listed in the U.S. and used the benefits of being public to reduce risk and accelerate their growth to become a decacorn or even a hectocorn. Other examples include:

ASML (Netherlands)
1995 IPO Valuation ~$600 Million
2026 Valuation $527 Billion
878x

Check Point (Israel)

1996 IPO Valuation ~$450 Million
2026 Valuation $20.3 Billion
45x

Lululemon (Canada)
2007 IPO Valuation ~$1.1 Billion
2026 Valuation $23.7 Billion
21x

Shopify (Canada)
2015 IPO Valuation ~$1.27 Billion
2026 Valuation$214.1 Billion
~168x

Atlassian (Australia)
2015 IPO Valuation ~$4.4 Billion
2026 Valuation $31.1 Billion
7x

As Atlassian co-founder Mike Cannon-Brookes said on the anniversary of their listing: "Ten years ago, we stood here and listed Atlassian under a ticker that says it all: TEAM. It just goes to show that anything's possible if you've got the right product and can identify a niche area to jump into. On an international scale, it's massive... it proves you don't have to be in Silicon Valley to build a Silicon Valley-sized company."

There is a signaling power for a U.S. listing. It is good to be associated with the high-growth venture-backed companies found in the U.S There is also evidence that companies with intangible-heavy business models find Wall Street more adept at pricing innovation.[13] Put another way, valuation multiple analysis across exchanges tends to not hold up to academic rigor, especially when used to predict multiples in the future. Multiples are constantly changing. Company size, sector and growth profile have huge implications on sample size and the data's predictive usefulness. However, for companies with intangible assets, the signal is clearer: U.S. investors tend to be more forward-looking. Perhaps because the U.S. indexes are dominated by new-economy companies reliant on intangible intellectual property like software, technical team, and discoveries that are not yet reflected in cash flows.

Choosing to be Foreign Private Issuer

Just because a company can list in the U.S. as an FPI does not mean it's the best choice. There are some benefits to listing as a U.S. company, or at least voluntarily adopting many of the practices required of a U.S. filler.

Basically, an FPI can choose to file a F-1 with the SEC as an FPI, adopting just some of the disclosure practices of a U.S. firm, or they can choose to become a U.S. issuer and file the stricter S-1 document and adhere to the associated disclosure and governance framework.

As with so much around an IPO, it is necessary to work with advisors who know the rules and best practices.

As an F-1 company, some governance-heavy funds, like pensions and insurance mandates, may have policies to cap exposure. On the flip side, local investors may look at the foreign company as an opportunity to diversify, and to get exposure away from domestic geopolitical or regulatory risks.

One important consideration is the impact on index eligibility. Filing via Form F-1, in itself, does not preclude index inclusion, but it introduces structural and eligibility considerations that often delay or disqualify foreign private issuers from being added to major U.S. indices, especially the Russell 1000/2000. The Russell does include foreign-domiciled companies in certain circumstances, but they must report in USD and meet other extra requirements.

F-1 companies may also scare away investors concerned about changes to U.S. tax treatment. The U.S. is running a massive deficit and has failed to demonstrate an ability to have a balanced budget. The government may unexpectedly subject its citizens to unfavorable tax treatment under PFIC

(Passive Foreign Investment Company Act) or other foreign entity classifications.

Companies viewed as foreign are often the first to be sold in a general crisis. In times of high-uncertainty, investors may demand higher expected returns.

Another consideration is complexity. Not all foreign companies are complex, but as a rule of thumb, investors prefer simplicity. Transitioning from a foreign company to a domestic company may be an opportunity to avoid overly complex or unfamiliar corporate structures.

The most important decision for F-1 companies is deciding how much to adopt U.S. norms, and then to clearly communicating the reasoning behind the decision. Investors need to have both properly set expectations and confidence in management's governance decisioning process.

The most successful FPIs, such as Shopify, ASML and MercadoLibre, understood this dual mandate. They used the FPI regime to streamline filings, but voluntarily adopted many U.S.-style practices to ensure investor comfort:

- Quarterly earnings calls and KPI disclosures, even though not required.
- Enhanced board independence, exceeding home country minimums.
- U.S.-standard investor relations and financial modeling support.

The biggest mistake companies make when filing an F-1 is underestimating the governance, disclosure, and investor trust premium embedded in U.S. capital markets, and then failing to adapt their structure, communication, and accountability to U.S. institutional expectations. Tailoring the F-1 is an excellent opportunity to show that management has good judgement, listens to investors and has surrounded the team with knowledgeable advisors.

As an FPI, the company may find the IPO process is faster,

and they can still choose the option to file confidentiality, just like local companies going public in the U.S.

Maintaining Foreign Private Issuer Status

Once listed, the FPI needs to reevaluate if it wants to transition to the more rigid U.S. filing regime. This may become appealing at a certain scale, based on the needs of a certain investor group, index inclusion objective, in response to a regulatory change or for other reasons. Best practice is to evaluate this option at least twice a year.

What a company must avoid is accidentally losing their FPI status. This could happen if a founder with super-voting triggers U.S. residency, if the board has too many Americans, if too many of the voting shares are held by U.S. shareholders including indices, or if too much of the company's assets are in the U.S. The good news is that the asset test is conducted on a predictable schedule, so a big customer wire going through the U.S. office should not suddenly invalidate FPI eligibility, so long as the assets are moved. Cloud infrastructure and IP locations may also have an impact. The SEC applies a fact-based legal test, usually evaluated as of the end of the second fiscal quarter.

Evolving Landscape

In the U.S., trial attorneys are a powerful lobby and they have a motive to see the Cheng Gap shrink. In 2026, the SEC was also trying to close the gap. New regulations made the friction of suing foreign firms much lower. For example, the Multilateral Memorandum of Understanding Network (MMoU) allows the SEC to get audit papers from foreign countries in days, not years. The Holding Foreign Companies Accountable Act (HFIAA) is forcing foreign insiders to report their trades (Section 16), which provides plaintiffs' lawyers with insider trading triggers that were previously hidden.

HFCAA, signed into law in 2020, also makes it harder to use accounting firms that cannot be inspected by the U.S.

Public Company Accounting Oversight Board (PCAOB). The law stipulates that if inspection is not possible for three consecutive years, the company is subject to delisting from U.S. exchanges. The law also requires more disclosure related to government ownership.

Foreign issuers must disclose whether they are owned or controlled by a foreign government, particularly if based in a "non-cooperating jurisdiction" (e.g., China).

As always, the public markets are ever-evolving, and global companies need to monitor exchange regulations that may impact them, their exchange, or their shareholders. The teams that do that will have superior flexibility, resilience, and access to capital.

For foreign companies listing in the U.S., the key is to use available regulatory flexibility without sacrificing investor trust. Companies need to capitalize on regulatory flexibility while maintaining the transparency, governance, and investor alignment necessary to earn and preserve institutional trust.

Chapter 12
Life as a Public Company

Congratulations! Your company is now public. The company is on its journey of enhanced credibility, visibility and prestige. The team should now be in a superior position to attract talent, customers and partners. The cap table is simplified and flexible; ready to change if there is a need for a pocket acquisition or follow-on financing.

Furthermore, the company is now in a stronger strategic position. But, as with everything in business, the opportunity must be actively managed to fully realise its potential. Now public, the company holds the high ground as it battles the world.

"He who occupies the high ground... will fight to advantage."
Sun Tzu—*The Art of War*

This chapter will discuss management techniques to help business leaders make the most of their strategic public "high ground" position.

"The object of defense is preservation; and since it is easier to hold ground than to take it, defense is easier than attack."
Carl von Clausewitz—*On War*

And another important purpose of this chapter will be to discuss actions that business leaders should avoid in order to ensure that they don't lose the benefits of being a public company.

Your First Earnings Call

The single most important factor in your first earnings call is simple: don't miss your numbers. Exceeding expectations—not merely meeting them—is critical for your first, second and third earnings reports.[1] Public market investors are not like your private backers; they have no loyalty, no lock-ups, and very short memories.[2] As one seasoned public market investor put it: "A 5% miss will cost you 35% in valuation—and that pain can last two years."

To avoid this fate, it's essential to conduct a full dress rehearsal of your earnings call, ideally while you're still private.[3] This should include real-time feedback from someone with public markets experience—not just internal voices or private equity investors. The feedback you'll receive from public market professionals is fundamentally different: sharper, more skeptical, and laser-focused on narrative, guidance discipline, and forward-looking credibility.

Bringing in a coach or external advisor with deep IR and institutional investor experience is not optional; it's a strategic investment in how the Street perceives your leadership team from day one.

A common mistake on a company's first earnings call as a public company is failing to align messaging with market expectations, often by either overexplaining internal metrics or undercommunicating key strategic drivers that institutional investors care about.

Another common mistake is to overestimate or underestimate the audience. Some investors on the call will have heard management several times, and will be intimately familiar with the company, while other investors will be there to learn and may be hearing the story for the first time. Striking the right balance is important.

Transparent Financial Reporting

Trust is the currency of public markets. You don't earn a premium valuation or long-term institutional support without it.[4] Transparent financial reporting isn't just a compliance obligation; it's a tactical tool that underpins your credibility, narrative, and ability to navigate through volatility.

Years ago, I worked as a consultant for Brian Moynihan, who went on to run Bank of America. We implemented a wide range of financial and operational metrics to better understand his growing bank. We monitored financial metrics but, also critically important, we monitored how long it took to assemble the metrics. Over the years, I have come to believe that delay in getting financials inversely correlates with the accuracy, quality and utility of financials. Put another way, the faster a company generates financial reports, the better the financial operations are run. Speed is an indicator of quality.[5] My recommendation for public company leaders: don't just monitor your financials, continuously improve the speed and depth of your reporting infrastructure.

For your first filing as a public company, be sure to leave extra time. Over time, public disclosures and regulatory filings will become just another part of the operational rhythm, as routine as going to the gym. But that first time may feel like stepping onto the dojo floor in a crisp white gi, bare feet on polished wood, belt tied too tight, hampered by a slowness until the organizational muscle memory is built. Best to plan to file early.

If you list in a jurisdiction with a continuous disclosure regime, be sure that the management team understands what activity might require immediate disclosure.

Monitoring, Dashboards and Non-Financial Metrics

Most business leaders harden their financial infrastructure as a result of being public.[6] Knowing that many smart, and not so smart, finance professionals will be viewing the finances sharpens the mind in the same way that an athlete trains better once the competitions are scheduled.

What can be overlooked is metrics that are not specifically financial. As a public company, it is important not to let the financial elements distract from the non-financial. Each business is its own special snow flake, but example items to track could include:

- Headcount retention and turnover
- Time to recruit (in days)
- Customer satisfaction / Net Promoter Score (NPS)
- Defect rates
- Number of software releases
- Media and online sentiment
- Number of new products launched
- Customer support tickets per active user
- Supply chain resilience
- Sales cycle length
- Onboarding time to first value
- Bug resolution time
- Equipment utilization

Communications

It is easy to fall into the trap of compartmentalizing media relations and investor relations (IR). It is not uncommon to see PR rolling up to the head of marketing and IR rolling up to the head of finance. It is critical that communications efforts are coordinated, because the days where investors read *Barron's* and customers read Facebook are over.[7] Everyone has access to everything, and AI reorganizes information according to the needs of the media consumer.

One way to get better coordination is a unified news flow

calendar. Leaders can plan ALL key press releases (product launches, partnerships, key hire announcements, financial updates, annual meetings, investor days, etc.) as a team. Another approach is to involve the CEO, CTO, or CFO in providing commentary on major market events. Cross-functional team spokespeople signal stability and unified strategic intent.

This also includes communications to employees, as employees treated as investors are more likely to act like owners. I can think of multiple large investors who ran away from a public market investment because of a casual conversation with a current (or former) employee.

Earnings calls and public milestones are an opportunity to reinforce category leadership, just as investors may chat with customers or employees. Prospective customers and employees may be listening into an earnings call. Overall, managers should avoid unnecessary reinventions or jargon, unless it is central to businesses narrative and competitive advantage.

Investor conferences should be used to build relationships, not just to wave a participation flag. We recommend that management meets investors in another region of the world at least once a year. If they do that, they are more likely to stand out, get new feedback and understand regional opportunities. Management can use investor insights to refine product and expansion plans.

A common mistake is to silo communications with investors, customers and prospects. Unfortunately, this approach is both impossible and sub-optimal. Leaders should regularly review all touchpoints between the company and the broader community to ensure consistent messaging of vision and values. Ideally, management will spot opportunities to use the higher profile and credibility of the public markets to get the desired message out to customers, partners, regulators and proactive hires.

As a public company, it is important to communicate with

all stakeholders, but the management team needs to prioritize prospective investors with a long-term orientation. Long-horizon capital such as pensions, sovereign wealth funds, specific family offices and endowments should receive ongoing communication of status, strategy and progress.

A good head of IR will monitor the share register. They should be tracking the top-20 equity holders, liquidity, and churn. The best IR will also help management proactively target long-term institutional holders.

Keep to Your Narrative

Leaders need to consistently reinforce a clear, coherent story about what the company is, where it's going, and how it plans to get there. The narrative becomes a strategic tool, an anchor that shapes how investors, employees, media, customers, and partners perceive and value your business over time.

Management needs to guard against distractions or near-term priorities that prevent the ongoing drumbeat of a repeated, and then again repeated, story. The story must match the numbers, articulate a focused mission, vision and value proposition. Aligning messaging across earnings calls, investor decks, and filings should become a habit. Consistent narrative is how new and existing investors build long-term trust.

Enhanced Recruiting and Retention

A public company should use its improved access to media to raise its profile among potential employees.[8] Public companies typically have more structured and transparent compensation systems, which appeal to senior operators.[9] Prospective employees can model wealth outcomes more precisely, more thoroughly research the company, and trust that performance will be rewarded over time. Leaders should make the most of having public stock as currency, if they see opportunities to do acquihires (buying a company to acquire the team), incentivize acquired teams with liquid equity, or recruit top talent who want visibility into their equity outcomes.

As best practices for talent compensation evolve, the company's approach should evolve too. At least once a year, the company should benchmark their strategy given competition, regulations, operational footprint and market conditions.

Continue to Improve the Board

As a public company, you now have new opportunities to attract better board members. The best companies grow, and the perfect board member at one phase may be suboptimal later.

For founders, curating the right board is about more than meeting governance requirements; it's about building a strategic brain trust that can help the company endure and thrive over decades. If you are listed in the U.S., managers should expect to have robust Directors and Officers insurance (D&O), as the best board members understand the potentially high level of litigation. For companies listed outside the U.S., this considerable expense is usually unnecessary.

Another consideration is the expertise of the board members. They may be exceptional in many ways, but lacking in a specific area. Rather than expanding the number of board members, which risks reduced engagement and accountability, it can often be possible to supplement the existing board with outside expertise or training.

Investors should be on guard against companies that don't build a board that aligns with the long-term vision, and that does not have an appropriate level of independence, aligned incentive structure, industry and capital markets experience.

Disciplined Capital Allocation

"Capital allocation is the CEO's most important job; value per share is what counts, not overall size or growth.... Over the long-term, returns for shareholders will be determined largely by the decisions the CEO makes in choosing which tools to use." Christopher W. Mayer—Investor/Author

Starting in 1932 and continuing to 1971, investor Thomas Phelps analyzed every company that increased in value 100X in the public market.[10] Christopher W. Mayer extended this research through 2018 in his excellent book, *100 Baggers: Stocks That Return 100-to-1 and How To Find Them*. His conclusion was clear: these companies consistently made smart, disciplined decisions about how to deploy their cash and equity.

To become a 100-bagger, it's not enough to be a great operator—leaders also need to be a great capital allocator. The good news is that, as an operator, management is in a unique position to spot investment opportunities. Or as WarrenBuffet says: "I am a better investor because I am a businessman, and a better businessman because I am an investor."

The most exceptional business leaders are not just outstanding managers, they're exceptional investors. As a public company—whether it is investing in R&D, buying back shares or acquiring a company—management should be disciplined in how it allocates resources. As a leader, don't fall into the short-term trap of optics. Long-term investors realize that how leadership deploys capital is an indicator of how they think. Their decisions are huge indicators for the long-term prospects of the enterprise.

Acquisitions

As a public company, you now have greater flexibility as it relates to potential acquisitions—both in how you structure deals and how you finance them. You can use your publicly-traded equity as a liquid, market-valued currency, which often reduces friction in negotiations compared to illiquid private stock. Sellers are more willing to accept public equity, especially when it can be immediately valued and monetized. You also potentially gain access to lower-cost debt financing.

New disruptive industries tend to consolidate over time. Oracle, Salesforce and Cisco are all powerful examples of businesses that complemented their growth with acquisitions on their path to becoming massive companies.[11] Public companies have the strategic flexibility to drive consolidation, be the acquirer, not just be acquired. But management should be prepared. There can be many reasons why an acquisition could be of great value to the company and its shareholders. Whether it's a small accretive pocket acquisition, gaining a new strategic capability, an acquihire, or pushing into a new geographic region, it is best to be proactive not reactive.

We recommend that our portfolio companies build a framework defining what types of acquisitions would be appealing, and to do this long before acquisition opportunities present themselves or are discovered. In the heat of a deal, it's easy to make bad decisions, and so it is therefore best to think the process through in the sober bright light of a strategic planning session. I recommend having a document that predefines what types of acquisitions are worth pursuing, and updating that document at least once a year. Ideally, the document has example targets, and the target list expands over time.

Being able to articulate your interests and criteria saves time in the long run. The document will come in handy as you talk to industry and capital market participants. Even if the criteria is kept confidential, management and the board is less likely to get distracted by the noise of an enthusiastic banker.

Risk Management

Often companies improve their risk management process as a result of going public. There is no substitute for talking to a diverse group of investors to help identify potential threats to the business. Boards and company managers should make a regular process of re-underwriting risk.

One important element of risk management is having a crisis management plan in place before a crisis happens. Pre-defining the Who, How and When of crisis response can be the difference between a bad day and a bad year. A technique we have found effective in achieving this is a pre-mortem, a strategic planning technique in which a management or the board imagines that a company has already failed. The team then works backward to identify why it failed. When done right, a pre-mortem surfaces potential risks, blind spots, knowledge gaps and inaccurate assumptions.

Similar to pre-mortems, we also like to use Charlie Munger inversion technique. "Invert, always invert: Turn a situation or problem upside down. Look at it backwards."

Inversion technique is summarized as thinking of all the things you can do to cause a disaster, and then making sure you don't do them! But whatever process is used, as a public company success is no longer just about hypergrowth, it is also about durability. Investors will want to understand the diversity of the customer and supplier base. Ongoing contingency planning should result in a stronger company.

Stay Humble

A common pitfall for public company CEOs, particularly founders, is egotism. The market rewards bold vision and conviction, but it does not forgive arrogance. The best leaders possess a clear sense of direction, and the discipline to ignore short-term noise or misinformed advice. The fact that something worked in the past, or that the stock is hitting all-time highs, is no guarantee of future success.

Henry Ford was a canonical case study in how prior success can breed strategic blindness. In the early 20th Century, he revolutionized transportation with the Model T, introduced in 1908. It was affordable, reliable and mass-produced using the innovative moving assembly line. Ford gained 60% of the U.S. car market by the early 1920s. This success made him arguably the most influential industrialist of his era.[12] It also made him arrogant. He famously said, "Any customer can have a car painted any color that he wants so long as it is black."

Ford clung to the Model T, delaying the introduction of new

models until 1927. By contrast, General Motors under Alfred Sloan introduced a tiered brand strategy (Chevrolet, Pontiac, Buick, Cadillac), offering varied price points, colors, and annual updates. They soon grabbed market share. Ford's U.S. market share plummeted to less than 15% by the early 1930s. Ford's Founder was not humble enough to realize what worked in 1908 no longer worked in 1918.

The advice a mentor gave years ago also applies to public CEOs: "The risk is not failure; you will be successful. The risk is what you will do once you achieve incredible success. Look at all these rock stars and athletes, how many go out buy a fast car and drive off a cliff? You need to plan now how you will act then."

Or maybe it's better advice coming from Intel's co-founder, Andy Grove. "Success breeds complacency. Complacency breeds failure. Only the paranoid survive."

Follow-on Offerings

Follow-on offerings (also known as secondary offerings or subsequent equity raises) are a critical tool for public companies, particularly those in capital-intensive industries or with aggressive growth strategies.[13] On many stock exchanges, the capital raised in follow-on offerings far exceeds the capital raised in IPOs, or the private markets.

Management should be prepared to do opportunistic follow-on offerings. A well-timed follow-on, especially when earlier financings were oversubscribed, can signal market confidence and strong demand for equity. It can also help broaden the investor base, bringing in new institutions that missed the IPO.

Follow-on offerings can also fund a cash war chest whose mere existence reduces risk and increases optionality. The ability to do follow-on offerings also helps optimize the cost and availability of debt.
The process of follow-on offerings varies by exchange, so it is

important for management to understand the paperwork and relations that need to be put in place, empowering management to make the most of this powerful capital access tool.

New Exchange and Duel-Listings

As a listed company, the number of global investors who can invest is vast. But management might still consider listing on a new exchange, or pursuing a dual listing (listing on two or more exchanges simultaneously) for several strategic, financial, and operational reasons. While dual listings come with complexity, they can unlock significant upside in terms of investor access, valuation, and market positioning. Listing in certain jurisdictions may align with strategic geopolitical or regulatory goals. For example, a U.S. tech firm duel-listing in Singapore might improve access to Southeast Asian markets, show commitment to the region, and signal an openness to local oversight.

Some regional or regulated investors may need local or dual listing to participate. Changes in the business or applicable regulations could also cause a company to consider a different or an additional exchange. When done right, an IPO on one exchange should not preclude a company from changing exchanges or delisting if conditions change. The best regulator and exchanges realise they are competing, and competing globally. Managers should reevaluate the listing venue from time to time, in order to ensure that it's still optimal.

Monitor Index Eligibility

Once included in an index a company's stock is automatically bought by index-tracking funds and ETFs. This results in a steady, non-discretionary flow of capital—from pension funds, retail ETFs, and sovereign wealth vehicles.[14]

The company and the criteria of indexes change over time, so, again, leaders need to monitor this closely. There may be small changes that result in index inclusion, assuming that is desirable.

Generally, inclusion is favorable for the company and existing investors. However, passive investors often defer their shareholder votes to proxy advisors, who have no economic interest and are subject to political, regulatory or ideological capture.[15] Management may want to make small changes to avoid index inclusion. In all cases, management should monitor the criteria for passive funds and affiliated indexes.

Summary

- **Nail your earnings calls** Don't miss numbers. Rehearse thoroughly, get outside IR/public-market coaching, and align messaging to market expectations.

- **Be transparently fast with financials** Build reporting systems that are accurate and quick; plan extra time for your first public filings and follow continuous disclosure rules.

- **Track both financial and non-financial metrics** Use dashboards for revenue and for things like hiring, NPS, release cadence, bug fixes, supply resilience and onboarding time.

- **Unify communications** Coordinate PR, IR and employee messaging; use earnings and press conferences to reinforce a single, clear narrative and target long-term investors.

- **Allocate capital with discipline and plan M&A** Have a written framework for acquisitions, use equity and follow-on offerings strategically, and regularly reassess listing/exchange choices and index implications.

- **Strengthen governance, risk and humility** Build a fit-for-purpose board, run pre-mortems and crisis plans, avoid complacency, and protect long-term durability over short-term optics.

Going public is not the finish line, it's the starting point for a new strategic chapter. As a public company, you now occupy the high ground. Public company life brings new tools, like follow-on offerings, index inclusion, dual listings, and institutional investor relationships. As Sun Tzu reminds us, those who occupy the high ground fight to their advantage. The rest of this journey is about holding that ground with discipline, foresight, and integrity, before using it to build something truly enduring.

Welcome to public company leadership! Now the real work begins. In the next and last chapter we dive into the future of capital markets.

Chapter 13
The Future of Global Capital - Challenges & Opportunities

"The best way to predict the future is to create it."
Alan Kay—computer scientist

Most of this book is for practitioners of management and investment. This section takes a step back with an eye towards futurists, exchange operators and policy professionals. Capital formation policies have a huge impact on innovation, productivity, economic prosperity and society, and so this chapter aims to address some of the inevitable tradeoffs as the market evolves.

Designing the Market of the Future

For the first two decades of the 21st Century, the private markets out-innovated the public markets. Private capital under management grew from about $600 billion to over $12 trillion—20 times the AUM in just 20 years.[1] Globally, the number of public companies went down as companies chose to stay private longer.[2] As a consequence, capital formation shifted behind closed doors. Companies that were already public, choose to go private, and this trend became a global phenomenon. In Germany, for example, there are 40% fewer listed companies by 2025, compared with 2007.[3] Similarly, the U.S. number is also down by 40% since 1996.[4]

Capital and entrepreneurs go to where they are treated well, and in the first two decades of this century that was in the opaque private markets.[5]

When markets are opaque, resources are misallocated, innovation slows, and trust erodes—outcomes no healthy society can afford.[6] The good news is that technology such as AI, distributed ledger, mobile computing and cross-border telecommunications are combining with global demographic and geopolitical trends to restructure the public markets, ultimately leading to a new era of IPOs.[7] Together, these forces are steadily laying the groundwork for more transparent, inclusive, and resilient capital markets.

Why It Matters

But why should we care? As business leaders, investors, or as a society, what is at stake? Plenty:

Economic Mobility

Public markets democratize ownership.[8] Anyone with access to a smartphone can buy into the next Apple or NVIDIA. This enables ordinary people to participate in the upside of innovation and productivity, not just a small group of insiders. PE ownership is limited to accredited investors and institutions.[9] If companies stay private forever, only insiders and a narrow slice of capital holders see the upside. In a society where technology is driving an ever faster pace of change, do we really want to create a society where a few insiders profit from innovation while the public is merely disrupted? Public markets enable broad economic mobility. Regulators who want to repress their population should discourage companies from going public, and if listed, discourage the general population from investing.

For private markets, high "qualified investor" definitions can be used to increase the likelihood that only the rich get richer. Alternatively, jurisdictions that eliminate qualified investor gates, or allow private market participation based on exam-based criteria, are likely to find their markets more dynamic, and their population more self-reliant.

Greater Transparency

Public companies are subject to standardized disclosure rules, auditor oversight and shareholder votes.[10] This creates a layer of transparency and governance that drives reporting discipline and makes it possible for the broader public to understand how major institutions operate. In short, a robust public market fosters a democratic society of economically mobile owners. This is in contrast to a world where owners get richer via the awesome power of compounding, and everyone else works in serfdom for a paycheck.

Private and public equities underpin the balance sheets of insurance firms, sovereign wealth funds, university endowments and retirement systems.[11] A stable society needs valuation transparency, yet any student who has ever done a discounted cash flow might argue that these private assets get outside valuations. In the industry, outside valuations are called "NAVs" (Net Asset Valuations), yet, these "independent experts" have no skin in the game.[12] Indeed, if you have access to multiple private funds, you will quickly discover different experts put very different values on the exact same asset.[13] The opacity is further complicated by human nature; non-owner investment professionals are compensated based on the increased "paper value" of the portfolio.[14] Greed can decrease transparency in private markets, while greed increases transparency in public markets, as investors are incentivized to find underpriced assets.

Transparency also matters for geopolitical stability. Companies that are systemically important can now operate in the shadows. Private equity owns dozens of mission-critical businesses, yet no one really knows the health of those entities.[15] Opacity in sectors such as defence, education, healthcare, AI, Media, dual-use manufacturing or critical infrastructure is not prudent. Public markets afford important insights for citizen-voters, as information may relate to company ownership, health, capabilities and governance.

Better Resource Allocation

Inclusive public markets unlock the genius of the crowd to play a role in allocating society's resources. Promising companies get superior access to capital, based on the force of the market, not the mood of a few PE insiders.

Public markets enable efficient capital allocation and real-time price discovery.[16] Price discovery allows capital to flow to its highest-use, which enables investors to enter and exit positions without friction.[17] The wisdom of the market is a key enabler of financial planning and risk management.

Liquidity

Liquidity is the indispensable counterpart to effective risk management and resource allocation. How do you re-allocate capital locked in a private company? In the first two decades of the 21st Century, recirculating capital was not a problem.[18] Near-zero interest rates simply meant a private owner could convince a lender that an asset was valuable and borrow against it.[19] Assets could also easily be sold to other private investors because their cost of borrowing was near zero, too!

As an investor who bought his first bond as a child during the Carter Administration, I can assure you that zero interest rates are not normal.[20] I worked hard raking leaves, squirreling away the earnings in a security that yielded 14.5%. For our international readers, Jimmy Carter served as U.S. president from January 1977 to January 1981. Predicting interest rates for the next half-century is beyond the scope of this book, or my expertise, but we can safely say "*not zero.*"

Despite the narrative that PE takes the long view, in practice firms are often optimizing for a three-to-seven-year exit.[21] This can encourage aggressive cost-cutting, underinvestment in long-term innovation, or financial engineering, over durable value creation. Public markets, by contrast, make it possible for both companies and investors to optimize for what makes sense given their specific circumstances.[22] Ultimately, public markets are the most efficient way to empower all investors with the ability to recirculate capital—and at a time and place of their choosing.

Scalable Capital

Public markets are also the most scalable form of capital formation. In the 1800s, the public markets played a critical funding role in fueling the transition of society to rail connectivity. Again, in the 1910s, the deep pools of wealth in the public markets fueled the transition to the automobile. In the decades ahead, society faces another series of infrastructure transformations. Next generation energy infrastructure, Artificial Intelligence, on-demand electric aviation, humanoid robotics and advanced manufacturing will all likely require massive investment.

Readers will be forgiven for thinking that private equity is big. This is a sector that attracts an enormous amount of press. Funds like the Carlyle Group, Andreessen Horowitz, Silver Lake, Blackstone and KKR all manage tens of billions. Yet, all their limited partners are also public market investors. The depth of investable dollars in the public market is about one order of magnitude bigger.[23] Yes, the public markets are about 10 times bigger than private markets.

IPOs, and more important, follow-on offerings, enable companies to raise vast amounts of capital relatively efficiently. Public markets remain one of the only venues where you can raise billions of dollars in a single day. Tesla's secondary offerings are a perfect example; the company netted about $226 million in their 2010 IPO. Since listing, and the last time I checked, the company has raised an estimated $19 billion as a public company.[24]

Debt Loads

PE often relies heavily on debt to enhance returns.[25] While this can create efficiency, it also loads companies with risk. PE often uses 5–7× EBITDA leverage; public companies average closer to 1–2×.[26] That makes PE-backed companies more fragile to economic downturns, policy changes or interest rate hikes. For regulators concerned about taxpayer funded bailouts, less leverage should be attractive.

Sometimes the PE firm also profits from organizing the debt, ensuring fees regardless of how the company performs. Large debt loads can prove fatal, as pointed out by the Oracle of Omaha: "Having a large amount of leverage is like driving a car with a dagger on the steering wheel pointed at your heart."[27]

I am not going to argue that bankruptcy is bad. Quite the opposite, I always say: "Bankruptcy is the white blood cells of capitalism: it cleans out the system," or put more dramatically by CEO-astronaut Frank Borman: "Capitalism without bankruptcy is like Christianity without hell."

That said, I would argue that public markets do a better job of restructuring poorly run assets. In the public realm, investors can force change (board replacements, divestitures, spinoffs), whereas in private markets, those checks are largely internal and slower. There is greater incentive to "pretend and extend" debt. In contrast, public markets enforce discipline through liquidity and visibility; the punishment is swift, continuous, and usually occurs financially long before it becomes existential.

Look at what happened to Toys"R"Us, which couldn't sustain operations under its PE-designed debt load. In 2005, a consortium of three PE firms (KKR, Bain Capital, and Vornado Realty Trust) bought it for $6.6 billion, taking it private. The deal was financed with about $5.3 billion in debt, and only about $1.3 billion in equity.

But technology shifted. Amazon and Walmart were able to invest in e-commerce and data systems, which enabled them to significantly outperform what had been a big and established brand. For Toys-"R"-Us, the debt load left no flexibility to invest in innovation, and the company's market share eroded to the innovators who offered customers superior convenience, lower prices and faster logistics.

By 2017, Toys"R"Us was paying $400+ million a year in interest on its debt. The company filed for Chapter 11 bankruptcy in September 2017, and less than a year later, it liquidated entirely. The result is less choice for consumers, as Toys"R"Us closed all 800 U.S. stores, laying off 33,000 workers.[28]

If Toys"R"Us had remained public, management could have used the flexibility of the public markets to make the needed investment. Equity holders would have most likely suffered dilution, but both consumers and those employed by the company would have most likely ended up better. Arguably, it would have been a win-win situation for everyone involved.

A diverse set of strategies, risk tolerances, hold periods and backgrounds is critical for the proper allocation of society's resources. If we are not going to rely on the wisdom of the crowd, we might as well just trust a Soviet style politburo to plan our economy, and any student of history knows how well that works. Clearly there are many societal benefits to a broad and inclusive public capital market. The good news is coming... fast.

Today's legacy public markets are best thought of as a layer cake of geographically-defined intermediaries:

- Investors have to go through exchanges.
- Exchanges go through clearing houses.
- Clearing houses go through custodians.

The legacy architecture creates delays, resulting in a lack of transparency and fostering systemic risk. As Kyle Samani, the

Co-Founder of Multicoin Capital explained in 2025:

> "Each of these players takes a cut. They add a fee, they add a delay, they create complexity, and they also create inertia in the status quo so that it's harder to remove them later. They add a fee, they add a delay, they create complexity, and they also create While the intent of these legal protections are generally pretty good, their evolutionary path over the last 100 years has produced in our modern system of bloat and crust, markets still close at 4pm, fees are still high. Access is still limited. Inefficiency is baked into the system by design. It still takes two days to settle a stock trade in 2025.

> "If you asked a group of engineers and traders to redesign capital market infrastructure from first principles in 2025, you wouldn't be recreating all of these intermediaries. You'd be building something based on modern software. You'd build something that's global in 24/7 that's programmable and permissionless, and that's secured, most importantly, by cryptography. You'd build one global ledger that can support internet scale capital markets. Until recently, these global ledgers, or as we like to call them, blockchains, couldn't actually scale to support internet capital markets."

The good news: the disruptors are delivering. The technology is mature, corporate leaders are aligned, investors are engaged, and policy thinkers are quickly catching up.

The U.S. Congress passed the GENIUS Act, which created a foundation for tradable tokens that are 100% backed by government bonds.[29] Tokens fully backed by publicly-traded equity are also proliferating in many jurisdictions.

> "Digital assets will speed-run centuries of financial evolution within a few decades"
> James Glasscock—fintech investor

These new tokens are denominated in fiat currency and backed by real assets. With the introduction of the GENIUS Act, the United States defined a clear path for the regulation of stablecoins. The act has moved this trend into overdrive and stablecoin initiatives have been announced by Walmart, Amazon, Coinbase, Shopify and Bank infrastructure provider FinServ.

The tokenization of currency has moved from fringe finance to a near-fait accompli. Finance insiders call this the tokenization of real world assets, or RWA for short. In accordance with this, the tokenization of public equities is now within reach. The concept has moved into what is often referred to as "the adjacent possible"—the set of new things now just one step away from what actually exists.

In the case of tokenized equities, the technologies already exist; indeed, multiple companies have announced equity tokenization initiatives. As Thomas Cowan, who worked at the Boston Federal Reserve and served as the Head of Tokenization, Galaxy Digital pointed out, "Discussion around tokenizing equities has taken off in 2025."

In the mid-2020s, equity token availability is limited, but non-US investors already trade tokens backed by shares in Microsoft, Nvidia, MicroStrategy, Intel, Tesla and Apple. In a cyberpunk ode to William Gibson, I say: "The future is here, and it's distributed; it's just unevenly distributed."

But it's not just cryptography, tokenization and blockchains. A huge range of technologies are making the world smaller. New technology such as smartphones, Artificial intelligence, open protocols, application programming interface (APIs) and social media are all playing an important role. An inclusive and transparent world is rapidly evolving. A world not driven by rent-seeking intermediaries, but instead by the proliferation of a truly global and inclusive marketplace, beyond the reach of any single regulator.

Technology is about to do for capital what the internet did

for information.

In Kevin Kelly's outstanding 1992 book, *Out of Control*, he provided a perfect framework for understanding how the internet would impact information. At the time, information was in physical books, stored in local libraries. I am paraphrasing, but, basically, Kelly recommended imagining a world where any piece of information could be quickly found by anyone. He went on to explain that this would never happen, but the future would look more like that than the world of 1992. He was right! Working backward from that vision, investors could have predicted the impact on the information intermediaries of the era, such as newspapers, television and magazines. His framework empowered investors to predict Yahoo, Google, Starlink, and even OpenAI.

Today, we are in the same place, but this time it is involving capital intermediaries, not information intermediaries. Our society will never reach a world with a truly open market, just as the flow of information is not truly free. We are moving ever closer to a world in which all money moves at the speed of light. A word where any consumer can sell their Hershey stock and buy a Hershey candy bar, 24 hours a day, and all in the time it takes to check out at a 7-11 convenience store.

We may never reach that level of frictionless commerce, but working backwards from that world will provide a better framework than by imaging successive incremental improvements from legacy intermediaries. To be clear, I am not saying today's stock exchanges, custody providers and trading houses are going away. Not all information intermediaries followed the fate of Blockbuster, but everyone had to compete at a new level. The Nasdaq, for example, has petitioned the SEC to approve their proposed blockchain-based architecture. The SEC chairman told his team to prepare for "the digital finance revolution."[30] Expect issuers and investors to benefit from the competition, just as consumers benefited from cooperation in the era of Blockbuster.

In the traditional financial world, an IPO is often treated like a "Grand Reveal." A transition from when a private company hides its messy books in the dark, then suddenly turns on the lights (disclosures) to prove it's worthy of public money. Thanks to distributed ledger technology (DLT) and blockchain, that paradigm is shifting. Private companies will increasingly become "pre-lit," meaning they can maintain public-market-grade data long before they ever ring the bell.

What has historically differentiated public and private markets is not ownership, but verifiability. Public companies are trusted not because they are public, but because their disclosures are standardized, audited, time-stamped and comparable. That gap is now closing. Advances in data provenance, cryptographic verification, and continuous attestation make it possible for private companies to publish disclosure-quality data without listing. In effect, verifiable data becomes a substitute for public disclosure, enabling trust to emerge before liquidity. Regulators need to adjust to a binary public/private worldview.

For the incumbents and regulators that can adapt fast, cryptographic blockchain technology is their friend. The same is true of AI.

Artificial Intelligence

One powerful example of an opportunity for incumbents is AI. Data is the fuel that powers AI and incumbents already have a critical mass of data, both in the form of historical information and ongoing feedback loops. AI is especially good at standardizing information and streamlining predictable workflows. A domain incumbents clearly have room to improve.

Exchanges everywhere have suffered from a proliferation of paperwork. Disclosures, filings, and legal reviews have all ballooned while the number of companies willing to battle the red tape dragon has withered. With this in mind, AI offers enormous opportunities for regulators, companies and service providers to drastically reduce the time and costs associated with being public.

AI is also great at translating information into the format investors expect. Whether it's Spanish to English or GAAP to IFRS, AI is about to make the world smaller. Companies, regulators and investors should all expect lower disclosure costs associated with being public.[31]

Artificial Intelligence also has incredible analytical capabilities. In a world where it is expensive for humans to analyze companies, professional investors typically must focus on large companies in which they can invest a lot of money to justify the cost of analysis. But the economics of equity research changes with AI, as much of the analytical heavy lifting can be offloaded to AI agents. For amateur investors, or as I like to say, "up and coming" investors, AI lowers the barrier to explore, test and implement investment approaches. Not just locally, but anywhere an investor lives or a company is public. AI is an onramp for new equity analysts, with the rapid iterations of new and diverse investment strategies. AI is proving to be a democratizing influence, empowering a whole new class of global investors who now have vast analytical resources at their disposal.

For institutional investors, many of whom are already thinking globally, AI improves productivity, allowing more stocks to be identified and analyzed. Some institutions will use this new power to increase the amount of research they publish, further lowering the friction for the broader market to analyze public companies.

AI also has a profound impact on financial media too. Bloomberg, Reuters, and Dow Jones all use AI summarization models to increase media depth and diversity. AI-driven newsletters and "explainers" are scaling. Text, audio and video content is widely available. Investor education is proliferating without armies of high paid analysts.

As a result of AI, as the marginal cost of an insight approaches zero, anyone can publish a financial report instantly. Regional regulations curbing investment research, such as MiFID II and the Spitzer Settlement, are losing relevance. AI enables hyper-personalized financial media feeds, tuned to each investor's holdings or interests. Products like Alphasense, Koyfin and Notion-style AI dashboards tailor information flow the way Spotify personalizes listening to music. The line between financial data platforms and a media company is disappearing.

As AI lowers research costs, local governments who try to censor equity research through litigation (Spitzer) or regulations (MiFID) will increasingly find their policies out of step with a global market for securities and financial information.[32] Regulatory turf wars may become unwinnable. Local institutions constrained by what research they can review will be at a disadvantage to investors domiciled in other jurisdictions. Wealth will be redistributed to freer markets.

AI is great for growth companies looking to go public. AI can help not just the cost and distraction of the disclosures. AI can aid in the identification of appropriate investors to pitch based on rigorous analysis of their other investments. AI will result in broader exposure and more research coverage including new geographies and languages. IPOs will see broader and more rigorous analysis should result in better pricing, which, in itself, better reflects the bid-ask spread in the weeks that follow the IPO. Less value leakage through mispricing means less dilution for founders, employees and early investors.

AI agents are going to play an important role, not just capital markets, but society as a whole. Just like the non-human corporate joint-stock entities pioneered in the 1600s, these non-human entities will have a profound positive impact on the world. Yet AI entities have other characteristics in common with companies as well. For example, AI actors consume and allocate resources; in short, these entities will need to be paid. But the legacy financial system is not equipped to fuel the growth in AI agents. How do you fulfill the regulatory requirement to know your client (KYC) if an agent is self-governing, spawned by code, and may only exist for a few minutes?

Artificial intelligence will not simply analyze markets—it will participate in them. Autonomous agents will price risk, rebalance portfolios, execute trades and allocate capital continuously. These agents cannot operate efficiently in batch-based settlement systems, human-centric compliance models or fragmented custody rails. AI requires machine-readable assets, programmable compliance, atomic settlement and verifiable data feeds. Markets that fail to adapt to AI will not just be slower; they will be unusable to the fastest-growing class of economic actors. The proliferation of AI agents will accelerate the need for innovation on how value is priced, transferred and traded.

Small Investors

Smartphone access to the financial markets is here to stay. The worlds of regulated financial services, entertainment, media and permissionless crypto protocols are converging. This is going to open up access to capital markets for people all over the world. Policymakers should seek to use these technologies to educate, inform and engage their investing public. Policymakers who try to limit access will find themselves out of step with the needs and expectations of a modern public. Societies that don't encourage investments risk evolving into a population where the elderly are dependent on the government, at a time when the public finances may be far from healthy.

It is important for public exchanges to be a level playing field that attracts a wide range of both investors and speculators. Regulators that limit market access to wealthy investors risk institutionalizing structural barriers to economic mobility. They also risk creating a market that underperforms its core function of pricing risk and allocating resources.

Shared Ownership: Multilateral DOAs, Mutuals and Co-ops

The first stock exchange was launched in 1601, which means stock exchanges have been around for well over 400 years. One defining characteristic you almost always see is that they're membership organizations, sometimes called seats, sometimes called associations. Over the last 400 years, 90% of that time was dominated by organizations that are run by and for their members.[33]

Up until very recently, communal ownership was the trend. Think about that: capitalists—some of the most market-oriented and *pure* capitalists in the world—agreed that working together would create a better environment to serve themselves and the community. The markets were self-regulated; if the exchange members screwed the investors, then the investors would go elsewhere, and the same is true of the companies. Greed and the pursuit of profit kept the system in balance.

It wasn't until the end of the 20th Century that we started to see these "for the benefit of the community organizations" become for-profit organizations. This has been a disaster. Companies are choosing to stay private; concentrating ownership in the hands of a few, increasing opacity, reducing accountability, and limiting broader public participation in wealth creation.

There is a huge opportunity in going back to a membership-oriented organization. The supranational nature of capital markets may even require multilateral cross-border structures to achieve optimal market efficiencies. Maybe the market of the future is a federation of international exchanges working together. Shared ownership of exchanges is good for society, good for companies listing, and good for all ecosystem participants.

The first problem with today's hyper-centralized stock-exchange model is that it creates a single point of failure. Whether the threat is geopolitical, technological, or simply bad governance, the entire system hinges on just one company, unlike the federated member-owned exchanges of the past. This critical infrastructure is run at the whims of a single leader, a King with no need to consult others. A bad decision can drastically affect the market and society as a whole. Historically, exchanges were not kingdoms. They were parliaments. The clubby "seat on the exchange" approach ensured that important decisions were deliberated, and incorporated multiple perspectives.

The centralization of exchange ownership makes them susceptible to what Cory Doctorow calls "enshittification." He describes the gradual decay of platforms over time, following a three-stage process.[34] Initially, a system is for the benefit of all users, then platforms prioritize their largest institutional customers, before finally moving to a phase of extracting all value for themselves, degrading the experience for everyone involved to maximize profits. Stock exchanges are too important to how society allocates resources to be owned by one corporation. Their concentrated ownership causes a systemic risk to the world's financial system.

The second problem with this centralized, single-owner organization structure, is that it lends itself to bad regulation because the owner is in one location. There is one regulator who feels they have full control and authority over how the exchanges are run.

It is hard to be global with a centrally-owned exchange, because the entity is tied to a sole jurisdiction and regulatory authority. Regulators tend to think about their own jurisdiction. Yes, there are exceptions—the FSA in England, the MSA in Singapore, the Barbados regulators—these all tend to think more globally. Often the exchange sets rules that are appropriate for one jurisdiction, but inappropriate, or, in some cases, illegal in other jurisdictions. This turns off participants and reduces liquidity.

Furthermore, central ownership can result in a lack of stakeholder dialogue and this lack of transparency then turns off regular investors, creating an uneven playing field between insiders and outsiders.

An exchange run by its members is undoubtedly preferable. Those who have members (once called seats) from diverse jurisdictions are more likely to act in a manner that is the optimal solution for all parties involved. The exchanges of the future should operate more as a global federation of participants.

Technology makes all of this possible on a global scale. Smart contracts and modern blockchains are designed to be transparent, but limit execution access to seat holders, who are members of the exchange. What is old can be new again. Markets can go back to their roots, as membership-driven, member-regulated global exchanges, allowing a broader set of participants and more equitable access globally. Local exchange seat holders can be regulated by the local authority, providing local policy authorities with the power to put whatever consumer protections in place that they deem to be suitable.

Most important, a globally-connected equity exchange better serves the entrepreneurs and innovators who depend on capital to build our future.[35] The solution is to return to our roots: a member-driven, member-regulated global exchange that opens participation, broadens access, and channels investment to talent wherever it emerges.

Blockchains are the perfect infrastructure for member-driven organizations. First and foremost, they foster transparency, increasing trust in what will need to be geographically-diverse groups. Anyone, anywhere, can see exactly what has happened equally, anywhere they can see the settlement.

The second benefit is the restriction of access. One of the controversies of blockchain technology is that it can be the Wild West, but we don't often hear how the technology can also be the precise opposite. Blockchains can be deployed that easily restrict who has access to certain capabilities. The technology can ensure regulators that all participants are reputable, have skin in the game, and are properly regulated in their home jurisdiction. This ties right into enforcement. A blockchain run through a membership organization, can essentially restrict or remove members, restrict the ability to perform certain actions, or even all actions. This root-level, code-level ability to enforce rules and monitor what's going on is absolutely critical when operating in our low-trust, geopolitically-diverse multijurisdictional world.

Blockchain infrastructure is often framed as a replacement for existing exchanges. In practice, it can function more like a pre-market layer. Assets can form, mature, attract global participation, and establish governance before graduating to the most liquid public venues. Rather than displacing exchanges, this architecture expands the funnel - allowing more assets to get on the Global IPO path.

Transparent Real-time Settlement

There are many tenuous examples of how blockchains are helpful. Stock ownership ledgers are the opposite of tenuous. If ever there was a need for the transparency of an immutable ledger, confirming the transfer of share ownership is a perfect fit.

Modern, high-volume blockchains are perfect for transparent real-time stock settlement. The legacy global settlement systems have massive systemic risk due to the delays in settlement. It is not uncommon for traded stocks to be traded multiple times in a day, and no one knows for sure who owns them. Even worse, bad actors are able to overwhelm the system and use the confusion to sell or borrow against shares they don't possess. This distorts markets and creates systemic risk. Settlement that is clear, cryptographically confirmed, and conducted in a timely manner, will greatly improve the global equity markets.

Blockchain-based settlement will reduce risk, increasing fairness and transparency, which is critically important, because

80% of the world's equities by value are publicly traded.[36] Most equities are thinly traded. This means that the markets are not yet reaching their full potential. They can do a better job of their core purpose: providing continuous price information to support society's need to properly allocate resources, drive innovation and manage risk.

The legacy systems will last longer than anyone expects, but it does not matter. Assuming you are not a U.S. citizen, you can trade tokens that are 100%-backed by public stock. Nvidia, Coinbase and Apple tokens are just a few examples. As Philipp Pieper, founder of trading platform Swarm, points out: "Markets don't fail because of too much innovation, but because innovation outgrows the rails it runs on."

Speeds Impact on Fairness and Liquidity

Another problem with centralized markets is the speed of light. Essentially, traders closer to the exchange are able to frontrun the broader market. This reduces fairness and diminishes trust in the market. Distributed smart-contract empowered blockchain settlement is one solution. Markets can be slowed down so binding bids and offers are collected cryptographically. Bid and Asks can be matched based on a predetermined optimization algorithm that benefits both willing buyers and willing sellers. The market becomes a continuous series of sealed auctions, where the results are published transparently seconds after the auction is completed.[37]

Investors no longer need high-speed computers just feet away from a centralized exchange in order to get the best execution. With a distributed ledger, even the trader, in the most remote corner of the world, with the slowest internet connection, on a second-grade smartphone has an equal shot in that auction. The auction takes place at the exact same time everywhere in the world.

Furthermore, by slowing down the process to provide time to build a confidential binding order book, you can increase liquidity by speeding up or slowing down the pace of auctions based on global demand. It could be that there are some publicly-traded stocks that would experience the best liquidity by having their trading auction just a few times a day, for other stocks a few auctions every minute might be the right pace. With modern software, cryptography and telecommunications this level of adaptive liquidity is not just possible, it may be inevitable.

Threats to the Future of Stock Exchanges

We rely on free markets to allocate resources, manage risk and drive up productivity, and this improves standards of living. Or, as Milton Friedman put it, "The great achievements of civilization have not come from government bureaus… but from individuals pursuing their own interests. In well-functioning markets, this pursuit aligns private incentives with public benefit—fueling innovation, efficiency and rising living standards."

Markets decentralize intelligence, unleash incentives and build a more resilient society. In a market economy, prices act as a signal firing through the neurons of the crowd. The price reflects supply, demand, scarcity, and risk. When something becomes more valuable or scarce, its price rises, attracting more resources and innovation. Economist Friedrich Hayek called prices "a system of telecommunications"—a way for millions of people to coordinate without central direction.[38]

One hundred years of history has proven market-based economies outperform the central planning of a Soviet-style politburo. In the 1990s, countries everywhere got the memo. There was a wave of privatizations, where state-owned enterprises were superseded by a new structure of ownership, forcing management to become more efficient and accountable.

Free Markets Under Siege

Ownership was distributed and diverse market feedback was continuous. But open and transparent markets are under siege:

Rising Economic Nationalism & Protectionism Tariffs, export controls, reshoring mandates, and industrial policies that favor national champions over competitive markets.

Censorship, Speech Regulation, Content Moderation & "Online Safety" The wisdom of the crowd only works if there is free speech. Capital markets depend on transparency, trust and the efficient flow of information. The power of the crowd is its ability to process massive amounts of uncertainty, and that wisdom is impeded with information suppression.

Free speech helps reduce information asymmetry between insiders and ordinary investors. Free media helps democratize access to insight, offering investors a better shot at informed participation.

Without the free exchange of views—including dissent, criticism, and minority opinions—prices cannot reflect all available information, leading to mispricing of risk and value. Think of stock prices as collective predictions—those predictions require debate, analysis and disagreement.

The internet has increased the flow of opinions, but governments everywhere are pushing back. It is no surprise that authoritarian countries like China have limited speech, but what's more surprising is persecution in traditionally liberal markets such as Australia, Canada, the UK, and even the USA.

Policy professionals take note; limiting speech to protect political control inherently limits capital formation, market efficiency, economic advancement and innovation.

Concentration via Private Equity PE is buying publicly-traded companies, and is moving ownership decisions from the hands of the many, to the hands of the few. As a result, society loses the wisdom of the crowd. One of the core characteristics of PE is that it's more centralized than public ownership.[39] If too much of the economy is controlled by a small group of investors, society loses out. Markets are most efficient when there is the greatest diversity of participants.

For regulators, centralization is always attractive, because it is easier to regulate a few entities than many. Regulators could be tempted to support neverending consolidation via PE. For aspiring dictators, it is easier to seize control of a few big entities than trying to control many small ones.

Consolidation via PE is also appealing for aspiring monopolists as regulatory capture is easier when orchestrated from the shadows of the private market.

Policymakers must ensure that markets remain open and inclusive, supporting a polarity of participants; large and small, public and private. Efficient resource allocation must reflect broad-based opportunity, rather than concentrated privilege. Jurisdictions who get this wrong should expect underperformance relative to their economic rivals.

Anti-competitive Regulatory Barriers Globally, we are seeing a rise in complex, expensive compliance regimes that entrench incumbents and shut out startups and smaller innovators. Policymakers seeking to protect incumbents risk distorting the market and worse delaying the productivity gains that are vital to preventing a sovereign-debt spiral.

Indexing and Passive Capital's Dark Side When trillions flow passively, price discovery weakens, reducing the role of markets as real-time, truth-seeking mechanisms. Index investing is a type of passive investment which involves purchasing a portfolio designed to mirror the performance of a market index, like the S&P 500, NASDAQ-100, or MSCI World. Instead of trying to pick individual stocks or time the market, index investors aim to own the whole market (or a slice of it) and benefit from its long-term growth.

Understanding individual equities is hard work. For many investors, delegating that responsibility to others is simply easier. Indeed, the last two decades have seen massive increase in passive investment. By some estimates, more than half the investment in the public markets is passive.

This works great for the largest companies, the so-called "big end of town." These companies have sufficient liquidity to attract the index funds that buy and sell the underlying stocks, not on an informed opinion, but instead based on pre-defined formulas. Companies are able to tap near limitless capital from investors, while investors are able to own some of the biggest companies without the added expense of professional management.

Smaller companies often don't yet have the liquidity to be eligible for index inclusion. Index funds need to be able to quickly enter and exit companies. This means passive investors don't get exposure to smaller, often more innovative companies. It also means these companies have less access to capital. One estimate out of Australia observed that a company gets a 30-40% increase in price[40] in anticipation of being included in an index.

There is a risk if too much of the market is passive. IPOs by their nature need active investors to figure out correct prices. Furthermore, their lack of public trading history usually makes them ineligible for passive fund inclusion. It is possible if too much of the market is passive that there will be insufficient active investors to price IPOs; some would argue this is already happening in some markets. Self-driving markets won't work! If everyone buys the index, nobody's doing the analysis to determine what companies are truly worth.

Furthermore, companies with too many passive investors can use the low cost of capital and lack of shareholder oversight to buy smaller competitors. Regulators should expect increased monopolization.

Another risk in passive investment is self-amplifying, resulting in volatility that scares off some investors. When a stock goes up, it becomes a bigger part of an index, this means index investors need to own more of the stock, driving up the stock. This dynamic has been of great benefit to some companies, but this amplification also happens in reverse too.

If markets become too disconnected from the value of the underlying companies, it is possible this will scare off a group of investors, resulting in a smaller and less efficient market.

Another risk with passive investment is a lack of "skin in the game." Capitalism works because investors are putting their own money at risk, but this is not happening with passive investment. As trillions of retirement and pension dollars are pooled into passive funds, real economic power is separated from democratic owner oversight. Vanguard or BlackRock may vote your shares on issues like climate policy, executive compensation, or corporate lobbying—without your direct owner input.[41]

Creeping Capital Controls The jurisdictions thriving under capitalism today tend to have *few* capital controls. Why? Because open markets harness the wisdom of the crowd—more people making decisions about scarce resources.

In contrast, too many governments can't match spending with tax revenue. That gap spells long-term trouble. And here's the danger: weak leaders, cornered by deficits, may turn to capital controls as a desperate fix. Capital controls are never a sign of strength. They're a blinking red light, a government admitting it can't compete on a level playing field, eroding the efficiency of properly functioning markets. Participation is less robust. Resources get misallocated.

Although capital controls are generally in decline, that could change. Capital controls take many forms: foreign ownership limits, investment approval requirements, divestment approvals, lock-in periods, jurisdiction-related dual-class shares, voting restrictions, stamp taxes, repatriation restrictions and exchange controls. Investors, policy professionals, and voters need to remain diligent.

Policy Mandates That Conflict with Fiduciary Duty When governments impose investment frameworks designed to advance political or social agendas, they risk distorting capital allocation and compromising fiduciary obligations. Rigid mandates, particularly those imposed at the state level, can force capital away from sectors that, while politically contentious, offer superior risk-adjusted returns. This subverts the core principle of markets: leveraging decentralized decision-making to efficiently allocate resources.

A clear example emerged in the mid-2020s, when ESG mandates in certain jurisdictions led to widespread divestment from sectors like energy and defense. Ironically, these sectors later delivered strong performance, and those investors constrained by regulatory edicts missed out. For pensioners and retirees dependent on long-term compounding, these opportunity costs are real and irreversible. Some savers will need to work longer and retire later. Meanwhile, governments that suppressed capital formation in critical industries found themselves underprepared when geopolitical realities demanded energy security and defense readiness.

Summary

- Private capital has grown massively over the last 20 years.
- As a consequence of this, many companies have stayed private for longer, so fewer firms list on public markets.
- An advantage of public markets is that they enable ordinary people to buy stock, supporting wider economic mobility.
- Public companies must disclose more information and face stronger governance; private valuations are often opaque and inconsistent. Private markets also offer real-time price discovery and liquidity, making it easier to allocate capital to its best uses and for investors to enter or exit.
- Conversely, private equity often utilizes high debt and shorter exit horizons, which can increase risk, hurt long-term investment, and sometimes lead to business failures.
- New technologies—especially blockchain, tokenization and mobile connectivity—are making tradable, transparent digital versions of assets possible, furthering the de-

mocratization of markets.

- Artificial intelligence will lower the cost of research and disclosure, broaden investor analysis, and help price IPOs more accurately.
- The goal of this development must be to preserve diverse, transparent, and inclusive public markets (backed by technology and smart policy), so that capital can fund innovation, protect investors, and support a healthy economy.

New technologies and smarter policy can rebuild more open, fairer markets. Blockchains, tokenization and AI potentially speed settlement, widen access, lower disclosure costs, and enable exchanges to be run as member-led, global platforms with adaptive auctions. But these opportunities come with threats: information suppression, too much concentration of ownership, passive investing, capital controls, and politicized investment mandates. It is only when technology is combined with inclusive policy to keep markets diverse, and true respect is given to transparency, that the next wave of innovation will emerge.

Appendix

About the Author

Jeffrey Stewart offers a rare vantage point on IPOs. He's a serial founder who built Inc. 500 companies, an investor who's backed ambitious entrepreneurs, and a FinTech CEO who successfully scaled across borders. After seeing the corrosive impact of companies staying private for too long, Jeffrey became somewhat obsessed with understanding the opportunity of multi-jurisdictional public offerings.

By 2018 he co-founded the Global Public Offering Fund, a growth-stage venture capital firm focusing on founder-lead, disruptive businesses that can benefit from accelerated international expansion and public market access.

Jeffrey made his first public market investment and started his first company before high school. He started his career at Ernst & Young consulting for the Nasdaq regulatory group, the predecessor to FINRA, an experience that later proved invaluable as a Fin-tech founder who worked with regulators across two dozen countries.

As an adjunct professor at Columbia University School of International and Public Affairs (SIPA), Mr. Stewart has lectured on the impact of technology, such as AI and blockchain, on global capital markets and international policy affairs.

Having been on both sides of the table—raising capital as a founder and deploying it as an investor—Jeffrey understands what it takes to build great companies and back them at the right time. He believes passionately in the power of startups to drive innovation and create wealth, not just for founders but for investors who recognize their potential early.

Timeline of Public Markets (1602 - 2025)

1602	Dutch East India Company was formed, the first joint stock company.
1611	Inauguration of the Amsterdam Stock Exchange, the first to include equity trading.
1621	Dutch West India Company is formed.
1698	Stock trading in London began informally in coffee houses, especially Jonathan's Coffee House, where brokers and jobbers met to trade stocks and commodities.
1783	Bank of North America went public in Philadelphia, It was one of the first IPOs in the newly formed United States.
1790	Mississippi Company was initially issued by Law's Banque Générale in Paris, and later became wildly speculative as demand soared due to promises of enormous wealth from the Louisiana Territory.
1792	The Buttonwood Agreement, which evolved into the formal New York Stock & Exchange Board, precursor to today's NYSE.
1801	Formal Establishment of The London Stock Exchange (LSE)
1817	NYSE Constitution adopted, building on the Buttonwood Agreement of 1792.
1827	Baltimore & Ohio Railroad kick off the railroad stock infatuation, The technology of steam is hot.
1852	Toronto businessmen met to form the Association of Brokers, the predecessor to the Toronto Stock Exchange (TSX), formed in 1878.
1867	First ticker tape Invented by Edward Calahan, revolutionizing real-time financial information dissemination.
1869	Thomas Edison develops a more practical (& popular) ticker tape machine.

1870	The first U.S. corporation that would only own other companies, a holding company, kicking off the era of the trust.
1876	Alexander Graham Bell patented the telephone.
1878	NYSE installs its first telephone.
1884	Tech Pioneer Eastman Kodak goes public, attracting 14 investors.
1891	Hong Kong Stock Exchange (HKEX) founded under the name The Association of Stockbrokers in Hong Kong.
1899	AT&T first offering ($7 million of bonds, organized by Kidder Peabody).
1906	Sears Roebuck offers common and preferred stock to the public.
1916	General Motors goes public on the NYSE, giving them a foundation to consolidate the nascent industry of automotive technology
1919	Coca-Cola goes public.
1924	Mutual Funds in the US unlocked Wall Street for the middle-class.
1929	Wall Street Crash (Black Tuesday: Oct 29) marked the beginning of the Great Depression and led to many regulatory reforms.
1933	US Securities Act of 1933, governs IPOs for US offerings, requires companies to register securities with the Securities and Exchange Commission (SEC).
1940	Disney goes public.
1940	Investment Company Act in the USA, "40s Act" mandated transparency, reducing conflicts of interest and bolstering trust in mutual funds.
1946	Formation of American Research and Development Corporation (ARDC), Led by Georges Doriot, this was the first publicly-owned VC firm.
1952	Harry Markowitz Publishes Modern Portfolio Theory, introduced the concept of efficient diversification.

1956	Ford goes public, one of the largest IPOs of its time, raising over $600 million.
1957	Fairchild Semiconductor founded, it birthed the "Fairchild Eight" and seeded Silicon Valley's ecosystem. Many founders of major VC firms trace their lineage to Fairchild.
1957	Silicon Valley-based Hewlett-Packard goes public.
1960	Green Shoe Manufacturing Company when public, using an overallotment option for the bankers, originating the term "greenshoe".
1971	NASDAQ trading system founded, Over time, NASDAQ became synonymous with technology stocks, hosting some of the most influential companies in the world, including Apple, Microsoft, and Amazon.
1971	Wells Fargo launches its first institutional index fund (for Samsonite pension), Roger Gibson and John McQuown pioneer the first institutional product tracking the S&P 500.
1971	Index funds exposed active management fees, encourage market exposure without fees.
1971	Nine year-old Walmart goes public in the US, Founder uses proceeds to fuel growth.
1973	Stock Exchange of Singapore (SES) formed in 1999 merged with the Singapore International Monetary Exchange (SIMEX) to become the Singapore Exchange (SGX).
1973	Creation of Black-Scholes Model & the Chicago Board Options Exchange (CBOE) massively expanding the options markets by formalizing pricing.
1973	Burton Malkiel publishes *A Random Walk Down Wall Street*, which popularized the efficient market hypothesis and advocated for low-cost indexing to the masses.

1975	John Bogle launched the first retail index fund (Vanguard 500) widely mocked at the time ("Bogle's Folly"); it catalyzed the democratization of passive investing.
1979	The U.S. Department of Labor reinterpreted the "prudent man" rule under the Employee Retirement Income Security Act (ERISA) kicking off a flow of pension funds LP investment into venture capital and private equity funds.
1994	ERISA Act in the USA further accelerated adoption, integrating index funds into retirement plans.
1979	Venture capital-backed Federal Express Corporation (FedEx) goes public, founder users proceed to accelerate growth.
1980	Apple goes public on the NASDAQ.
1980	Genentech becomes first biotech company to go public.
1985	Institutional Shareholder Services (ISS) is founded to provide institutional investors advice on voting, proxies and governance.
1987	Australian Stock Exchange Limited (ASX) is formed.
1990	Cisco IPOs and raises about $50 million, Like General Motors they were especially good at using their public stock to make acquisitions and consolidate the network equipment industry.
1991	India's economic liberalization, opening to global capital markets.
1992	AOL goes public, IPO investors investing $10,000 would have $1.7 million when they merged with Time Warner in 2000.
1993	First ETF in the US - transforming index investing with easier exposure to sectors and broad trends.
1993	European Union (EU) was formally established, kicking off a range of initiatives for increased interconnectivity between regional exchanges.

1995	Netscape Communications Corporation IPO, viewed by many as the beginning of the internet tech bubble.
1996	National Securities Markets Improvement Act passed in the U.S., designed to promote efficiency, reduce regulatory burdens, and better coordinate federal and state oversight.
1997	Amazon IPO, Raised $54 million, laying the foundation for the future of e-commerce.
2000	Dubai Financial Market (DFM) exchange formed, first Sharia-compliant exchange in the UAE.
2000	Abu Dhabi Securities Exchange (ADX) formed to focus on UAE domestic and foreign investment.
2000	Euronext formed, which combined exchanges in Paris, Amsterdam, Brussels, and later Lisbon, creating a pan-European stock exchange.
2000	Regulation Fair Disclosure (Reg FD) from the SEC, changed how (and when) companies share information with investors for US exchanges.
2001	Enron scandal, created an atmosphere in the US for increased regulation and disclosure
2001	Desilimization, NASDAQ stock market transitioned to trading in penny increments (100th vs 8th), radically changing the economics of market making.
2002	Sarbanes-Oxley Act of (SOX) Regulation increases the initial and ongoing cost for companies listing on US exchanges.
2003	The EU introduces the Prospectus Directive as the Union's core legal framework for companies raising capital publicly across member states.

2003	The first set of International Financial Reporting Standards (IFRS) was published to establish a global framework for financial reporting. These standards promote consistency and comparability in financial statements for international investors. Some stock exchanges require companies to use IFRS or to reconcile their financial reports with U.S. GAAP.
2003	The Global Research Analyst Settlement, commonly known as the Spitzer Settlement, mandated the separation of research and investment banking departments. Changed how U.S. banks create and distribute research. Radically changed the cost and benefit associated with generating sell-side research.
2004	Google, (now Alphabet) Innovative Dutch auction method approach to IPOs, developed by Bill Hambrecht.
2007	Saudi Exchange (Tadawul) formed, largest Middle Eastern exchange.
2007	The EU passes the Markets in Financial Instruments Directive (MiFID) to harmonize rules for securities trading across EU markets. Allowed investors to trade seamlessly across borders with consistent rules, improving liquidity.
2008	Financial Crisis, Bear Stearns goes under. The sub-prime mortgage market suffers. Equity markets worldwide plummet.
2010	Dodd-Frank Act, enhanced disclosure requirements for financial institutions and IPOs, especially around executive compensation and risk, Added compliance complexity for IPOs.
2012	Facebook (now Meta) IPO was significant because it was an example of companies staying private longer, $16 billion raised at IPO.
2012	Jumpstart Our Business Startups (JOBS) Act, created the Emerging Growth Company (EGC) category, exempting smaller IPOs from certain regulatory burdens, Allowed confidential filing of IPO paperwork.

2013	Robinhood founded, aimed to democratize finance by offering commission-free mobile-first trading, a model made viable by payment for order flow (PFOF).
2014	China best Alibaba Group lists on the NYSE, prime example of a cross-border IPO where the company is seeking a 'size appropriate' listing venue.
2014	NYSE changes rules to allow unprofitable companies to list, begins to compete directly with NASDAQ for unprofitable venture-backed growth companies.
2016	SoftBank Vision Fund I, with ~$100 billion, marked a new era of late-stage capital and blurred lines between VC, PE, and sovereign wealth.
1018	Smaller reporting company (SRC) framework expanded in the U.S. Designed to reduce compliance burdens and encourage IPOs among smaller companies with less than $100 million of revenue.
2019	The EU introduces Prospectus Regulation (EU) as the Union's core legal framework governing how companies raise capital publicly across EU member states.
2019	Saudi Aramco, IPOs on the Tadawul (Saudi Stock Exchange), it was the largest IPO in history, raising $25.6 billion.
2021	Meme Stock Mania (GameStop/AMC) signaled a new era of 'wired and mobile' retail investor power and equity narratives.
2021	Robinhood went public via direct listing on the NASDAQ.
2023	BlackRock and Vanguard each exceed $10 Trillion AUM, highlighting the concentration of power among passive giants which impacts corporate governance.

2025	Swiss exchange group SIX acquired Aquis Exchange (London-based challenger bourse), making SIX the sole operator with listing venues in Switzerland, the EU, and the UK.
2025	U.S. Passes the U.S. Stablecoins Act (GENIUS Act), accelerating the integration tokenized assets infrastructure into traditional financial systems.
2025	U.S. Commodity Futures Trading Commission (CFTC) approved Polymarket in the U.S. Polymarket acquired U.S. licensed exchange/clearinghouse, accelerating prediction markets integration into capital markets.
2025	Robinhood Markets launched a "prediction markets hub" within its super app, allowing users to trade event-outcome contracts. Gaming platform DraftKings Inc. counters by acquiring Railbird Technologies to accelerate its entry into prediction markets.
2025	Intercontinental Exchange (ICE), the owner of the NYSE, committed up to $2 billion into Polymarket, infrastructure integration with prediction contacts and tokenization.

Related Books

Founder vs Investor: The Honest Truth About Venture Capital from Startup to IPO / by Elizabeth Joy Zalman

The IPO Playbook: An Insider's Perspective on Taking Your Company Public and How to Do It Right / Steve Cakebread

Mastering the VC Game: A Venture Capital Insider Reveals How to Get from Start-Up to IPO on Your Terms / Jeffrey Bussgang

IPOs for Everyone: The 12 Secrets of Investing in IPOs / Linda R. Killian

Going Public: How Silicon Valley Rebels Loosened Wall Street's Grip on the IPO and Sparked a Revolution / Dakin Campbell

The Entrepreneur's IPO: The Insider's Roadmap to Taking Your Company Public / Peter Goldstein

Running a Public Company: From IPO to SEC Reporting / Steven M. Bragg

From Alchemy To IPO: The Business Of Biotechnology / Cynthia Robbins-Roth

IPO Readiness A Complete Guide - 2021 Edition / The Art of Service

Initial Public Offerings: The Mechanics and Performance of IPOs / Arif Khurshed

IPO: A Global Guide by Philippe Espinasse

Global IPO Readiness Checklist

Timing & Mindset

- ☐ Begin IPO preparation early, incorporating it into ongoing planning.
- ☐ Treat IPO as a long-term strategic transformation, not a one-time financing event.
- ☐ Allocate sufficient executive time while avoiding all-consuming distraction.

Equity Story & Vision

- ☐ Craft a clear, simple, and compelling equity story that can be explained in 2 minutes.
- ☐ Evolve the narrative from the VC story to one tailored for public investors.
- ☐ Incorporate origin story and long-term founder vision.
- ☐ Highlight vision-driven strategy and durable competitive advantage.

Financial Discipline & Unit Economics

- ☐ Prove robust, improving unit economics; clearly define the "unit."
- ☐ Establish a track record of meeting financial targets and benchmarks.
- ☐ Conduct annual audits and quarterly financial closes.
- ☐ Implement a fast month-end close process (goal: <5 business days).
- ☐ Build FP&A capabilities for high-quality forecasts and scenario modeling.

Corporate Governance & Legal Structure

- ☐ Set up a public-company-ready board, with at least one public board veteran.
- ☐ Establish key committees: audit, compensation, nominating/governance.
- ☐ Install governance provisions (dual-class shares, staggered board, etc.) while still private.
- ☐ Define policies for shareholder approvals (e.g., M&A, equity issuance).
- ☐ Complete any necessary restructuring or change of domicile early.

Management & Human Capital

- ☐ Conduct a self-audit of leadership gaps; build a talent roadmap.
- ☐ Institute scalable, globally harmonized compensation and equity plans.
- ☐ Avoid excessive founder pay or poorly structured evergreen option plans.
- ☐ Ensure tax-advantaged treatment of equity across jurisdictions.

Global IPO

Growth Strategy & Market Position

- ☐ Articulate a clear growth strategy (organic, M&A, international, etc.).
- ☐ Define TAM and its growth trajectory; show how company expands TAM.
- ☐ Understand and communicate relevant public comps and differentiation.

Capital Strategy

- ☐ Explain use of IPO proceeds with clarity (growth, R&D, etc.).
- ☐ Anticipate need for follow-on capital; highlight capital efficiency.
- ☐ Justify the reason for going public beyond liquidity.

Investor Engagement

- ☐ Begin building relationships with institutional investors early.
- ☐ Gather feedback and iterate on equity story and metrics.
- ☐ Track consistency in KPIs shared over time to avoid "moving goalposts."

Brand & Communications

- ☐ Align all customer, media, and investor touchpoints with equity story.
- ☐ Train all employees on consistent messaging; enforce social media policy.
- ☐ Develop experiential branding that lets investors feel the product/service.
- ☐ Set a consistent PR/Media cadence well before the quiet period begins.

Strategic Positioning

- ☐ Connect equity story to known investor frameworks and sectors.
- ☐ Establish geographic credibility through clients, partnerships, or operations.
- ☐ Prepare for cross-border expectations if listing internationally.

Advisory Team

- ☐ Meet key IPO advisors early: bankers, lawyers, auditors, IR, tax. Study their readiness guides.
- ☐ Evaluate investor relations professionals; simplify story with their input.
- ☐ form top accounting, legal and banking firms.

Global IPO

Selecting an Exchange Checklist

Strategic Intent & Fit

- ☐ Treat exchange selection as a foundational "stack" decision—evaluate fit like you would with infrastructure or technical architecture.
- ☐ Avoid defaulting to domestic exchanges out of habit or historical legacy.
- ☐ Confirm alignment with company's growth path, long-term capital strategy, and visibility goals.

Exchange Trade-offs

- ☐ Compare capital access vs. regulatory burden.
- ☐ Weigh valuation upside vs. governance scrutiny.
- ☐ Assess liquidity potential vs. founder control.
- ☐ Evaluate branding halo vs. reporting load.

Size & Institutional Alignment

- ☐ Ensure exchange scale fits your offering size, avoid getting lost among large-caps or overburdened by overhead costs.
- ☐ Identify regional or size-appropriate institutional investors more likely to anchor your IPO.

Comparables & Positioning

- ☐ Map your closest public comps across exchanges.
- ☐ Choose a venue where comps are well-understood and receive strong multiples.
- ☐ Consider contrarian positioning where differentiation may attract attention (e.g., tech in resource-heavy markets).

Connective Tissue

- ☐ Leverage customer base, operations, partnerships, or early investors tied to the target market.
- ☐ Use "boomerang" ties—early backers or founders with local roots—for additional credibility.
- ☐ Avoid zero-connection listings which may raise red flags with investors.

Legal & Regulatory Environment

- ☐ Prefer exchanges governed under English Common Law if your incorporation matches for legal efficiency and investor confidence.
- ☐ Assess the venue's treatment of dual-class shares, free-float rules, disclosure cadence, and litigation risk.

Global IPO

Pre-IPO Optionality

- ☐ Evaluate whether exchange jurisdiction supports pre-IPO rounds (popular outside the U.S.).
- ☐ Use pre-IPO to test demand, clean cap table, and improve pricing at IPO.

Exchange Structure

- ☐ Identify if the exchange is self-regulated vs. government-regulated (e.g., ASX vs. LSE Main Board).
- ☐ Choose between main board, junior board, or industry-specialty exchanges based on company maturity and sector.

Pricing Control & IPO Mechanics

- ☐ Understand the likelihood of underpricing and greenshoe dilution in each venue.
- ☐ Evaluate level of pricing influence and ability to prevent excessive first-day "IPO pops."

Cost & Operational Burden

- ☐ Model upfront costs: underwriting fees, legal, audit, D&O insurance, and roadshow.
- ☐ Estimate ongoing costs: compliance, IR, governance, and quarterly reporting.
- ☐ Factor in cost of management distraction, litigation risk, and governance complexity.

Timeline & Capital Flexibility

- ☐ Determine lead time-to-list on each exchange.
- ☐ Assess ease of raising follow-on capital post-IPO.
- ☐ Review ability to conduct quick secondary offerings or strategic placements.

Additional Considerations

- ☐ Reporting cadence (quarterly vs. continuous disclosure).
- ☐ Shareholder spread and index eligibility.
- ☐ ESG and climate disclosure standards.
- ☐ Lock-up structure flexibility.
- ☐ Delisting optionality and required shareholder thresholds.

Life as a Public Company Checklist

First 90 Days

- ☐ Nail the first earnings call: Exceed guidance and rehearse thoroughly with external public markets experts.
- ☐ Craft balanced messaging: Avoid insider jargon or overexplaining; appeal to both new and familiar investors.
- ☐ Build muscle for transparent reporting: Prepare early and move toward fast, accurate quarterly closes.

Financial & Operational Reporting

- ☐ Maintain dashboards with financial and non-financial KPIs (e.g., NPS, time-to-hire, bug resolution, onboarding to value).
- ☐ Monitor reporting speed as a quality signal—faster close equals better ops.
- ☐ Ensure readiness for continuous disclosure regimes, if applicable.

Unified Communication Strategy

- ☐ Create a cross-functional news calendar across IR, PR, and internal comms (communications).
- ☐ Align narratives across earnings, product launches, hires, and media.
- ☐ Use earnings and press to reinforce category leadership and long-term vision.
- ☐ Proactively engage global investors annually, not just U.S.-based.

Narrative Discipline

- ☐ Maintain one consistent story across all investor materials, media, and internal docs.
- ☐ Avoid sudden shifts in message or KPIs—stick to what was promised pre-IPO.

Talent Strategy

- ☐ Use public company status for recruiting visibility and compensation clarity.
- ☐ Update talent strategy and benchmarking annually.
- ☐ Consider acquihires or equity-based retention plans.

Board & Governance

- ☐ Upgrade board composition for scale and capital markets experience.
- ☐ Evaluate gaps in expertise and consider external advisors or targeted training.
- ☐ Ensure board independence and incentive alignment.
- ☐ Be prepared to act on follow-on offerings when market conditions are right.

Capital Allocation & M&A

- ☐ Use a written capital allocation framework to prioritize between R&D, M&A, buybacks, and growth initiatives.
- ☐ Maintain a running M&A strategy doc: what, why, when, and targets.

Risk Management & Durability

- ☐ Conduct annual pre-mortems and crisis simulations.
- ☐ Use inversion thinking (what could cause failure?) and address accordingly.
- ☐ Develop a formal risk register and contingency plans.

CEO Mindset

- ☐ Cultivate humility despite success—avoid Ford-style blind spots.
- ☐ Stay paranoid (in the Grove sense)—anticipate change even during strong quarters.

Global Positioning & Expansion

- ☐ Reassess exchange and listing strategy periodically.
- ☐ Explore dual listings to access new investor pools or align geopolitically.

Index & Investor Monitoring

- ☐ Monitor index eligibility and understand criteria.
- ☐ Balance index benefits with governance risks of proxy-driven voting.
- ☐ Target long-horizon investors (pensions, sovereigns, endowments) for strategic stability.

Global IPO

Endnotes

Chapter 1
Rise of the Global IPO

1 Kharas, H., 2017, The unprecedented expansion of the global middle class. Brookings Institution.

2 Ha, A., 2010. Breaking: Groupon acquires German clone CityDeal. TechCrunch, 7 May.

3 Vaiman, V. & Collings, D. G., 2014. Global talent management. In: D. G. Collings, G. T. Wood & P. M. Caligiuri, eds. Routledge Companion to International Human Resource Management. London: Routledge, Chapter 15.

4 Collins, J., 2001. Good to Great: Why Some Companies Make the Leap... and Others Don't. HarperBusiness.

5 Choi, R., 2022. What startup hiring looks like in 2021 - and during a pandemic. Y Combinator Blog, 17 January.

6 Ernst & Young, 2025. EY Global IPO Trends

7 Business Chief, 2023. Xero to hero – New Zealand's most valuable company. Business Chief Asia, 1 August.

8 Botsari, A., Kiefer, K., Lang, F. & Pal, K., 2021. Scale-Up Financing and IPOs: Evidence From Three Surveys. EIF Working Paper 2021/69.

9 BlackRock, 2023. How AI is transforming investing. BlackRock Institutional, 15 June.

10 Encyclopaedia Britannica, 2025. Michael R. Milken. Encyclopaedia Britannica.

11 A&O Shearman, 2025. Merger control frustrates more M&A, but are the tides turning?. A&O Shearman Global Trends in Merger Control Enforcement Report, 27 February.

12 Horton, D., 2024. Interest Rates Continue to Depress Valuations - Impacting Private Equity and IPO Markets. Anchin, 17 July.

13 Financial Times, 2025. Private market funds lag U.S. stocks over

short and long term. FT.com, 11 June.
14 Bain & Company, 2025. Global Private Equity Report 2025. Boston: Bain & Company.
15 Investec, 2024. Five reasons why Private Equity deal valuations are decreasing. Investec.
16 Cherry Bekaert, 2025. Private Equity Mid-Year Trends in 2025. Cherry Bekaert.
17 Lewis R, 2025. Burger King Corporation. Encyclopædia Britannica.
18 Bank Secrecy Act, 1970, Pub. L. 91-508, 84 Stat. 1114.
19 UK Parliament, 2018. Gold and Foreign Exchange Reserves: Venezuela, UIN HL11737, answer by Lord Bates, 6 December 2018.
20 Government of Canada, 2022. Canada invokes the Emergencies Act to limit funding of illegal blockades and restore public order. 15 February 2022. Department of Finance Canada news release.
21 Council of the European Union, 2025. EU sanctions against Russia explained.
22 Government of the United States, 2022. Treasury Prohibits Transactions with Central Bank of Russia and Imposes Sanctions on Key Sources of Russia's Wealth, Press Release, 28 February.
23 Government of Canada, 2022. Canada and G7 partners prohibit Russian Central Bank transactions, News Release, 28 February.
24 HM Treasury & Office of Financial Sanctions Implementation, 2022. UK Statement on Further Economic Sanctions Targeted at the Central Bank of the Russian Federation, GOV.UK, 28 February 2022.
25 The Government of Japan, 2022. Japan joins sanctions on Russian central bank, says 'Japan is with Ukraine', Nippon.com / Reuters, 28 February 2022.
26 Swiss Federal Government, 2023. Switzerland holds Russian central-bank assets and reserves, press release via Anadolu Agency / Bern (reported May 10 2023).
27 Australian Government, 2022. New sanctions on Russian banks and oligarchs, media release, 18 March 2022. Department of Foreign Affairs and Trade.
28 Congressional Research Service, 2025. Enforcement of Remedies Against Unfair Foreign Taxes (Section 899).
29 International Monetary Fund, 2002. Demutualization of Securities Exchanges: A Regulatory Overview, IMF Working Paper WP/02/119.
30 Federal Register, 2006. Statement regarding completion of merger creating NYSE Group, Inc., Federal Register, 29 August 2006.
31 Nasdaq, 2006. Nasdaq: demutualization and transition to a for-profit public company, Investor Relations materials.
32 Securities and Exchange Commission, 2005. SEC Adopts Regulation NMS and Provisions Regarding the National Market System, Press Release, 6 June 2005.
33 SEC Historical Society, 2025. Transformation & Regulation: Equities Market Structure, 1934 to 2018 - Consequences of NMS.
34 Ernst & Young, 2025. Global IPO Trends Q2 2025.

Chapter 2
Why Go Public

1 Forbes, 2025. Forbes Releases 23rd Annual Global 2000 Ranking Of The World's Largest Companies.
2 Benioff, M. & Adler, C. (2009). Behind the Cloud: The Untold Story of How Salesforce.com Went from Idea to Billion-Dollar Company – And Revolutionized an Industry. Wiley.
3 Allard, A.-F., Farkas, M., Pedio, M., Rubio, S. & Tonks, I. (2025). A Survey of the Consequences of Passive Investment Funds for Financial Markets: Report for Financial Conduct Authority. University of Bristol Business School.
4 Sullivan, K. & Seaman, J. (2023). Do investors care about a messy cap table? SeedLegals.
5 Goldman Sachs Asset Management. (2024). Distribution Drought: The Quest for Liquidity in Private Markets. Goldman Sachs Asset Management.
6 Intel Corporation (2025). Intel Corporation Historical Annual Reports
7 Heal, A. (2024) 'Buyout executives say distributions are 'magic word' after exit slowdown', 13 September. Financial Times.
8 Massa, Massimo and Xu, Moqi (2013). The value of (stock) liquidity in the M&A market. Journal of Financial and Quantitative Analysis, 48 (5). pp. 1463-1497.
9 Cisco Systems. (1990). Annual Report 1990.
10 Kerravala, Z. (2015). 'John Chambers' 10 most memorable quotes as Cisco CEO', Network World, 24 July.
11 Aggarwal, D., Eldar, O., Hochberg, Y. V. & Litov, L. (2021). The Rise of Dual-Class Stock IPOs. ECGI Finance Working Paper No. 806/2021.
12 Barr, A. (2012). Facebook's Zuckerberg says mobile first priority. Reuters.
13 Hurt, B. (2015). The pivotal tale from Facebook's history. Wharton Magazine.
14 Miller, R. (2020). CIO Cynthia Stoddard explains Adobe's journey from boxes to the cloud. TechCrunch, 26 June.
15 WIRED (2011). Qwikster Deleted From the Queue: Netflix Cancels Spinoff. WIRED, 10 October.
16 WIRED (2017). How Satya Nadella helped Microsoft get its groove back. WIRED, 30 September.
17 U.S. Government Accountability Office. (2025) Sarbanes-Oxley Act: Compliance Costs Are Higher for Larger Companies but More Burdensome for Smaller Ones. Washington, DC: U.S. Government Accountability Office.
18 Reuters (2024). TikTok preparing a U.S. copy of the app's core algorithm, sources say. Reuters, 30 May.
19 Calo, R. & Rosenblat, A., (2017). The Taking Economy: Uber, Information, and Power. Columbia Law Review, 117(6).
20 Franklin, J & Somerville, S. (2018). Uber makes confidential filing for long-awaited IPO. Reuters, 8 December.

21 Center for Public Integrity (2015). Hotel industry targets upstart Airbnb in statehouse battles. Center for Public Integrity, 15 July.
22 Amazon.com, Inc., (1997). Amazon's original 1997 letter to shareholders.
23 Business Insider, (2021). Jeff Bezos returns Amazon stock investment after selling 1997 house.

Chapter 3
Myths & Misconceptions

1 Ewens, M. & Farre-Mensa, J. (2019). The Deregulation of the Private Equity Markets and the Decline in IPOs, NBER Working Paper No. w26317, National Bureau of Economic Research.
2 Gao, X., Ritter, J. R., & Zhu, Z. (2013). Where Have All the IPOs Gone?. Journal of Financial and Quantitative Analysis, 48(6), 1663–1692.
3 OECD. (2025). Equity Markets for Growth Companies. Paris: OECD Publishing. doi: 10.1787/bbffd4f7-en.
4 Doidge, C., Karolyi, G. A. & Stulz, R. M. (2017). 'The U.S. listing gap', Journal of Financial Economics, 123(3), pp. 464–487. doi: 10.1016/j.jfineco.2016.12.002. Note: Doidge, Karolyi, & Stulz introduced the concept of the "U.S. listing gap," showing that the U.S. developed an unusually low number of publicly listed firms compared to other countries after 1999.
5 Forbes. (2001). 'A Decade of New Issues', Forbes, 05 March.
6 Bartlett, R. P., Rose, P. & Davidoff Solomon, S. (2017). The Small IPO and the Investing Preferences of Mutual Funds. Journal of Corporate Finance, 47, 151–173.
7 Fleming, R. A. (2017). Enhancing the Demand for IPOs. Speech presented at the NASAA Public Policy Conference, Washington, D.C., U.S. Securities and Exchange Commission.
8 Ernst & Young. (2025, July). EY Global IPO Trends Q2 2025. EY.
9 Pinto, G. The cost of going public and financial constraints. Financ Mark Portf Manag 38, 443–464 (2024). Springer.
10 Caglio, C. R., Hanley, K. W. & Marietta-Westberg, J. (2013). Going Public Abroad. Finance and Economics Discussion Series 2013-68, Board of Governors of the Federal Reserve System.
11 Brennan, P. & Hudgins, C. (2022, November 15). Large-cap U.S. stocks have increased dominance of public markets. S&P Global Market Intelligence.
12 Siev, S. & Qadan, M. (2022). Call Me When You Grow Up: Firms' Age, Size, and IPO Performance across Sectors. Journal of Risk and Financial Management, 15(12), Article 586.
13 OTC Markets Group. (2017, June 28). Small-caps failing to target small investors, survey shows. IR Impact.
14 Kaboth, J., Lodowicks, A., Schreiter, M. et al. Same same but different: how preferential claims trigger valuation discounts in equity tranches of VC-backed firms. Rev Quant Finan Acc 60, 877–914 (2023).
15 PwC. (2025). Roadmap for an IPO: A guide to going public.

16 London Stock Exchange. (2025). Corporate Governance - Guide to Listing & Disclosure Standards. London Stock Exchange.
17 Securities and Exchange Commission. (2019). Comment Letter Regarding File No. S7-26-18: Request for Comment on Earnings Releases and Quarterly Reports. SEC.
18 Related outstanding books on lean processes: "The Machine That Changed the World (1990) by James P. Womack, Daniel T. Jones, Daniel Roos, The Toyota Way by Liker, Jeffrey K. McGraw-Hill, 2004 and The Goal: A Process of Ongoing Improvement by Eliyahu M. Goldratt, North River Press (1984)
19 Der Marderosian, L., Johnson, B., Robinson, E. & Westenberg, D. (2017, May 25). 2017 IPO Report: U.S. Market Review and Outlook. Harvard Law School Forum on Corporate Governance & Financial Regulation.
20 Baker McKenzie. (2024). Presence in the jurisdiction – London Stock Exchange Main Market. Baker McKenzie Cross-Border Listings Guide.
21 Bebchuk, L. A., & Kastiel, K. (2017). The Untenable Case for Perpetual Dual-Class Stock. Harvard Business Law Review, 7, 1–61.
22 Vogelsang, O.J.T. (2019). The Effect of the Sarbanes-Oxley Act on Litigation Risk and Securities Class Action Lawsuits, Master's Thesis, European Master in Law & Economics, Warsaw School of Economics.
23 CNBC. (2020). Companies are paying big bucks to insure boards against liability as class-action suits soar, CNBC, 9 January.
24 London Stock Exchange Group. (2024). The U.S.: A More Litigious Place to List?, LSEG Issuer Services, 12 February.
25 Holt, R. and J.-H. Lee. (2018). The inherent risks associated with newly traded biopharmaceutical firms, Drug Discovery Today, 23(9), pp. 1680–1688.
26 National Bureau of Economic Research (2019) 'Differences in the Borrowing Behavior of Public and Private Firms', NBER Digest, 29 January.
27 Zhang, H. (2022). Cliff Asness Questions Whether Investors in Private Equity Are Being Rewarded - or Penalized - for Taking Illiquidity Risk. Institutional Investor, 2 June.
28 Bezos, J.P. (2000). Letter to Shareholders. Amazon.com, Inc., 2000.
29 CFA Institute. (2012). Dark Pools, Internalization, and Equity Market Quality. CFA Institute. (October 2012).
30 European Commission. (2025). Investment services and regulated markets (MiFID / MiFIR). European Commission.
31 Arcot, S., Black, J. & Owen, G. (2007). From local to global: the rise of AIM as a stock market for growing companies - a comprehensive report analysing the growth of AIM. London School of Economics and Political Science.
32 Coakley, J., Dotsis, G., Kourtis, A. & Psychoyios, D., 2022. The S&P 500 index inclusion effect: Evidence from the options market. International Journal of Finance & Economics, 29(1), pp. 1157–1171.
33 S&P Dow Jones Indices. (2025). S&P Dow Jones Indices An-

nounces Update to S&P Composite 1500 Market Cap Guidelines. S&P Global. (1 July 2025).
34 FTSE Russell. (2025). FTSE UK Index Series: Fast Entry and Trading Currency – Ground Rule Update. FTSE Russell, 3 March.
35 Kerzérho, R., 2025. The Passive vs. Active Fund Monitor: Year-end 2024 Data Update. PWL Capital. (Winter 2025).
36 Investopedia, (2025). Foreign Exchange Markets (Forex) – What Is Forex?. Investopedia.
37 Dahlquist, M. & Ibert, M. (2024). Equity Return Expectations and Portfolios: Evidence from Large Asset Managers. Review of Financial Studies, 37(6), pp.1887–1928.

Chapter 4
Historical Perspective

1 Petram, L. O. (2011). The world's first stock exchange: how the Amsterdam market for Dutch East India Company shares became a modern securities market, 1602-1700. PhD thesis, Universiteit van Amsterdam.
2 London Stock Exchange Group. (2025). The history of LSEG.
3 New York Stock Exchange. (2025). History of NYSE.
4 Nasdaq. (2025). About Nasdaq.
5 Shenzhen Stock Exchange. (2025). About SZSE / History.
6 Wikipedia. (2025). Singapore Exchange – History.
7 Long Term Stock Exchange. (2025). About LTSE.
8 TXSE. (2025). Home Page.
9 Global Growth Market. (2025). Global Growth Market website https://www.globalgrowth.market/
10 Payne, S.J. (1982) 'The Rise and Fall of the British Provincial Stock Exchanges', in The Development of British Capital Markets, 1919–1945, Business History, 24(1), pp. 1–20.
11 Mackintosh, P. (2021). Nasdaq: 50 Years of Market Innovation, Nasdaq, 11 February.
12 Lux, M. & Pead, J. (2018). Hunting High and Low: The Decline of the Small IPO and What to Do About It, M-RCBG Associate Working Paper No. 86, Harvard Kennedy School.
13 Gao, X., Ritter, J. R. & Zhu, Z. (2013). Where Have All the IPOs Gone?. Journal of Financial and Quantitative Analysis, 48(6), pp. 1663–1692.
14 Fleming, R. A. (2017). Enhancing the Demand for IPOs, speech at NASAA Public Policy Conference, 9 May. U.S. Securities and Exchange Commission.
15 U.S. Securities and Exchange Commission. (2021). PitchBook-NVCA Venture Monitor - Q1 2021.
16 Futunn. (2024). Nasdaq tightens rules for small-cap stocks to prevent pump.
17 Chicago Tribune. (2000). 'Bid farewell to an eighth', Chicago Tribune, 6 September.
18 Segal, T. (2025). Tick Size: Definition in Trading, Requirements, and Examples. Investopedia.
19 Bartlett, R.P. III and McCrary, J. (2013). Shall We Haggle in Pen-

nies at the Speed of Light or in Nickels in the Dark? How Minimum Price Variation Regulates High Frequency Trading and Dark Liquidity. University of California, Berkeley School of Law.
20 Farago, A. & Hjalmarsson, E., 2023. Small Rebalanced Portfolios Often Beat the Market over Long Horizons. The Review of Asset Pricing Studies, 13(2), pp. 307–342.
21 Cornell Law School Legal Information Institute. (2025). Securities Act of 1933.
22 Office of the Federal Register. (1972). Rules and Regulations: Part 230 - General Rules and Regulations, Securities Act of 1933; Part 239 - Forms Prescribed under the Securities Act of 1933; Adoption of Rule 144 (17 CFR 230.144). Federal Register, 14 January 1972, 37 (9), pp. 591–600.
23 Brav, A. & Gompers, P. A. (2003). The Role of Lockups in Initial Public Offerings. The Review of Financial Studies, 16(1), pp.1–29.
24 Cheung, Y.-L. & Liu, Y. (2007). 'IPO price performance and block-trading activities: Evidence from Hong Kong', Pacific-Basin Finance Journal, 15(3), pp. 276–291.
25 Kao, L., Chen, A. & Lu, C.-S. (2022). 'Retail investor attention and IPO prices with a pre-IPO market', International Review of Economics & Finance, 82, pp. 416–432.

Chapter 5
IPO Readiness and Preparation for the Global Stage

1 British Business Bank. (2025) Your journey to IPO.
2 Almazan, A., Swem, N., Titman, S. & Weitzner, G. (2024). Access to Capital and the IPO Decision: An Analysis of U.S. Private Firms. Working paper, Federal Reserve Board / University of Texas at Austin / McGill University, November.
3 Bradford, G. (1918). The whys and wherefores of navigation. New York: D. Van Nostrand Company
4 OECD. (2025). OECD Corporate Governance Factbook 2025. OECD Publishing, Paris.
5 Hidayat, S. E., Bamahriz, O., Hidayati, N., Sari, C. A. & Dewandaru, G. (2022) 'Value drivers of startup valuation from venture capital equity-based investing: A global analysis with a focus on technological factors', Borsa Istanbul Review, 22(4), pp. 653-667.
6 Schoenmaker, D. & Schramade, W. (2023) 'Valuing Public Equity', in Corporate Finance for Long-Term Value. Cham: Springer. DOI: 10.1007/978-3-031-35009-2_9.
7 Rüdiger Fahlenbrach, ‹Founder-CEOs, Corporate Governance, and Shareholder Value', Journal of Securities and Financial Analysis, vol. 44, no. 3, 2009
8 K. J. Martijn Cremers, Lubomir P. Litov and Simone M. Sepe, 'The Life-Cycle of Dual-Class Firm Valuation', The Review of Corporate Finance Studies, vol. 13, no. 2, 2024
9 Ning Gao and Bharat A. Jain, 'Founder Management and IPO Underpricing', Journal of Corporate Finance, vol. 17, no. 5, 2011
10 Chemmanur, T. J., Hu, G. and Huang, J. (2015) 'Founder-CEOs

and Innovation: Evidence from S&P 500 Companies', Review of Financial Studies, 28(6).
11 Chris Zook and James Allen, The Founder's Mentality: How to Overcome the Predictable Crises of Growth, Boston, Harvard Business Review Press, 2016, page 2.
12 Note: Excellent content on the importance of category vision from: Andrew Chen, Christopher Lochhead A Pirate's Guide to a Legendary IPO: How to Write an S-1 That Tells a Story of a DIFFERENT Future, March 17, 2021
13 Lochhead, C., Yoon, E. and Cole, N. (2021) A pirate's guide to a legendary IPO: how to write an S-1 that tells a story of a DIFFERENT future. [e-book] Category Pirates.
14 HarbourVest Partners. (2024). How does the size of private markets compare to public markets?. HarbourVest Insights, 2 October.
15 Fahlenbrach, R. (2009) 'Founder-CEOs, Investment Decisions, and Stock Market Performance', Journal of Financial and Quantitative Analysis, 44(2), pp. 439–466
16 Garg, S., et al. (2025). Directors in new technology-based ventures: An empirical inquiry. Journal of Business Venturing, Volume 40, Issue 2, March 2025, 106431.
17 Lambert, C., Molestina Vivar, L. and Wedow, M. (2024) 'Is home bias biased? New evidence from the investment fund sector', ECB Working Paper Series, No. 2924.
18 Local Support or Structural Barriers? Unpacking Local Bias in Equity-Based Crowdfunding (University of Tokyo, 2025).
19 Deschenaux, M. R. (2024). The IPO "Quiet Period" under U.S. Securities Law.
20 American Bar Association / Association of Corporate Counsel. (2015). Initial Public Offerings: Pre-Filing Period.
21 Wired. (2004, August 14). Play Boys: Google IPO a Go Anyway.
22 HM Government. (2024). The Public Offers and Admissions to Trading Regulations 2024 (SI 2024/105).
23 Rajah & Tann Singapore LLP. (2022). Initial Public Offerings: Singapore – Publicity and marketing restrictions.
24 Hong Kong Exchanges and Clearing (HKEx). (2025). Listing Rules - publicity material restrictions for new applicants.
25 Perkins Coie. (2025). Corporate Structural Defenses to Takeovers – Chapter 11, Public Company Handbook.

Chapter 6
Selecting an Exchange

1 Christiansen, H. & Koldertsova, A. (2009). The Role of Stock Exchanges in Corporate Governance. SSRN.
2 Cornell Law School Legal Information Institute. (2025). Securities Exchange Act of 1934.
3 Financial Conduct Authority. (2024). UK Listing Rules (UKLR).
4 Australian Securities Exchange. (2025). About ASX.
5 Leisinger, B., Costa, C. M. & Quillen, C. (2024). Listing venues for high-growth companies - using the capital markets as an alternative

funding tool. International Bar Association.
6 U.S. Securities and Exchange Commission. (2017). Enhancing the Demand for IPOs (speech by Rick A. Fleming, Investor Advocate).
7 Willis Towers Watson / Thinking Ahead Institute. (2024). World's largest investment managers see assets hit USD 128 trillion in return to growth.
8 "Fidelity Investments."
9 Willis Towers Watson / Thinking Ahead Institute. (2025). World's largest asset managers' AUM surges to record USD 140 trillion, driven by North America and passives.
10 Capital Group. (2025). ADV Ratings.
11 Financial Services and Markets Act 2000: Official Listing. (2025) – Explanatory Notes. n.d. Financial Services and Markets Act 2000 (c. 8) Part VI: Official Listing.
12 Australian Securities Exchange (2025). ASX regulatory framework.
13 Johannesburg Stock Exchange (2025). Issuer Regulation.
14 Singapore Academy of Law. (2025). Ch. 17 Corporate Finance and Securities Regulation. SingaporeLawWatch.
15 Singapore Exchange (SGX). (2025). Investor Relations.
16 Chemmanur, T.J. & Fulghieri, P. (2006) 'Competition and cooperation among exchanges: a theory of cross-listing and endogenous listing standards', Journal of Financial Economics, 82(2), pp. 455–489.
17 Baker, H. K., Nofsinger, J. R. & Weaver, D. G. (2002). 'International cross-listing and visibility', Journal of Financial and Quantitative Analysis, 37(3), pp. 495–521.
18 Williams, T. (2012). 'Exploration and the Listed Resource Sector', RBA Bulletin, September, pp. 37–42.
19 Australian Government. (1992). Superannuation Guarantee (Administration) Act 1992.
20 Australian Prudential Regulation Authority (APRA). (2016). APRA releases annual superannuation statistics for June 2015.
21 The Motley Fool Australia. (2021). 'Afterpay (ASX:APT) share price cracks $151 record high', The Motley Fool, 8 February.
22 Azevedo, M. (2021). "Square to buy Australian buy-now-pay-later giant Afterpay in $29B deal", TechCrunch, 1 August.
23 On-Market BookBuilds Pty Ltd. (2020). OnMarket Annual IPO Report 2019.
24 Cogman, D. & Orr, G. (2013). How they fell: The collapse of Chinese cross-border listings, McKinsey & Company, 1 December.
25 Wang, H. & Bao, Y. (2015). Reverse Migration in Contemporary China: Returnees, Entrepreneurship and the Chinese Economy. Basingstoke: Palgrave Macmillan. Doi:10.1057/9781137450609.s
26 Kiralfy, A.R. & Glendon, M.A. (2025). 'Common law', Encyclopædia Britannica.
27 Moses, A. (2018) 'The Development of Common Law in England – from 1066 to the 19th Century', iPleaders Blog, 9 April.
28 Burset, C. R. (2023) An Empire of Laws: Legal Pluralism in British Colonial Policy. New Haven & London: Yale University Press.

29 Daniels, R. J., Trebilcock, M. & Carson, L. D. (2011) 'The Legacy of Empire: The Common Law Inheritance and Commitments to Legality in Former British Colonies', American Journal of Comparative Law, 59(1), pp. 111–178.
30 Beck, T., Demirgüç-Kunt, A. & Levine, R. (2003). 'Law and finance: why does legal origin matter?', Journal of Comparative Economics, 31(4), pp. 653–675.
31 Touchton, M. & Tyburski, M. (2022) 'Judging the Market: Judicial Independence, the Rule of Law, and Economic Development', International Journal of Innovation and Economic Development, 8(3), pp. 12–26.
32 Anderlini, L., Felli, L. & Riboni, A. (2019) 'Legal efficiency and consistency', European Economic Review, 121, article 103323.
33 World Bank Group. (2025). Key Features of Common and Civil Law Systems, Public-Private Partnership (PPP) in Infrastructure Resource Center, World Bank.
34 Cantillon, E. & Yin, P.-L., 2011. Competition between Exchanges: A Research Agenda. International Journal of Industrial Organization, 29(3), pp. 329–336.
35 Hwang, S. (2020). The rise of the special purpose acquisition company. Cambridge Judge Business School, 18 December.
36 FinanceFacts101. (2025). Pre-IPO Placements: Understanding the Pre-Initial Public Offering Process. FinanceFacts101, 16 May.
37 Imagine Capital Group. (2025). Unlocking Liquidity: A Guide to Founders and Founding Teams Selling Secondaries. Imagine Capital Group, 12 February.
38 Investopedia. (2025). Understanding Pre-IPO Placements: Definition, Process & How They Work. Investopedia, 25 August.
39 IPO Platform. (2024). What Is Pre IPO Investment and Role of IPO Advisors. IPO Platform, 7 November.
40 Cleary Gottlieb Steen & Hamilton LLP. (2024). Post-IPO Liquidity Roadmap for Pre-IPO Equity Investors (Client Memo). 4 January.
41 International Forum of Sovereign Wealth Funds (IFSWF), 2021. Sovereign Wealth Funds - Investments in Private Markets (Survey & Report). IFSWF.
42 Morgan Stanley. (2025). The Growing Opportunity in Private Markets. Morgan Stanley.
43 Boston Consulting Group (2021). Does Your IPO Need an Anchor or Cornerstone Investor? BCG, 29 June.
44 PwC. (2025). Roadmap for an IPO: A guide to going public, PricewaterhouseCoopers.
45 Corporate Finance Institute. (2025). Bridge Financing - Definition, How it Works, Example.
46 U.S. Securities and Exchange Commission. (2019). SEC Adopts New Rule to Allow All Issuers to "Test-the-Waters", 26 September 2019.
47 McGuinness, P.B. (2014). IPO firm value and its connection with cornerstone/cornerstone-like investors (study on cornerstone investor signalling). ScienceDirect / Elsevier.
48 EY. (2018). Guide to going public - Strategic considerations before, during and post-IPO (PDF).

49 Investopedia. (2025). What a Roadshow Is and How It Creates a Successful IPO.
50 Orrick. (2018). Selecting an Underwriter for an IPO - guidance on choosing and evaluating investment banks and bookrunners.
51 DLA Piper. (2025). Bridge/pre-IPO financings reduce dependency on timing of IPO window and improve readiness; see DLA Piper, An overview of bridge financing.
52 U.S. Securities and Exchange Commission. (2013). Rule 144 - Selling Restricted and Control Securities. SEC.
53 Kish, R.J., Nayar, N. & Weng, W. (2012). IPO pricing: a case of short-sale restrictions and divergent expectations. Quantitative Finance, 12(9), pp.1439–1451.
54 Bajaj, M., Denis, D., Ferris, S. & Sarin, A. (2001). Firm Value and Marketability Discounts. New York University.
55 Steil, B. (2002). 'Changes in the Ownership and Governance of Securities Exchanges: Causes and Consequences', Brookings-Wharton Papers on Financial Services, vol. 2002, no. 1, pp. 61–91.
56 U.S. Securities and Exchange Commission. (1996), Report Pursuant to Section 21(a) of the Securities Exchange Act of 1934 Regarding the NASD and the Nasdaq Market, SEC, Washington, DC.
57 Nasdaq Stock Market, Inc. (2006). NASDAQ Becomes Operational as a National Securities Exchange, press release, 1 August.
58 Lannoo, K. (2010). Self-Regulation in Securities Markets, World Bank Policy Research Working Paper 5542, World Bank, Washington, DC.
59 Baker, M., & Gompers, P. (2000). Stock Listing Changes: Timing or Signaling?. ResearchGate.
60 Infotel. (2018). CSE: Marijuana and Blockchain Drive Growth, Infotel, 4 January.
61 Ritter, J.R. & Welch, I. (2002). A Review of IPO Activity, Pricing, and Allocations, Journal of Finance, vol. 57, no. 4, pp. 1795–1828.
62 Smith, T. (2023). Greenshoe Option, Investopedia.
63 Croft, A. (2019). What is a greenshoe option? How it affects Aramco's IPO, Fortune, 24 November.
64 Saini, M & Nishant, M. (2025). Strong market debuts raise questions over cautious IPO pricing by Wall St banks, Reuters, 21 August.
65 Perkins Coie. (2023). Chapter 12: Follow-on Offerings and Shelf Registrations, Public Company Handbook, Perkins Coie LLP, Seattle, WA.
66 Bebchuk, L.A. & Kastiel, K. 2017, 'The Untenable Case for Perpetual Dual-Class Stock', Harvard Business Law Review, vol. 7, pp. 1–52.
67 New York Stock Exchange (NYSE) 2023, NYSE Initial Listing Standards Summary, NYSE, New York.
68 Charltons. (2018). HK Stock Exchange consults on listings of emerging and innovative companies. Charltons.
69 London Stock Exchange. (2025). Global exposure and best execution: why London is a centre for global securities trading. London Stock Exchange.

Chapter 7
The IPO Process

1 Bank for International Settlements (2020), "Global liquidity - concepts, measurements and trends," BIS Papers.
2 FINRA (2003) 2003 Global Settlement. Available at: https://www.finra.org/rules-guidance/guidance/reports/2003-global-settlement FINRA
3 U.S. Securities and Exchange Commission (SEC) (2003) Federal court approves global research analyst settlement. Available at: https://www.sec.gov/enforcement-litigation/litigation-releases/lr-18438 SEC
4 Oehler, A. (2004) The existence and effectiveness of price support activities. Available at: https://ideas.repec.org/p/zbw/bamfin/30.html IDEAS/RePEc
5 Jenkinson, T. (2007) IPO syndication conflicts and the naked short puzzle. Available at: https://ora.ox.ac.uk/objects/uuid%3Adde15e4b-65e4-47f6-9be4-a052b42f82f6 Oxford University Research Archive
6 Saadah, S. (2016) The Green Shoe Option's effectiveness at stabilizing the IPO's stock price. Available at: https://pdfs.semanticscholar.org/af06/... Semantic Scholar
7 Spotify Technology S.A. (2018) Form F-1 - Registration statement (as filed 28 Feb 2018). Available at: https://www.sec.gov/Archives/edgar/data/1639920/000119312518063434/d494294df1.htm SEC
8 Credible Labs Inc. (2017) Prospectus (Credible IPO, ASX, December 2017). Available at: https://www.asx.com.au/asxpdf/20171208/pdf/43q0bk7g1lrh5z.pdf Australian Securities Exchange
9 Slack Technologies, Inc. (2019) Form S-1 - Registration statement (as filed 26 Apr 2019). Available at: https://www.sec.gov/Archives/edgar/data/1764925/000162828019004786/slacks-1.htm SEC
10 Reuters (2019) Murdoch's Fox Corp to buy fintech Credible Labs in $397 million deal (4 Aug 2019). Available at: https://www.reuters.com/article/business/murdochs-fox-corp-to-buy-fintech-credible-labs-in-397-million-deal-idUSKCN1UV0FE/ Reuters
11 SEC (2020) CF Disclosure Guidance Topic: Special Purpose Acquisition Companies (22 Dec 2020). Available at: https://www.sec.gov/rules-regulations/staff-guidance/disclosure-guidance/disclosure-special-purpose-acquisition SEC+1
12 Cleary Gottlieb (2020) Going public: A guide to U.S. IPOs for founders, officers, directors and other market participants. (Guide PDF). Available at: https://www.clearygottlieb.com/
13 Coinbase Global, Inc. (2021) Form S-1 - Registration statement (as filed 25 Feb 2021). Available at: https://www.sec.gov/Archives/edgar/data/1679788/000162828021003168/coinbaseglobalincs-1.htm SEC
14 SPAC market tallies and tracker (2020–2021) - industry tracker summary (SPAC Research / Dealogic). Available at: https://dealogic.com dealogic.com+1
15 Industry analyses of SPAC redemptions & PIPE stress (2022–2023) - SPAC Research / SEC staff observations. Available at: https://www.sec.gov SEC+1
16 Jay Ritter (2024) IPO-Statistics 1980–2024. Available at: https://

site.warrington.ufl.edu/ritter/files/IPO-Statistics.pdf Websites
17 NBER (various authors) - literature on earnings surprises and cost of capital (examples and surveys). Available at: https://www.nber.org NBER
18 Investopedia (no date) Bookbuilding. Available at: https://www.investopedia.com investopedia.com
19 PitchBook / DFIN practitioner guides on IPO pricing & timing (no date/guides) - PitchBook and DFIN resources. Available at: https://www.pitchbook.com / https://www.dfinsolutions.com/knowledge-hub PitchBook+1
20 Investopedia (no date) Greenshoe option. Available at: https://www.investopedia.com investopedia.com
21 SEC / FINRA material on stabilization & overallotment mechanics (no date / practice notes). Available at: https://www.sec.gov and https://www.finra.org SEC+1
22 Empirical/academic work on underwriter behaviour and greenshoe usage (e.g., Ellis 2006 and others). Available at: https://www.sciencedirect.com ScienceDirect
23 Norton Rose Fulbright / Practical Law (no date) Dual-track processes (IPO vs M&A). Available at: https://www.nortonrosefulbright.com Mayer Brown
24 DFIN (2024) Navigating the IPO Process: timeline for going public (practical guidance). Available at: https://www.dfinsolutions.com/knowledge-hub/thought-leadership/knowledge-resources/ipo-timeline-process Donnelley Financial Solutions (DFIN)
25 ESMA (Prospectus Regulation / Final Report) (2024–2025) Final report on format & content of EU prospectuses (12 Jun 2025). Available at: https://www.esma.europa.eu/sites/default/files/2025-06/ESMA32-117195963-1417_Final_Report_Listing_Act_Advice_on_Prospectus.pdf ESMA
26 UK Financial Conduct Authority (FCA) (no date) Prospectus rules and guidance. Available at: https://www.fca.org.uk FCA
27 PwC (no date) Choosing where to list - cross-border IPO considerations. Available at: https://www.pwc.com PwC
28 Deloitte (no date) Roadmap to initial public offerings - cross-border considerations. Available at: https://www2.deloitte.com Deloitte
29 Kraken (no date) xStocks - tokenized stocks (examples of tokenized equities). Available at: https://www.kraken.com/en-gb/xstocks

Chapter 8
Knowing the Players to Understand the Game

1 Munger, C.T. (2005) Poor Charlie's Almanack: The Wit and Wisdom of Charles T. Munger. Edited by P.D. Kaufman
2 PwC (2025) A guide to floating on AIM – Listing in London (PwC PDF guide). Available at: https://www.pwc.co.uk/risk/assets/pdf/guide-floating-aim-listing-london.pdf PwC
3 Baker McKenzie (2025) Guide to IPOs for Technology Companies (PDF). Available at: https://www.bakermckenzie.com/-/media/files/insight/guides/2025/guide-to-ipos-for-tech-companies.pdf Baker McKenzie

4 Gibson Dunn (2024) IPO Guidebook (October 2024 PDF). Available at: https://www.gibsondunn.com/wp-content/uploads/2024/10/Gibson-Dunn-%E2%80%93-IPO-Guidebook-10.2024.pdf Gibson Dunn

5 Beatty, R.P. and Ritter, J.R. (1986) 'Investment banking, reputation, and the underpricing of initial public offerings', Journal of Financial Economics, 15(1/2), pp. 213–232. Available at: https://www.sciencedirect.com/science/article/pii/0304405X86900553 ScienceDirect

6 The Marshmallow Test is a famous psychological experiment first conducted in the late 1960s by Walter Mischel at Stanford University. It was designed to study delayed gratification—the ability to resist an immediate reward in favor of a larger, future reward.

7 Benveniste, L.M. and Spindt, P.A. (1989) 'How investment bankers determine the offer price and allocation of new issues', Journal of Financial Economics, 24(2), pp. 343–361. Available at: https://www.sciencedirect.com/science/article/pii/0304405X89900512 ScienceDirect

8 Carter, R. and Manaster, S. (1990) 'Initial public offerings and underwriter reputation', Journal of Finance, 45(4), pp. 1045–1067. Available at: https://onlinelibrary.wiley.com/doi/10.1111/j.1540-6261.1990.tb02426.x Wiley Online Library

9 SEC (2003) 'Ten of Nation's Top Investment Firms Settle Enforcement Actions Involving Conflicts of Interest Between Research and Investment Banking' (SEC press release). Available at: https://www.sec.gov/news/press/2003-54.htm SEC

10 FINRA (2003) 2003 Global Settlement overview (FINRA). Available at: https://www.finra.org/rules-guidance/guidance/reports/2003-global-settlement FINRA

11 Loughran, T. and Ritter, J. (2000/2002) 'Why don't issuers get upset about leaving money on the table in IPOs?', working paper / published discussion. Available at: https://papers.ssrn.com/sol3/papers.cfm?abstract_id=243145 SSRN

12 Cornelli, F. and Goldreich, D. (2001/2002) 'Bookbuilding and Strategic Allocation' (working paper).

13 FCA (2016/2019) 'Quid pro quo? What factors influence IPO allocations to institutions and retail investors?' (FCA Occasional Paper / research). Available at: https://www.fca.org.uk/publication/occasional-papers/occasional-paper-15.pdf FCA

14 Aggarwal, R. (2003) 'Allocation of initial public offerings and flipping activity', Journal of Financial Economics (abstract). Available at: https://www.sciencedirect.com/science/article/abs/pii/S0304405X02002507 ScienceDirect

15 Investopedia (2025) 'Flipping: Definition, Strategies, Types, and Risks Explained'. Available at: https://www.investopedia.com/terms/f/flipping.asp Investopedia

16 European Commission / EUR-Lex (2017) Regulation (EU) 2017/1129 - Prospectus Regulation.

17 ESMA (2025) 'Prospectus - issuer disclosure' (ESMA guidance on prospectus publication).

18 SEC (2025) 'The Regulation of Securities Offerings' (overview and proposals; communications).

19 HKEX (Rulebook) 'Publication and prospectus rules & market-maker programs' (HKEX rulebook and market maker program pages).
20 Deutsche Börse / Xetra (2025) 'Designated Sponsors and Market Makers - Xetra' (requirements and role of designated sponsors).
21 Nasdaq (2025) 'Market Maker process - NasdaqTrader' (definition and market-maker role).
22 O'Hara, M. (1998) Market Microstructure Theory. John Wiley & Sons (classic reference on market-making and spreads).
23 APRA (2025) 'APRA releases superannuation statistics for December 2024' (Australian Prudential Regulation Authority).
24 SMC / market analysis (2025) report / research note on global pension rankings (Australia's Superannuation position).
25 EY (2025) Guide to going public (EY IPO guide PDF - practical steps, including IR and advisor selection).
26 PwC (2025) Roadmap for an IPO: A guide to going public (practitioner guide and checklist).
27 IR Society (UK) (2025) Best Practice Guidelines for Investor Relations (IR Society standards / playbook).
28 NIRI (National Investor Relations Institute) (2025) - official site and resources on IR best practices.
29 IR-Impact / research (2025) The Ultimate Guide to Investor Relations (2023 edition) (practical IR checklist for IPOs).
30 ESMA (2019/interactive) 'Article 21 - Publication of the prospectus' (how and where to publish prospectuses).
31 Practical Law / Thomson Reuters (2025) 'Prospectus Regulation - Practical Law overview' (UK/EU prospectus practical guide)
32 WilmerHale (2003) 'Global Research Analyst Settlement - commentary & implications for issuers' (law-firm analysis).
33 SEC (2002/2003) '$1.4 Billion Global Settlement - SEC Litigation Release' (overview of the global research analyst settlement)
34 Cornelli, F., Goldreich, D. and Ljungqvist, A. (2003) 'Bookbuilding: How Informative Is the Order Book?', Journal of Finance (study overview).
35 FCA (2025) 'Submit a prospectus or circular' (FCA procedural guidance for UK listings).
36 PwC (2016) Executing a successful IPO - Markets for technology (PwC sector guidance PDF).
37 ESMA / EU rule text / central bank pages (2025) - Prospectus Regulation guidance (formal EU guidance).
38 Investopedia (2025) 'Market Makers - role and how they make money (bid-ask spread explanation)'.
39 Citadel Securities (2025) 'What is a market-maker?' (practitioner overview of market-making and liquidity provision).
40 Maureen O'Hara (1998) Market Microstructure Theory - theory underpinning market-maker incentives and spreads.
41 Montague Law (2023) Understanding Pre-IPO Converts and Their Implications.
42 'Designated Sponsor Requirements' - Deutsche Börse (detailed guide and criteria for designated sponsors / market-making).

43 HKEX (2025) 'List of Market Makers / Liquidity Providers' (practical list showing participants for Hong Kong listings).
44 'The Pricing of IPO Audit Specialization and Subsequent Issuer Outcomes' - Accounting Horizons / academic work on audit specialization and IPOs (implications for Big-4 selection).
45 'Accents' is a term some founders to describe variations of accounting standards; no professional accountant would use the term.
46 'The Evolution of the Big Four Accounting Firms' - UK Government / industry working paper on audit suppliers (historical merger context from Big-8 to Big-4).
47 Rosati, P., et al. (2017) 'The Effect of Data Breach Announcements Beyond the Stock Price' - event studies on bid-ask spread and volatility (QUB / academic).
48 Skadden (2023) 'Hong Kong's new listing rules for specialist technology companies - prospectus & disclosure guidance' (law-firm note illustrating jurisdictional disclosure differences).
49 Investor Relations Society (2025) Best Practice Guidelines: Section 1 – IR strategy and investor targeting.
50 IR-Impact (2023) The Ultimate Guide to Investor Relations - 2023 edition.
51 GetIRwin / IR resources (2023) Top tips and perspectives on investor relations compensation and incentives.
52 EY (2021/2023) Guide to going public: Strategic considerations before, during and post-IPO (Guide).
53 Edelman (2025) IPOs & Spinoffs - Financial communications & capital markets.
54 Dubai Financial Market (DFM) (2016) DFM Guide on IPO Communications.
55 LSEG / industry guidance (2025) The critical role of cybersecurity and technology in IPO preparation (penetration testing and vulnerability assessments).
56 Aon (2025) Red Team Testing to Meet Regulatory Requirements.
57 European Commission (2016) Regulation (EU) 2016/679 – General Data Protection Regulation (GDPR).
58 Disclosure: The author has, or has had financial ties to FiscalNote.
59 Milhaupt, C. J., & Ringe, W.-G. (2025) The Political Economy of Global Stock Exchange Competition, Harvard Law School Forum on Corporate Governance.
60 HSBC (2025) The 2025 Global Founder-Led Equity Report: Navigating Disruption. London: HSBC Global Research.
61 Lee, S., Chang, J. and Wang, Y. (2024) 'Founder-CEOs and innovation in the age of AI', Journal of Business Venturing, 39(4), pp. 106–125.
62 PwC (2017) Considering an IPO to fuel your company's future? Insight into the costs of going public and being public. PwC Deals, November 2017.
63 LSEG Issuer Services (2024) The critical role of PMO in navigating an IPO.
64 Accordion (2019) Structuring the IPO PMO for exit success.

65 PwC (2022/2024) Roadmap to IPO / IPO readiness guidance (Project management & PMO

Chapter 9
Attracting the Right Investors

1 Gwern, E. (2025) Adobe: company history & early financing (incl. Hambrecht & Quist). Available at: https://www.gwern.net/
2 Oracle Corporation (2025) Company history - Oracle Timeline (includes 1986 IPO and underwriters). Available at: https://www.oracle.com/
3 Salesforce.com, Inc. (2004) Form S-1 Registration Statement (SEC filing).
4 Nasdaq (2020) Nasdaq Listing Qualifications / Initial Listing Guide (listing rules and market-cap tests).
5 Ritter, J.R. (1991) 'The Long-Run Performance of Initial Public Offerings', Journal of Finance, 46(1), pp. 3–27.
6 Gompers, P., Ishii, J. and Metrick, A. (2003) 'Corporate Governance and Equity Prices', Quarterly Journal of Economics, 118(1), pp. 107–156.
7 Bushee, B.J. (1998) 'The Influence of Institutional Investors on Myopic R&D Investment Behaviour', Accounting Review / Journal of Financial Economics (see Bushee works on institutional investor incentives).
8 HKEX / practitioner guides (e.g., PwC, Linklaters) - Cornerstone / Anchor investors: definition and practice (practice note: disclosure in prospectus; regional norms).
9 PwC / Ernst & Young / law-firm IPO guides - Cornerstone investor disclosure and prospectus practice (typical guidance/articles on public disclosure). Example: PwC (2025) Hong Kong IPO Guide (cornerstone investors explained)
10 PwC / market practice commentary - Cornerstone investor lock-ups (typical 3–6 months outside U.S.). Example guidance: PwC IPO guide / Hong Kong IPO practice notes.
11 Bebchuk, L. & Kastiel, K. (2017) 'The Untenable Case for Perpetual Dual-Class Stock', Harvard Business Review / Harvard Law Review (governance risks of concentrated control and investor responses).
12 GlobalSWF / Sovereign Wealth Fund Institute (2025) Overview and list of sovereign wealth funds (Temasek, GIC, Khazanah, QIC, Future Fund, EPF, KIC, KfW, ADIA, PIF etc.).
13 BCG / FT / practitioner pieces on strategic investors in IPOs and cross-jurisdiction differences (corporate participation more common in Asia / Middle East / parts of Europe). Example: Linklaters / Clifford Chance notes on strategic allocations
14 ARM Holdings plc (2023) Prospectus / filings and press coverage describing allocations to Apple, NVIDIA, Samsung, Intel, TSMC, AMD in its 2023 IPO. Example press: Reuters/FT coverage of ARM IPO allocations.
15 U.S. Securities and Exchange Commission (2025) Rule 144 - Selling restricted and control securities
16 Cleary Gottlieb (2024) Post-IPO liquidity roadmap for pre-IPO

investors (practitioner memo discussing Rule 144 impacts on pre-IPO participation).

17 PwC / EY / McKinsey / practitioner reports on pre-IPO rounds and benefits to pricing & dilution (discussion of how a pre-IPO round can support IPO pricing).

18 Deal reports / market surveys (typical pre-IPO discount ranges) - practitioner sources (e.g., Cooley, Wilson Sonsini, law-firm and boutique pre-IPO surveys)

19 WilmerHale (2017) Legal considerations in pre-IPO crossover financings

20 FTSE Russell / Russell (2025) Russell U.S. Indexes methodology and index inclusion criteria (Russell 3000 / index eligibility - why smaller companies miss larger index flows).

21 S&P Dow Jones Indices / ETF provider documentation - How index data feeds drive ETF and passive flows; operational mechanics of passive funds and index-driven buying.

22 Academic and industry literature on passive flows and index-tracking behaviour (e.g., BIS, NBER, and journal articles) - evidence that passive flows respond mechanically to index inclusion and rebalancing.

23 Appel, I.R., Gormley, T.A. and Keim, D.B. (2016) 'Passive Investors, the "Big Three," and Corporate Governance', Journal of Finance / working papers on Big Three influence.

24 Deloitte (2024) and other industry forecasts - family office AUM / $10 trillion+ by 2030 projection (industry commentary and forecasting in Deloitte report summary).

25 FCA / Jenkinson et al. (2018) "Quid Pro Quo? What factors influence IPO allocations to hedge funds?" (FCA / academic working paper) - research on hedge funds' role in bookbuilding and aftermarket.

26 BIS / ECB / academic literature on hedge-fund leverage and market impact

27 Muddy Waters Research (2011) Sino-Forest report as example); Reuters coverage and follow-up (Sino-Forest collapse). Or Hindenburg Research (2023) Adani report.

28 International Securities Lending Association (ISLA) / securities-lending and market-structure reports

29 ASX (Australian Securities Exchange) (2025) Listing Rule 3.1 - Continuous Disclosure (explains continuous disclosure regime vs. quarterly reporting).

30 Reg S / cross-border offering rules & U.S. retail investor restrictions (practitioner guidance) - example: Norton Rose / Skadden / InvestIndia notes on Reg S / cross-border offering compliance (how to limit U.S. retail participation to avoid triggering SEC registration/exposure).

31 Legal / regulatory commentary and case law on U.S. cross-border listing risk and litigation exposure - practitioner notes explaining why uncontrolled U.S. retail participation can increase SEC/regulatory and litigation risk for U.S.-domiciled companies listing abroad. Example: law-firm guidance on "Cross-border listings and U.S. investor participation." Available at: https://www.lawfirm.com/ (search "cross-border IPO U.S. retail

Reg S litigation risk")

Chapter 10
Smartphone-Fueled Animal Spirits

1 Xu, M. (2025) 0DTEs Decoded: Positioning, Trends, and Market Impact. Cboe Global Markets
2 Lysandrou, P. & Ranjbaran, T. (2021) 'Financialisation reinforced: the dual legacy of the COVID pandemic', Review of Evolutionary Political Economy, 2(3), pp. 589–606.
3 Lindzon, H. (2023) You Say Entertainment-ification of Sports... I Say 'Degenerate Economy'... Same Thing, Trends With Friends.
4 Lindzon, H. (2024) An Update On The Degenerate Economy and Some Rules and Advice, Trends With Friends, 21 June
5 Lindzon, H. (2023) You Say Entertainment-ification of Sports... I Say 'Degenerate Economy'... Same Thing, Trends With Friends.
6 Lindzon, H. (2025) You Are NOT On Your Own... A Refresh Of The Degenerate Economy.
7 ECMI (2023) Digital-Savvy Retail Investors – How Can the Financial Industry and Regulation Help Them to Prosper
8 Soros, G. (2003) The Alchemy of Finance: Reading the Mind of the Market. New York: Wiley.
9 Financial Times (2025) 'South Korean investors pile into U.S. equities as domestic stock market languishes', Financial Times, 2 January.
10 Peter Lynch and John Rothchild, One Up on Wall Street: How to Use What You Already Know to Make Money in the Market, New York, Simon & Schuster, 2000
11 Yogonet (2025) 'Kalshi tops $4.4 billion, Polymarket rebounds: October data highlights prediction markets' momentum', Yogonet International, 6 November.
12 Schwartz, H. (2025) Options Activity Review and Preview. Cboe Global Markets
13 Xu, M. (2025) 0DTEs Decoded: Positioning, Trends, and Market Impact. Cboe Global Markets.
14 Ghosh, P. (2021) 'Robinhood To Let Retail Investors Buy Into Initial Public Offerings', Forbes, 20 May.
15 Cboe Global Markets (2025) The State of the Options Industry: Quarter Three 2025.
16 Roy, S. (2025) 'Bring On The 5x ETFs', ETF.com, 23 October.

Chapter 11
Coming to America - The Double Standard

1 Deloitte (2025) DART Topic 6: Foreign Private Issuers. Available online.
2 Ewens, M., Xiao, K. and Xu, T. (2024) 'Regulatory costs of being public: Evidence from bunching estimation', Journal of Financial Economics, 153(2), p. 103775.
3 Morgan Stanley (2025) Investment Outlook 2026: U.S. Stock Market to Guide Growth.

4 PwC (2026) US Capital Markets 2026 Outlook: PwC Capital Markets Watch.
5 Ernst & Young (2025) 2025 Global IPO market key highlights and 2026 outlook.
6 Uyeda, M. (2025) Statement on the Global Research Analyst Settlement. Washington D.C.: U.S. Securities and Exchange Commission.
7 Burson (2026) Burson Quantifies the Value of Reputation, Revealing a $7 Trillion Global "Reputation Economy".
8 U.S. Securities and Exchange Commission, A Brief Overview for Foreign Private Issuers, Division of Corporation Finance, SEC (13 February 2013).
9 Securities Litigation Risk for Foreign Companies Listed in the U.S. Authors: Beiting Cheng (Harvard University), Suraj Srinivasan (Harvard Business School), and Gwen Yu (University of Michigan). Revised in 2014
10 Woodruff Sawyer (2025) D&O Looking Ahead Guide 2026: D&O Liability and Insurance Insights.
11 Hasan, I. and Waisman, M., 2010. Going public: An empirical investigation of U.S.-bound Israeli IPOs. Financial Markets, Institutions & Instruments, 19(3), pp.215–244.
12 EY Global IPO Trends Q1 2025 report
13 Costa, R., 2024. Overseas primary listing: U.S. stock markets as a global hub for IPOs? SSRN Working Paper No. 4980187.

Chapter 12
Life as a Public Company

1 Bartov, E., Givoly, D. & Hayn, C., 2002. The rewards to meeting or beating earnings expectations. Journal of Accounting & Economics, 33(3), pp.221–241.
2 Morgan Stanley, 2025. An Introduction to Private Equity Basics. Morgan Stanley Investment Management.
3 IR Impact, 2023. Nine Best Practices for Hosting an Effective Earnings Call. IR Impact Report. (p. "Schedule time to rehearse")
4 Polak, E., Scholtens, B. & Wang, J., 2024. Impact of investor trust on public firms' stock price efficiency and cost of capital: Insights from a firm-level measure for investor trust. International Review of Economics & Finance, 89, 106799. ScienceDirect
5 Shemshad, A. & Karim, R.G., 2023. The Effect of Managerial Ability on the Timeliness of Financial Reporting: The Role of Audit Firm and Company Size. Journal of Operational and Strategic Analytics, 1(1), pp.34–41.
6 Ball, R. & Shivakumar, L., 2005. Earnings quality in UK private firms: comparative loss recognition timeliness. Journal of Accounting & Economics, 39(1), pp.83–128.
7 Rohrbach, T. & Makhortykh, M., 2024. A Matter of Mindset? Features and Processes of Newsroom-based Corporate Communication in Times of Artificial Intelligence.
8 Ojha, N. & Vaishnaw, H., 2024. Employer Branding Tactics for Elevating Attractiveness in Recruitment. European Economic Letters,

14(1).
9 Pfeiffer, I. & Jarchow, S., 2024. The determinants of compensation report transparency: manager incentives and firm characteristics. Journal of Business Economics, 94, pp.659–691.
10 Phelps, T.W., 1972. 100 to 1 in the Stock Market. New York: Random House.
11 Ioramashvili, C., Feldman, M., 2024. "Gathering round Big Tech: How the market for acquisitions concentrates the digital sector", Cambridge Journal of Regions, Economy and Society, 17(2), pp. 293–312.
12 Tedlow, R.S., 1988. The Early Years of Ford and General Motors. Business and Economic History, 17, pp.49–62.
13 Kim, W. & Weisbach, M.S., 2008. 'Motives for public equity offers: evidence from seasoned equity offerings', Journal of Financial Economics, 87(1), pp.179–207.
14 Greenwood, R. & Sammon, K., 2024. Passive Investing and the Rise of Mega-Firms. Review of Financial Studies. OUP Academic.
15 Bebchuk, L. & Hirst, S., 2019. Index Funds and the Future of Corporate Governance: Theory, Evidence, and Policy. Columbia Law Review, 119, pp.2029–2127.

Chapter 13
The Future of Global Capital - Challenges & Opportunities

1 McKinsey & Company, 2023. Global Private Markets Review 2023: Private markets have expanded dramatically. McKinsey & Company.
2 Oxera, 2020. Primary and secondary equity markets in the EU - Are we witnessing the decline of public equity markets? Oxera.
3 TheGlobalEconomy.com, 2025. Number of listed companies - Germany (historical series).
4 Doidge, C., Karolyi, G. A. & Stulz, R. M., 2017 (updated 2025). The U.S. listing gap (and updates).
5 Bain & Company, 2022–2024. Global Private Equity / Private Markets reports - drivers of capital flow to private markets.
6 International Monetary Fund (IMF), 2021. Global Financial Stability Report - risks from opaque markets and non-bank finance.
7 PwC / EY / Nasdaq analyses (2023–2025). Reports on tokenization, AI and technology as drivers for IPOs and capital-formation. Example: PwC, "Global IPO Watch" (2024).
8 OECD, 2020–2024. Reports on retail share ownership and the democratizing effects of public equity markets.
9 U.S. Securities and Exchange Commission (SEC), 2024. Accredited Investor Definition & Rules.
10 U.S. Securities and Exchange Commission (SEC), various. Public company disclosure obligations (Form 10-K, 10-Q, audit requirements, shareholder votes). SEC - EDGAR & investor guidance.
11 OECD / IMF / SWF Institute, 2023–2024. Institutional investors' balance sheets - insurers, SWFs, endowments and pension funds and their public/private allocations. Example: OECD, Pension Markets in Focus.
12 International Private Equity and Venture Capital Valuation

(IPEV) guidelines and FCA/SEC reviews, 2018–2024. Discussion of NAV practices and valuation challenges in private funds. Example: IPEV Guidelines.
13 Financial Conduct Authority (FCA), 2019–2023. Findings on valuation divergence and NAV subjectivity in private funds.
14 IOSCO / IMF research, 2020–2023. Incentives, fee structures and valuation-linked compensation in asset management. Example: IOSCO thematic reports.
15 Financial Times / IMF commentary (2020–2025). Private equity's ownership of mission-critical firms and opacity concerns. Example coverage: Financial Times investigations into PE ownership of critical sectors.
16 Fama, E. F., 1970. Efficient Capital Markets: A Review of Theory and Empirical Work. Journal of Finance. (Classic reference on price discovery and market efficiency).
17 Fama, E. F., 1970 and later literature on price discovery and liquidity. Price discovery and frictionless entry/exit in markets.
18 Federal Reserve / FRED data (St. Louis Fed), historical policy rates (2000–2021). Evidence of near-zero interest-rate era and its macro impact. FRED (Effective federal funds rate series).
19 Financial Times / academic analyses (post-2008). How low rates enabled leveraged buyouts and higher private leverage - LBO finance in low-rate era.
20 Federal Reserve Economic Data (FRED), U.S. Treasury yields (10-year) historical series - Carter era yields (late 1970s/early 1980s) showing double-digit yields (c.14%–15%).
21 PitchBook / Bain / Preqin reports (2020–2024). Median private-equity holding periods and empirical industry analyses showing 3–7 year exit horizons.
22 Asker, J., Farre-Mensa, J. & Ljungqvist, A., 2015. Corporate Investment and the Going Public Decision.
23 World Federation of Exchanges / IMF market-capitalization statistics (2023).
24 Tesla investor relations and SEC filings (post-listing).
25 Academic literature and industry reports (e.g., Kaplan & Strömberg; PE capital structure reviews PE's use of debt to enhance returns).
26 Empirical studies on leverage multiples for PE-backed vs public comps (Bain, PitchBook, academic). PE-backed deals historically use higher leverage (commonly reported ranges 4–7x EBITDA) vs public company averages. Available at: https://www.bain.com/insights/topics/private-equity/.
27 Buffett, W. (1997). The Essays of Warren Buffett (compilation). Lawrence A. Cunningham.
28 Toys "R" Us SEC filings and bankruptcy disclosures (2017). Interest expense figures (c.$400m/year by 2017), Chapter 11 filing in September 2017 and liquidation reporting.
29 Congress.gov - S.1582 GENIUS Act (2025). Text and legislative status of the GENIUS Act.
30 SEC communications and speeches (2025). SEC Chair Paul S. Atkins - "American Leadership in the Digital Finance Revolution" and

Project Crypto statements urging agencies to prepare for tokenization / digital finance.
31 McClure, C. G., Shi, S. X. & Watts, E. M. (2025) 'Information acquisition costs and price informativeness: global evidence', Review of Accounting Studies, 30: 2468–2507
32 Mirishli, S. (2025) Regulating AI in Financial Services: Legal Frameworks and Compliance Challenges, preprint (arXiv).
33 Aggarwal, R. (2002) 'Demutualization and corporate governance of stock exchanges', Journal of Applied Corporate Finance, 15(1), pp. 105–113.
34 Doctorow, C. (2019) 'Enshittification', Pluralistic, 30 September.
35 OECD (2023) Financing SMEs and Entrepreneurs: An OECD Scoreboard.
36 OECD (2025) OECD Corporate Governance Factbook 2025. Paris: OECD Publishing
37 Cargill, J. (2022) 'Crypto trading reimagined - batch auctions are the answer', Cargill Insights.
38 Hayek, F.A. (1945) 'The use of knowledge in society', American Economic Review, 35(4), pp. 519–530.
39 Harvard Business Review (2016) 'How Private Equity Differences Create Value', Harvard Business Review, March.
40 Chaney, M. (2021) Capital Markets and the Passive Investment Revolution. Sydney: Australian Institute of Company Directors (AICD).
41 Klein, M. & Mills, D. (2022) 'Index-fund investing and the disconnect between ownership and control', SSRN Electronic Journal.

Additional Resources

The Law firm, Norton Rose, has an excellent guide to various exchanges called "Navigating the IPO"

Venture Impact 2007, 2008, 2009 & 2010 by IHS Global Insight.

America's Roster of Public Companies Is Shrinking Before Our Eyes Wall Street Journal, by Maureen Farrell Jan. 6, 2017

Squaring Venture Capital Valuations with Reality, July 2017, by Will Gornall, Sauder School of Business, University of British Columbia, Ilya A. Strebulaev, Graduate School of Business, Stanford University and NBER

The Evolution of New Markets, Oxford University Press 2009 by P.A. Geroski

For more on the role of public listing in category creation: Play Bigger: How Pirates, Dreamers, and Innovators Create and Dominate Markets, 2016 by Al Ramadan, Dave Peterson, Christopher Lochhead, Kevin Maney

University of Florida Professor Jay Ritter https://site.warrington.ufl.edu/ritter/ipo-data/

"Where you list isn't necessarily where you trade anymore"
Adena Friedman, CEO Nasdaq - Bloomberg Interview, July 24th, 2019

The Global Public Offering - The coming decentralization of global equity capital markets, Public Draft: May 1, 2018 https://docsend.com/view/dpakvau

How Unicorns Grow Harvard Business Review Jan/Feb 2016

Jay Ritter and Ivo Welch, "A Review of IPO Activity, Pricing, and Allocations," Journal of Finance 57 (2002): 1795–1828.

A Wake-up Call for America (November 2009), by D. Weild and E. Kim

S. Torstila, "The Clustering of IPO Gross Spreads: International Evidence," Journal of Financial and Quantitative Analysis (September 2003) citing a 2002 study by Ljungqvist et al.

Grant Thornton; Market structure is causing the IPO crisis; By David Weild and Edward Kim; October 2009

Harvard Law School Forum on Corporate Governance and Financial Regulation https://corpgov.law.harvard.edu/

GSV Capital Investor Letter 2017

David Weild, Edward Kim, Lisa Newport - OECD Corporate Governance Working Papers 2013 Making Stock Markets Work to Support Economic Growth Implications For Governments, Regulators, Stock Exchanges, Corporate Issuers And Their Investors

A. Ljungqvist, Handbooks in Finance: Empirical Corporate Finance, Chapter III.4: "IPO Underwriting," Salmon Center, Stern School of Business, New York University and CEPR, September 1, 2004.

A. Butler (University of Texas at Dallas) and H. Wan (University of South Florida), "Investment Bank Compensation and IPO Pricing," July 19, 2005.

L. Tian (Peking University) and W. Megginson (University of Oklahoma), "Extreme Underpricing: Determinants of Chinese IPO Initial Returns," March 15, 2007.

Rebuilding the IPO On-Ramp Putting Emerging Companies and the Job Market Back on the Road to Growth, Issued by the IPO Task Force October 20, 2011, Presented to The U.S. Department of the Treasury

S. Arco, J. Black, and G. Owen "From Local to Global—The Rise of AIM as a Stock Market for Growing Companies," London School of Economic and Political Science, www.londonstockexchange.com

"World Stock Exchanges," Globe Law and Business (May 2007)

"The Competitive Position of the U.S. Public Equity Market," Committee on Capital Markets Regulation, December 4, 2007.

Ernst & Young, "Growth During Economic Uncertainty: Global IPO Trends Report 2008," www.ey.com.

"The High Cost of IPOs Depresses Venture Capital in the United States," Ohio State University Moritz College of Law (August 2006).

U.S. General Accounting Office, Report to the Chairman, Committee on Small Business, U.S. Senate, Small Business: Efforts to Facilitate Equity Capital (2000).

"Final Report of the Advisory Committee on Smaller Public Companies" (April 23, 2006), http://www.sec.gov/info/smallbus/acspe.shtml.

W. Sjostrom, Jr., "Going Public through an Internet Direct Public Offering: A Sensible Alternative for Small Companies?" Florida Law Review, Vol. 53, 529 et seq. (2001).

Ritter, J.R. and Welch, I. (2002) 'A Review of IPO Activity, Pricing, and Allocations', The Journal of Finance, 57(4), pp. 1795–1828. doi: 10.1111/1540-6261.00478.

Committee on Capital Markets Regulation (2006) Interim Report of the Committee on Capital Markets Regulation: The Competitive Position of the U.S. Public Equity Market. Cambridge, MA: Committee on Capital Markets Regulation

World Federation of Exchanges Annual Report and Statistics www.world-exchanges.org/

Stephen Joyce, "NYSE Euronext Will Be First Traded Firm to List in U.S. and China, Niederauer Says," BNA, Inc. Securities Regulation & Law Report (July 28, 2008). Pros and Cons of a U.S. IPO

'Moving the Market: Oaktree Stock Sale Completed," Wall Street Journal, May 23, 2007.

For more on the history of betting see: Historical Presidential Betting Markets,
Paul W. Rhode and Koleman S. Strumpf - Journal of Economic Perspectives, Volume 18, Number 2, Spring 2004, Pages 127–142

Writing Process and Disclaimers

Going public requires a range of specialized experts. Lawyers, accountants, and bankers make their living following the ever changing landscape. Professional advisors can tailor their advice to the latest practices, newest rules and your specific situation.

This book is the product of extensive research conducted across the world's leading financial centers. To capture the full picture of how public markets are being reshaped, we interviewed a wide spectrum of market participants, from regulators, exchange executives, and policymakers to institutional investors, venture capitalists, and company founders navigating the path to going public.

I am grateful for the volumes of documentation provided by many of the world's stock exchanges.

Above all, I am deeply grateful to the many individuals and institutions who shared their time, insights, and candor with me. Without their openness and generosity, this book would not have been possible.

Limit of Liability/Disclaimer of Warranty

This book should not be used as a substitute to talking with professional advisors. While the publisher and author have made an effort to ensure the accuracy and completeness of this book, they make no representations or warranties, express or implied, regarding its contents. In particular, they disclaim any warranties of merchantability or fitness for a particular purpose. No warranty is created or extended by sales representatives or promotional materials. The information, advice, and strategies presented may not be appropriate for every circumstance. This is not investment advice. Readers should consult qualified professionals where appropriate. Neither the publisher nor the author shall be liable for any loss of profit or other commercial damages, including but not limited to special, incidental, consequential, or other damage.

Glossary

The terms used to describe all the parts of the IPO process vary by local customs or regulatory framework. As it relates to a multijurisdictional IPO, we have tried to provide some of the nuance on terms that may have different meanings to different market participants. We have also tried to highlight terms that may be common in some regions, but unused in others. The meaning of terms can change over time and by region, but hopefully this helps as a jumping-off point for navigating the ever-changing global public funding landscape.

Accelerated Bookbuild (ABB) Capital-raising mechanism used mainly in Europe, Asia, and Australia to sell a large block of shares very quickly (typically overnight, sometimes within hours). It's rare in the U.S.

Admission In the U.S.: 'Admission', 'IPO' and 'listing' are often used interchangeably. However in the UK and EU 'Admission to trading' has legal specificity under the Prospectus Regulation of the European Commission, and may or may not involve a public capital raise (direct listing).

Admission Document A short form of a prospectus written in plain English. Designed to be simple and used in the UK AIM market and Euronext Growth Exchange.

ATS (Alternative Trading System) – A type of U.S. securities trading venue. Introduced in 1998, under Regulation ATS. Basically America's framework for electronic trading platforms that aren't fully-fledged exchanges. ATS are the U.S. cousin of Europe's MTFs (Multilateral Trading Facilities). It includes dark pools (hidden block trading venues) and ECNs (Electronic Communication Networks).

Bookrunner Also known as the managing underwriter or lead underwriter. See lead underwriter.

Cheng Gap Term used in academic and legal circles to describe a specific phenomenon in securities litigation: Foreign firms listed on U.S. exchanges are sued at a lower rate than their U.S. domestic counterparts. Named after Harvard researcher Beiting Cheng.

Cleaning Up the Cap Table The process of simplifying and restructuring a startup's capitalization table (cap table) to make it more attractive to new investors, more manageable for legal and financial purposes, and better aligned with the company's strategic goals.

Clearing House Electronic Subregister System (CHESS) An electronic settlement and registration system used in Australia to manage the clearing, settlement, and ownership registration of securities traded on the Australian Securities Exchange (ASX). For foreign companies, CHESS Depositary Interests (CDIs) are used, where a CHESS entity acts as a depository nominee, but a local agent must also be appointed for ASX communications.

Confidential Filings This U.S. rule, first introduced in 2012, allows companies to keep their S-1 filing undisclosed until 15 days prior to their actual IPO. This keeps vital information away from competitors until the company and market are ready.

Concurrent Private Offering A capital raise that takes place at the same time as a public offering, but it targets a different investor base. Typically applicable to qualified institutional buyers (QIBs) or accredited investors under exemptions like Rule 144A or Regulation D.

Cornerstone investors Common in Asia and part of Europe: A distinct class of early-committed, large investors who agree to a lock-up in exchange for early allocation. This arrangement is often critical for deal marketing. This approach is rarer in the U.S, but PIPEs and anchor investors may play a similar role. Cornerstone structures are less common in the U.S.

Cross Listing A company lists its shares on more than one exchange, typically its home exchange and one or more foreign exchanges. Shares are fungible, often through mechanisms like ADRs or CDIs.

D&O or **Directors' & Officers' Insurance** Common in the U.S., this is additional liability insurance protecting company officers from claims made against them related to their role on the board of directors, or as an officer of the company. Most VCs will require D&O as a condition of investment, but the insurance premiums (cost) can be significant for U.S.-listed companies.

David F. Swensen (1954-2021) Yale University investor and portfolio manager who pioneered portfolio diversification through the Yale Model, which included alternate assets as an important element of portfolio design.

Dealer(s) They often trade on their own account, but they are not necessarily obliged to quote both sides or provide continuous liquidity. A dealer may take positions to profit from inventory management, price movements, or client facilitation. They can act as a principal (own-risk) or as an agent (on behalf of clients), depending on the applicable regulatory framework. See market maker.

Depository Receipts Umbrella term for negotiable financial instruments issued by a bank to represent shares in a foreign company. They are one of the mechanisms that allow investors to trade non-domestic equities on local exchanges. Examples include American Depositary Receipts (ADRs) Global Depositary Receipts (GDRs) European Depositary Receipts (EDRs) Brazilian (BDRs) Indian (IDRs).

Emerging Growth Company (EGC) Is a classification under U.S. securities law, and is specifically defined in the Jumpstart Our Business Startups (JOBS) Act of 2012. The term is legally and operationally specific to U.S. capital markets, particularly in the context of IPOs and public company disclosures. Generally these companies have under $1.2B of revenue and under $700M USD of float.

Firm Commitment Underwriting Underwriting method common in the U.S. where the underwriter (usually an investment bank) guarantees the sale of an entire securities offering by purchasing it from the issuer outright and then reselling it to investors. Outside the U.S., firm commitment underwriting is a hybrid tool, often backed by: 1.) Soft book pre-commitments and/or 2.) Anchor investor allocations. This means that risk is often 'engineered away' rather than fully absorbed. Outside the U.S., the structure may legally be a "firm commitment", but economically closer to a risk-mitigated syndication. The nuance matters because standard NVCA terms often stipulate a 'firm commitment' offering to remove the preferred preference stack.

FIX Protocol Short for *Financial Information eXchange Protocol.* A globally-standardized, electronic messaging protocol used to facilitate real-time communication of trade-related information between financial institutions. It's the *lingua franca* of global capital markets infrastructure, analogous to how TCP/IP powers the internet.

Follow-on Share Issues How much of the company can be offered in a follow-on offering without a shareholder vote.

Foreign Account Tax Compliance Act (FATCA) A U.S. rule requiring that many foreign financial institutions and certain other non-financial foreign entities report on the foreign assets held by their U.S. account holders, or be subject to withholding on withholdable payments. The rule matters for non-US investors because they may create substantial incentives to hold their listed equities outside of U.S. accounts.

Foreign Exempt Listing Refers to a type of listing status granted by certain stock exchanges to foreign companies that are already listed on a recognized foreign exchange (like NYSE, NASDAQ, TSX, LSE, ASX, etc.). It is designed to speed up dual-listing and streamline the compliance burden for these companies. It allows the company to follow it's primary exchange's rules, rather than the full local regulatory framework.

Free Float How much of the company is listed. Can also refer to the amount of a company that must be listed to be eligible for a specific exchange.

Generally Accepted Accounting Principles (GAAP) Is an accounting framework most commonly used in the U.S., and generally understood by domestic U.S. investors.

Globally Registered Shares (GRS) A type of equity security that allow a company to list and trade its shares on multiple stock exchanges across different countries. The concept behind GRS is to facilitate easier cross-border trading of a company's shares without the complexities often associated with other mechanisms like American Depositary Receipts (ADRs) or Global Depositary Receipts (GDRs). GRS can help boost liquidity by enabling investors from different regions to access the same shares on multiple exchanges.

Greenshoe (Overallotment Option) In a typical IPO, underwriters allocate more shares than are being sold by the company, creating a short position (e.g., 15% of the offering). To cover this, they can buy shares in the open market (stabilizing the stock) or exercise the 'greenshoe' option to purchase additional shares from the company or sell at the IPO price for up to 30 days after pricing. This mechanism is designed to facilitate trading, and provides reassurance to investors that the stock won't immediately fall below the IPO price.

Greenshoe Option An over-allotment option for the bankers, a mechanism used during an IPO (or sometimes a follow-on offering) that allows underwriters to purchase up to an additional 15% of shares at the offering price, typically within 30 days of the offering. In some markets, this option is either not permitted (e.g., until recently in India), structured differently (e.g., China uses a 'price stabilization fund'), or executed with more regulatory oversight (e.g., in Hong Kong). Named after the Green Shoe Manufacturing Company IPO of 1960.

Indexes A statistical measure that tracks the performance of a specific market, segment, or asset class. Inclusion may or may not be determined by countries of operation.

Indian Depository Receipts (IDRs) A type of financial instrument that allows foreign companies to raise capital in India by offering their equity shares to Indian investors, without listing directly on an Indian stock exchange.

International Accounting Standards Board (IASB) A global organization that establishes International Financial Reporting Standards (IFRS) used in many parts of the world.

International Financial Reporting Standards (IFRS) Is an accounting framework used by many investors. It is also used by regulators in over 120 countries, including the EU, UK, Canada, Australia, and parts of Asia. IFRS is an alternative to GAAP (Generally Accepted Accounting Principles). IFRS is principles-based accounting, in contrast to GAAP which is rules-based. Many exchanges allow reporting in either format.

Institutional Shareholder Services (ISS) A proxy advisory firm providing institutional investors with data, research, and voting recommendations. Their recommendations can be important, as they can shift shareholder votes especially significant in markets with large passive or index investor strategies.

Issuer The entity that offers securities to investors. In an IPO, it is the company. In the U.S., it is used more among industry professionals. In Europe and Asia, it is a dominant term, used widely in the securities niche.

Lead Managers Responsible for a subset of the bookbuild. Outside the U.S. and U.K., it's not unusual to see 'lead managers' responsible for specific regions, coordinating local investor outreach, regulatory compliance, and distribution strategies in line with regional norms.

Lead Underwriter Also known as the bookrunner or managing underwriter. It is the investment bank or financial institution that takes primary responsibility for orchestrating an initial public offering (IPO) or secondary equity issuance. Their duties span structuring, underwriting, marketing, pricing, allocation, and supporting aftermarket trading.

Managing Underwriter Also known as the bookrunner or lead underwriter. See lead underwriter.

Market Maker and Dealer These terms are often used interchangeably in global finance, but there are important distinctions in function, obligation, and regional interpretation, especially across jurisdictions like the U.S., UK, and EU. Market makers provide liquidity by quoting both buy and sell prices for a security, profiting from the bid-ask spread. Some markets require market makers to offer a bid ensuring ongoing price transparency.

Minimum Shareholder Count The minimum number of shareholders that an exchange requires a company to have in order to be listed (and stay listed). It's designed to ensure a broad investor base, adequate liquidity, and fair price discovery.

Moratoriums A term used for SGX offerings, moratoriums are similar to lock-ups for some pre-IPO shareholders (e.g., founders, early investors), depending on financial criteria. Note: in the U.S., founder and early shareholder lock-ups are contractual and negotiated with underwriters, not exchange-mandated.

MTF (Multilateral Trading Facility) A type of European securities trading venue, which was first introduced in 2007. Basically, Europe's alternative trading system's (ATS) framework. The EU/UK cousin of U.S. dark pools or electronic communication networks (ECNs).

Nominated Adviser (nomad) Unique to London's junior AIM market. A nomad is a firm approved by the London Stock Exchange responsible for overseeing a company's suitability for admission and compliance with AIM Rules. They act as both gatekeeper and advisor, akin to a regulator within a self-regulated framework.

NVCA Standard Terms Refer to the model legal documents and term sheet templates published by the National Venture Capital Association (NVCA), a U.S.-based trade group representing the venture capital industry. These voluntary standards lay the foundation for governance standards, and importantly often contemplate the elimination of share preference as part of a qualified IPO.

OTC or **Over-the-Counter** In the U.S., refers to a decentralized quotation market where securities not listed on U.S. formal exchanges are traded directly between parties, typically through broker-dealers.

Placing Agents The term is used in relation to a pre-IPO, but also IPOs. The term carries different nuances depending on the country and exchange. In some markets, placing agents may be distinct from bookrunners and focused only on allocation to specific customers. This is unlike the U.S. where underwriters both price and place deals.

Placing Tranche A specific portion of securities (sometimes preferred shares) that are offered to a particular group of investors during a private placement or bookbuilding process, potentially at the same time as the IPO. It can be a subset of an overall offering that is 'placed' with selected investors, often institutional, under negotiated terms. This tranche may differ in size, pricing, or timing compared to other tranches in the same issuance. These securities can be tailored to long-only funds, high-profile investors, sovereign wealth funds, or strategic investors.

Preference overhang Happens when the liquidation preferences attached to preferred stock (e.g., 1x, 2x, participating preferred) represent a large portion of the expected exit value. This means that common shareholders may receive little or nothing unless the exit valuation is very high. Based on standard NVCA deal terms, preference overhang disappears at a properly designed IPO.

Preference Stack Term used in venture capital and startup finance to describe the hierarchy of liquidation preferences among different classes of investors in a startup's cap table. It's essentially the priority order in which investors are paid when there's a liquidity event.

Primary Offering A securities offering in which all of the proceeds of the sale of previously unissued stock goes directly to the company.

Prospectus Directive Was the European Union's core legal framework governing how companies raise capital publicly across EU member states from 2003 until it was replaced in 2019 by the Prospectus Regulation (EU).

Prospectus Regulation (EU) EU-wide framework that governs when and how companies must publish a prospectus if they want to offer securities to the public in the EU, and/or seek admission to trading on an EU-regulated market such as Euronext or Deutsche Börse. The 2019 rule was designed to harmonize disclosure standards across the EU and increase cross-border capital mobility.

Quiet Period A regulatory framework for listing in the U.S. The rule dates back to an era when information traveled slowly and most households did not own a phone. The rule reduces information flow. Companies and underwriters are restricted from making public communications that could be seen as 'conditioning the market' (e.g., promotional media, interviews). The period is during 30 days prior to the IPO filing and lasts until 25 days after the IPO pricing.

Re-IPO Refers to a securities offering that has the size, structure, or strategic intent of an IPO. It is found in many Asian capital markets, used most in Hong Kong, Singapore, Korea, and parts of China, with slightly different meanings depending on the jurisdiction.

Red Herring A term used to refer to a prospectus circulated to potential investors. The term dates back from a time when disclaimers were printed in red ink.

Restricted Securities Often these shares are held in escrow. In many markets, the term denotes shares that cannot be traded for a pre-defined period post-IPO. These are managed explicitly under local exchange rules, and they are typically excluded when calculating free float or shareholder spread.

Restricted Stock Sometimes referred to as "legended stock" or "lettered stock." Securities, usually issued in private placements, that have limited transferability.

Retail Tranche U.S.: retail investors typically access IPOs through brokerage allocations or platforms like Robinhood with no formal "retail quota." In other companies, retail participation is mandated. For example, India, Hong Kong, Japan: IPOs often have a mandated retail tranche, sometimes up to 35%, with lottery or proportional allocation systems.

Rights Issue Pre-emptive offering giving existing shareholders rights to buy discounted shares (Common in Europe and Asia). Rare in the U.S. but sometimes found in distressed offerings. U.S. investors might describe it as 'participation right but for public companies'. The rights are usually transferable, when the rights are non-tradable it is called an '**pen offer**'.

Sarbanes-Oxley (SOX) U.S. corporate governance and accounting law passed in 2002, in the wake of the Enron, WorldCom, and Tyco scandals. Added documentation and compliance costs. CEOs and CFOs must personally certify the accuracy of quarterly and annual reports. Increased criminal liability for executives who commit securities fraud.

Secondary Offering The term 'Secondary Offering' can have different meanings depending on jurisdiction, largely due to differences in securities regulation, market structure, and local terminology conventions. Outside the U.S., a 'Secondary Offering' often refers to any offering after the IPO, including: Placing of new shares, Sale of existing shares, or a combination of both. In the U.S., "Secondary Offering" typically refers to the sale of existing shares by current shareholders. "Secondary Offering" is also sometimes used to refer to the sale of an LP position that holds an equity, or the sale of an SPV claiming to have the rights to own shares in the future.

Shareholder Spread The distribution of shares among different shareholders, particularly focusing on how many individual shareholders own a company's stock, and how concentrated or dispersed that ownership is. Important in public markets and IPO contexts, as stock exchanges often require a minimum "shareholder spread" either before or at listing.

Shareholder Votes Certain actions trigger a shareholders' meeting or shareholders' vote

Smaller Reporting Company (SRC) A U.S. SEC term introduced for companies with revenue less than $100M USD. The SRC framework was expanded in 2018 as part of a broader capital formation agenda in the U.S., aimed at reducing compliance burdens and encouraging IPOs among smaller companies.

Staggered Board (also called a classified board) is a corporate governance structure where the board of directors is divided into separate classes, typically three. Instead of all directors standing for election every year, only one class comes up for election in a given year, usually serving multi-year terms (commonly three years).

Stamp Tax A local government-imposed tax on the transfer of certain assets. Most common in jurisdictions that don't want a globally-competitive capital market or seek to push investment transactions offshore. Also known as **Stamp Duty** or **Stamp Duty Reserve Tax (SDRT)** in some jurisdictions.

Testing the Waters (TTW) Is a legal framework that allows companies considering going public to **communicate with potential investors** before formally filing an IPO registration. These rules vary substantially by jurisdiction, with the U.S.

being especially restrictive, especially post-2000, when considering a U.S. IPO.

Transfer Agent Also referred to as a "share registrar" or "shareholder service agent," a transfer agent is a crucial third party that a company engages to maintain an official record of stock ownership. Their role extends throughout the listing process and into a company's life as a public entity. Responsibilities include; keeping the official record of stock ownership, detailing who owns shares and how those shares are held, share management for issuing, canceling, allotting, and transferring shares and stock certificates, dividend payments and managing some administrative tasks related to corporate action

Underwriting Agreement A contract defining the relationship between the company ("issuer") and the underwriters. While the core purpose is universal (allocation of risk, pricing, distribution mechanics, indemnification), the structure, terminology, and obligations vary meaningfully by jurisdiction and exchange. Well-informed negotiations can also have a significant impact on terms.

Up-C Structure A tax advantageous IPO structure, in which capital goes to a newly formed company that then uses the IPO proceeds to acquire an interest in a partnership along with the historical owners.

Up-Listing When a company that's already publicly trading on a smaller or less prestigious exchange moves its shares to a major exchange.

XBRL Short for **eXtensible Business Reporting Language.** A freely-licensable, open technology standard used to electronically exchange business information. This standard is increasing information sharing, and is a business reporting offshoot of the commonly used eXtensible Markup Language (XML).

Yale Model Pioneered by David F. Swensen, the Yale portfolio design used alternative assets to simultaneously reduce risk while increasing long-term returns.

Zombie Funds Johns Hopkins instructor Jeff Hooke coined the term to describe venture capital and private equity funds that are effectively 'dead' in terms of making new investments or generating meaningful returns, but haven't been formally shut down. For limited partners (LPs), zombie funds are a drag on capital and reporting. LPs are stuck with illiquid, underperforming positions and minimal transparency. In some cases, the GP may still be collecting fees based on the fund's committed capital or remaining NAV, which further drags returns.

The GPO Story: From Founders to Funders

We didn't set out to be VCs. We were founders first, hands dirty, sleeves rolled up. We built several venture-backed companies. We made angel bets. We lived in the adrenaline of scaling at speed.

Then we saw the pattern: staying private too long was killing value.

At the same time, we were building across borders. We saw up close, the global surge of demand for high-quality investments. Hundreds of millions joining the middle-class. Wealth becoming distributed. International Institutions hungry for access, not as venture insiders, but as public market investors.

The world's capital markets were being rewired. The IPO wasn't dead; it was going global.

So in 2018 we launched the Global Public Offering Fund. Not just to "invest," but to fix a problem. Our aim was to back the most ambitious founders. Leaders who wanted to take their companies public earlier in their lifecycle. Just like Oracle, Salesforce, and AOL did, long before "unicorn" became a buzzword.

We developed a playbook to go public "globally", by laying the foundation of institutional public market investors, around the world, and well before the IPO. We aimed to help our portfolio companies add the optionality of a multi-jurisdictional IPO, in the same way venture capitalists of the 1990s helped startups navigate Wall Street.

Our mission: help the best companies use the credibility, visibility, and financial flexibility of being public to build generation-defining global businesses.

Acknowledgements

This book is the product of four years of research, debate and ongoing conversations with some of the most thoughtful investors, operators and regulators in global finance. But its origin goes back further, to a 2018 research collaboration with Key Compton, *The Global Public Offering: The Coming Decentralization of Global Equity Capital Markets*. The 44 page paper laid the foundation for what would eventually become this book. That research was born not from academic curiosity alone, but from a desire to document, clarify, and challenge our own assumptions in advance of launching our venture capital firm the Global Public Offering Fund.

We were fortunate to have investors, partners, really, who demanded more than slogans. Their probing questions and intellectual generosity created the conditions for this book to exist. Without their engagement and encouragement, these ideas would have remained scattered in decks, memos, and late-night whiteboard sessions.

A special thank you goes to our LPs and co-investors around the world. Your desire to understand the deeper forces shaping markets pushed us to sharpen our thinking. You didn't just back our investment partnership, you backed the act of inquiry itself.

I would be remiss not to recognize the person who made my very first capital raise possible: Stephen Brown of MIT. In the early 1980s, Steve invested in a much smaller venture, my childhood lawn mowing business. His confidence (and check) allowed me to upgrade my lawn-trimming equipment, dramatically accelerating growth in that first enterprise. It was a formative experience. Without that first taste of earned success, I often wonder whether the dozen companies I founded since, would have happened at all.

To all those who helped shape this book, whether through conversation, critique, or capital, thank you. Together, let's go change the world for the better!

www.ingramcontent.com/pod-product-compliance
Ingram Content Group UK Ltd.
Pitfield, Milton Keynes, MK11 3LW, UK
UKHW020509061026
15625UKWH00033B/755/J

9 798218 877439